MAKING THE FARM PAY

MAKING THE FARM PAY

BY

C. C. BOWSFIELD

WILDSIDE PRESS

CONTENTS

PAGE

The Modern Farmer's Opportunity............ 9
One of the Great Questions of the Day.......... 12
Arguments for Diversified Farming............ 16
Farming More Profitable Than Ever........... 20
Aim to Get Above the Average............... 25
City Men Succeed on Farms................. 29
Results Which May Be Attained.............. 33
Succession Crops Feasible.................... 38
Earning Capacity of Land Requires Study....... 40
Learn How to Go Back to the Land........... 46
Avoid the Single Farming Interest............. 51
Getting the Most Out of an Acre.............. 53
Plans to Keep Young People Interested........ 57
Profit Sharing with Fruit and Vegetables........ 64
New Vocation for the City Family............ 66
Good Selling Is a Farmer's Need.............. 70
Parcels Post Brings Dinner Fresh from Farm.... 77
Soil Improvement and More Profitable Farming.. 80
Soil Conservation Easy to Understand......... 86
Lime as an Adjunct in Farming.............. 88
Phosphorus as a Soil Preserver............... 90

	PAGE
Making the Most of Manure	93
Growing Legumes for Soil Betterment	96
Large Profits in Potatoes	102
Growing Sweet Potatoes in the North	106
Money Making from Pork	108
Making a Dairy Farm Pay	114
Forage Problem Demands Attention	117
Cows Kept at a Loss	124
Importance of Cow Testing Associations	127
Dairy By-Products Are Important	130
How to Obtain a Good Stand of Corn	134
The Culture of Broomcorn	139
The Sugar Beet Industry	142
Irrigation by Wells Profitable	148
Advantages of Concrete on Farms	151
Important Points in Building Silos	155
Chance for Big Profits in Novelties	159
Pin Money in Pickles	164
The Lowly Onion a Profitable Crop	168
Give More Attention to Fruit	171
Care and Skill in the Orchard	176
Common Fruits Return Liberal Profits	179
Fruit Raising Suited to Amateurs	183
Small Fruits Pay Well	187
Have Early and Late Strawberries	192
Commercial Handling of Strawberries	196

PAGE

Thorough Cultivation Makes Gardening Pay..... 200

Practical Study of Gardening................. 204

Commercial Value of Garden Flowers.......... 214

Making and Care of Hotbeds and Coldframes.... 221

War on Field and Garden Pests.............. 225

Enemies of the Corn Crop.................. 232

Wealth in Honey Under Skillful Management... 235

Care and Marketing of Extracted Honey........ 241

Management the Key to Poultry Success........ 244

Winter Egg Production..,.................. 249

Egg Type in Hens......................... 252

Preservation of Eggs Until Prices Advance...... 256

Favorite Breeds of Ducks................... 259

Disease Injuring Turkey-Raising Industry....... 263

Parasites Cause Heavy Poultry Losses......... 266

Poultry Diseases and Remedies.............. 270

Neighborhood Social Centers................ 275

Selecting and Testing Seed Corn............. 277

Farm Bookkeeping 283

Useful Hints for Everyday Farm Life......... 290

Dates for Planting Vegetables.............. 306

Insecticides and Fungicides................ 308

Fertilizers for Farm and Garden............. 310

Index 312

MAKING THE FARM PAY

The Modern Farmer's Opportunity

MODERN farming, as the author views the subject, requires varied information as well as unflagging zeal and industry. It needs the application of commercial ideas. Real success in agriculture can only be attained by keeping up with changing conditions and developing a well-balanced business programme to go with the tilling of the soil.

The average land owner, or the old-fashioned farmer, as he is sometimes referred to, has a great deal of practical knowledge, and yet is deficient in some of the most salient requirements. He may know how to produce a good crop and not know how to sell it to the best advantage. No citizen surpasses him in the skill and industry with which he performs his labor, but in many cases his time is frittered away with the least profitable of products, while he overlooks opportunities to meet a constant market demand for articles which return large profits.

Worse than this, he follows a method which turns agricultural work into drudgery, and his sons and daughters forsake the farm home as soon as they are old enough to assert a little independence. At this point the greatest failures are to be recorded. A situation has developed as a result of these existing conditions in the country which is a serious menace to American society. The farmers are deprived of the earnest, intelligent help which naturally belongs to them, rural society loses one of its best elements, the cities are overcrowded and all parties at interest are losers. The nation itself is injured.

Farm life need not be more irksome than clerking or running a typewriter. It ought to be made much more attractive and it can also be vastly more profitable than it is. Better homes and more social enjoyment, with greater contentment and happiness, will come to dwellers in the country when they grasp the eternal truth that they have the noblest vocation on earth and one that may be made to yield an income fully as large as that of the average city business man.

This whole subject of making agriculture more profitable and enjoyable is approached in a spirit of sympathy. The author resides on a farm and has long been a land owner. He knows the difference between book farming and the actual work of tilling the soil or taking care of live stock. No one appreciates more fully than he what a great fund of information a person must possess to be even an ordinary farmer. As a rule people who dwell in the country are also well posted on political affairs and are patriotic citizens. They are above the average in these respects.

In the effort to show that farmers are lacking in commercial skill it is permissible to repeat that they are the only business people who have nothing to say either in fixing the prices which they get for their own goods or which they pay for other people's. This want of market ability is a result of their isolated life and the old method of raising a single crop, such as wheat or corn. With steady improvement in transportation facilities and other modern conveniences there will come greater diversity in agriculture and a general betterment in rural affairs. The tiller of the soil will be a business man, who will not only devote his land to products which naturally pay best, but who will have something to say about price making.

Prices of agricultural commodities are now on such a high level that land owners may enter upon a period of money making. It is not true, however, that farmers are to any great extent responsible for the high cost of living. Producers are not overpaid. High prices are mainly due to business conditions for which people in the rural districts have no responsibility. Consumers are at the mercy of a system which involves unreasonable expense and too many middlemen.

It would be to the advantage of farmers, however, to have the expense of handling agricultural commodities lessened. They may help toward the attainment of this end by adopting better methods of marketing than now prevail. Consumers as well as themselves would benefit by such a movement.

This book is published in the hope of assisting farmers to improve their position. There is a widespread and intelligent movement toward more diversified and intensive farming, which I heartily endorse. By this system the farm can be made to pay better than it does, because it aims at greater production on each acre cultivated and at meeting special market requirements. The one great point in commercial farming is to produce those articles which pay best.

There is a continual and expanding market for numerous products that are easily raised, and which, by their very diversity, are a guarantee against failure. The market has never been oversupplied with fruits, broilers, mushrooms, honey, squabs, berries and the like. There is the keenest sort of demand today all over the country for extra nice butter, eggs and poultry. The need of parsnips, beets, carrots, lettuce, cucumbers, beans and other kinds of vegetables is incessant, and in all of these lines there is a profit far exceeding that gained from large single crops or big dairies.

One of the Great Questions of the Day

IN common with thousands of others I am strongly impressed with the belief that the subject of better farming in America is the most important now occupying the attention of the commercial world. By better farming is meant a system that will produce larger profits and an easier living for those who till the soil, as well as a greater acreage production.

In discussing this subject I have in mind these salient propositions: Farmers who are not capitalists occupy too much land. They would do better farming and attain better results on smaller tracts. The little farm requires less drudgery than the large one.

It affords a more enjoyable existence and tends to stimulate the interest of the young people in progressive agriculture. To reduce the size of farms will make it easier for poor men to acquire land, consequently the number of owners must increase.

With more owners and renewed interest, our rural population will be augmented. By increasing the production of commodities per acre, we will have heavier exports, and the prosperity of the nation will be enhanced. These considerations are worthy of our attention and highest intelligence.

The little-farm proposition is appealingly strong, both to the man in the country and the resident of the city. It is, in fact, the hope of the American farmer, and of the business world today. Through this modern system the rural family is to escape much of its drudgery, and the city family is to obtain commodities at lower prices. By the new method of intensive and diversified agriculture, country life is to become easier and more attractive, both to the young and to the old.

Big farms are all right for those who are equipped to handle them properly, but they are not desirable for people who have not capital enough to hire plenty of help, and organize in a businesslike way, to secure good results.

It is the evolution that bothers the average farmer. How can he make the change without losses? If he sells off half his land to enable him to farm in the modern, intensive fashion, has he any guarantee that he will not fail in this, and so find himself at the end of a few years, minus both land and capital?

He can best satisfy himself on this point by making an easy comparison of crop values. Such a comparison will startle some of the old-fashioned agriculturists, who persist in running large farms on the one crop idea.

It requires methodical work and business methods to make any kind of a farm pay. As land increases in value the person with limited means will have to be contented with a small tract, and he must learn his business so well that a few acres will yield enough for a living. Better farming is the need of the hour.

The soil should be so handled that it will produce twice as much as it has in the past. Otherwise this nation will become an importer of foodstuffs instead of an exporter. The importance of diversified farming and intelligent agriculture cannot be overestimated.

It has been shown by competent authorities that the wheat crop of the country returns an average profit of much less than $10 per acre. In fact, many people agree that when the expense of equipment, the value of the land, the cost of seed, and the worth of labor are considered, there is no profit whatever in raising wheat.

The American farmer, as a rule, does not count his

own time, the value of his land, or the cost of his horses and machinery, in estimating his profits on grain.

If he has a crop of 100 acres of wheat that will clear $500 for him after reckoning the value of seed, the cost of help and the expense of threshing, he puts it down at $500 profit, though he has put most of his year's time into it, besides maintaining the land and an equipment of horses and machinery worth several hundred dollars.

The following table showing the relative value of crops is based on my own experience:

	GROSS	NET
Wheat per acre	$ 15.00	$ 8.00
Field-corn	30.00	20.00
Sweet potatoes	150.00	110.00
Potatoes	125.00	75.00
Onions	250.00	150.00
Cucumbers	200.00	150.00
Strawberries	300.00	200.00
Cherries	200.00	150.00
Apples	250.00	200.00
Clover	25.00	20.00
Alfalfa	45.00	30.00
Timothy	20.00	15.00
Millet	25.00	20.00

Live stock and dairying can be figured on the acreage basis, just as easily as grain or fruit. If a farmer with 50 acres handles 25 cows and clears $1,000 after paying for help, his net profit is $20 per acre.

A man with 20 acres can easily handle 100 hogs a year, which will net $1,000 to $1,500. A profit of $10 per head, or $1,000, is $50 per acre. This is at least treble as much as can be made from grain, and the work is a great deal less.

If the small farm will serve to render rural life more attractive, shorten the workday and arouse interest among the young people, it is the right system for the average person to adopt. If it will keep the young folk away from the cities and make them love their homes, it beats the old method immeasurably.

Furthermore, if these results are accomplished, the help question will no longer be a serious one. To gain so much is worth the best efforts of the American farmer.

With the ordinary family no help is needed on a little farm except where there is a considerable crop of fruit or vegetables, for which there is a ready cash, return sufficient to meet the expenses of operation.

The old method is driving young people away from the farm and it has become next to impossible to keep hired help. Men will not work on a farm when they come to understand that they can get employment in town or on the railroad at higher wages and with shorter days. Nine or ten hours a day will not do on the old-fashioned farm. It is fourteen or more and seven days in the week at that. The average in the city, taking all classes of employment together, is about nine hours.

Then again, clerkships are very alluring to boys and girls, especially after they have had a taste of farm life, where the family labors from daylight to dark. Under existing conditions it has come about that the farmer finds himself, in many cases, without hired help or the assistance which is ordinarily expected from his sons and daughters.

Arguments for Diversified Farming

FARMING is becoming a more serious proposition year by year. A long succession of drouths in certain localities and the consequent waste of a large acreage are forcing landowners to consider crop diversity.

The one weak spot in modern farming is the disposition to do big things with a single interest, such as wheat raising or dairying. When there is a failure either through seasonal causes or accident, the loss is heavy, discouraging, disastrous. The growing cost of land and labor and the increasing importance of the farmer's time cry out against the single crop idea.

I am confident that those who have in large part lost their wheat crops through drouth will give attention to my plea for a greater diversification on all farms.

Milk producers whose pastures are dried up by the intense heat of summer are also likely to be ready listeners. Furthermore, the young farmer and the student of agriculture who are observing the conditions described must soon reach the conclusion that it is bad policy to depend on a single crop.

While grain raising is an attractive scheme when figured on the basis of a dollar a bushel and twenty bushels an acre, it never has been a safe proposition for the person of limited capital. Capitalists in many cases have made it profitable, because through operating extensively the acreage cost is reduced and they are able to wait a year or two for profits.

There are also numerous instances of men of small means being fortunate enough to escape droughts and other destructive agencies and gaining substantial returns

16

from a wheat crop of one or two hundred acres. This
does not prove it a safe enterprise, however. It is always
hazardous; always more or less of a gamble. I am allud-
ing, of course, to non-irrigated lands.

Within the range of my own experience and observation a farmer with 200 acres feels that he is doing well
when he clears $500 to $1,000 a year either from grain
or a dairy. How many can show this profit, either in
cash savings or substantial improvements?

The man on such a tract of land who produces for
market 100 hogs, 20 beeves, 200 sheep, 500 chickens and
a variety of vegetables, with a small grain crop, will
double discount the exclusive wheat grower. Instead of
risking his year's time and his whole investment on one
product he divides his risks into eight or ten parts. Therefore, if his grain is a failure he can stand the loss because he has various other interests to fall back on. If
he has bad luck with his hogs and chickens, he still has
an assured income from many other sources.

Another almost equally important point is the distribution of labor over the year. The extra labor required during seeding and harvest on a grain farm eats a
big hole in the ordinary profits.

When one considers the teams and machinery involved,
together with the upkeep, it becomes doubtful whether
there is any actual profit in wheat raising. The investment in land, teams, machinery and labor is substantially
the same whether the yield is ten bushels or twenty.

With the other principle established, the amount of
labor required is pretty much the same at one time of
the year as another. Nobody knows better than the
farmer how vexatious and costly the uncertainty of labor
has become.

I claim without fear of successful contradiction that
the farmer who diversifies his products will accomplish
more on one hundred acres than a grain grower or milk

producer will on two hundred. For an illustration I will give a list of products which come within the capacity of 100 acres in a season.

100 hogs	$1,500
20 beeves	1,200
200 sheep	1,400
1 span horses	350
500 chickens	300
Eggs	250
1,000 bushels potatoes	500
Total	$5,500

The intelligent farmer can decide for himself whether it is possible or not to raise the fodder for this amount of stock on 100 acres, and whether any figures given are unreasonable. About $1,000 must be deducted from the gross amount for labor, and the help should be the same throughout the year. The program can be varied to suit tastes and conditions. A few acres might be devoted to strawberries, cherries, apples, sweetcorn, cucumbers, cabbage, etc.

There is immense profit in these lighter crops, and the acreage is so small, comparatively, that in a drought it is possible to save the product with well or slough water. There is a constant demand for fruit and vegetables at fair prices. This is also the case in regard to poultry and eggs.

Diversified farming cannot be carried on without intelligent effort. There is no end to the work, but even in this respect it beats a dairy, and for a certainty it makes for smaller investment, less risk, and greater chance to take advantage of market conditions.

Fruit raising and mixed farming make a good combination. The wheat is in the bins and the corn in the shocks or silos by the time the apples are ripe and fit for harvest.

Dairy farming and stock growing form an excellent combination, and one that will improve the fertility of the farm. Dairying and potato growing make another good combination. The potatoes may be grown in the same rotation of crops that is practised in growing food for the dairy cattle. The work may be done with the same help that is required to care for the dairy, and very little horsepower is needed to handle the additional crop.

Take the ordinary crops of corn and wheat as examples. The western farmer who grows a large acreage of corn and wheat finds he must plant his corn early and push its cultivation so as to have it well out of the way by the time the wheat is ready to harvest. Late planted corn and wheat need attention at the same time, and one or the other must suffer.

A second consideration in diversified farming should be to grow a rational rotation of crops, a rotation adapted to the needs of the live stock, and one that will not diminish the fertility of the soil for future crops. Corn, wheat and clover constitute an excellent crop rotation, and this may be lengthened a year to admit a cash market crop.

Farming More Profitable Than Ever

Viewed as a financial proposition, farming is more attractive today than ever before. All staples are selling at figures which give liberal profits. While the farmer is not being overpaid, compared to business people generally, he is in a position to make money faster than it has heretofore been made in agriculture. He is independent and secure.

A well located farm of 100 acres ought to show a net profit of $2,000 a year. It will do this if operated with fair business sagacity. It can be made to do more in the hands of a person who is able to apply scientific knowledge together with good business methods.

A person starting with sufficient capital and going in for fruit, flowers, fine poultry and some of the other fancy lines will clean up $2,000 or more on a tract of twenty to forty acres. This is being done in a few cases, and market demands are such that it can be accomplished by thousands of others.

Location may not determine the success of a farmer, but it has much to do with the kind of produce which is raised. Near a large city it is profitable to give special attention to dairy and poultry products, fruit, vegetables and flowers. In cases of less favorable location, when shipping is more difficult, live stock, grain, potatoes, onions and hay are the best staples to cultivate.

It is the general belief that farmers should diversify their crops, so that a failure of one crop or low prices for that crop would leave him other products to fall back on. There are other reasons. There is no single crop that keeps farm labor busy all of the time, but by a proper com-

20

bination of crops, employment of labor can be extended virtually throughout the year.

A dairy helps to balance up the labor of a farm. The milk herd requires attention morning and night through the summer, say an hour and a half each time, and the middle of the day is spent in cultivating fodder crops. In winter the work of feeding and cleaning takes more time than in summer, but there are still several hours to be devoted to the care of poultry, the marketing of produce and other incidental labor. Hogs and poultry go nicely with the dairy, not only to distribute the labor, but for the profitable use of skimmed milk or other surplus.

This diversity works well in many other ways. It is an advantage to raise early potatoes, and after this crop has been taken off, onions, cabbage, beets, corn, millet, cow-peas or soy beans can be grown on the same land. There is a cash demand for all such staples which improves with the growth of cities. The market improvement is due to the steady development of a non-producing population.

A few years ago garden truck was so cheap that farmers could not afford to give their time to it. Today a fine income is assured the person who has five or ten acres devoted to such common products as cabbage, onions, beans, lettuce and celery. No crops are more certain than these and with a variety of them the failure of one or two does not ruin the tiller of the soil.

No crop is easier to handle than strawberries or raspberries, and there is no investment for machinery or power in connection with their production, yet berries pay hundreds of dollars per acre, while grain crops which require expensive equipments return $10 to $30 an acre.

The increase of transportation facilities is another large factor in making farming profitable. The lack of train service in years past was a great handicap to farmers. This improvement not only helps farmers to do quick and regular marketing, but enables city people to live in the country. It has such an influence on the prosperity and comforts of rural life that land becomes a most desirable investment, being certain to advance in value.

If you are starting a country home, or planning to do so, make up your mind that farming as an avocation can be made both pleasant and profitable. Confine the work to reasonable hours and have such a variety of products that something will appeal to every member of the family.

This is necessary if boys and girls are to be held in the country. Farming has been plain drudgery in too many cases, and ambitious young people have been driven to the cities. Unmistakable signs of a change in this tendency are seen. The country eventually will be attractive both as to occupation and home-making.

There has been real progress in recent years in agriculture and the development of a broader and more hopeful rural life. Actual results are being accomplished along these progressive lines. It is apparent that the financial side of farming has reached a higher plane than it occupied five years ago.

Questions of selling and buying are receiving more attention than ever before, and the principle of co-operation is being applied in these and other matters pertaining to the farmer's business.

Telephones are breaking in upon the isolation and monotony of rural life; good roads can bring neighbors still closer and the outside world nearer by encouraging rural mail delivery. With a care for beauty in home surroundings, even on the prairie a vast change can be wrought—a change that not alone will increase the value of the farm, but with other conveniences will make a farm home ideal.

Just at present those living in cities, large and small,

consider a day or a week in the country a privilege. They are looking for but a glimpse of natural beauty that can be part of the farmer's home surroundings during the entire season.

At present 2,000 American high schools are teaching agriculture; 37,000 students in these schools are studying this subject. There is a great shortage of well-prepared high school teachers of agriculture, and such teachers receive 50 to 100 per cent greater salary than do teachers of other subjects. There is no reason why a part of the studies carried on in the agricultural colleges today could not be given to pupils in properly equipped rural schools, a greater portion of which equipment would be an experimental plot. '

We now recognize the need not only of knowing the general laws of nature and their application to methods of culture but that each farmer should be able to make the application under his peculiar conditions of soil, climate, topography, market and transportation facilities. So long as there are unsolved problems lying before our farmers, which can be solved only in the light of knowledge which the average farmer can not gain for himself, then the schools must help.

There is the problem of distributing products once grown; nearness to market, transportation, character of market, competition for the market, function and rewards of middlemen, development of agricultural credit, business co-operation among farmers, etc. These economic considerations, just because they are vital to the success of agriculture, are a subject for thorough investigation.

Our greatest concern is with the quality of people developed by the rural mode of living. Hence, the conditions of rural life—moral, religious, recreational—are of significance. Because these things are vital to the welfare of the nation they must be studied.

Next to this is the recognized need of stimulating

agricultural production in order to meet the growing call for supplies at home and abroad. The rapid growth in American cities has created a consumptive demand which is increasing far more rapidly than the output of the farms. The effect of this has been to cut down our export to such an extent that we have come to depend on the cotton crop and manufactured products to maintain the nation's balance of trade.

The wheat crop of this country is raised on 50,000,000 acres and averages 13.7 bushels to the acre, while several countries of Europe, on thousand-year-old farms, average 26 bushels. We have as good, or better, land, tools, brains, etc., but we are not yet properly employing any of these factors.

The corn average is only 28 bushels per acre, and yet in some twelve experiments last summer a yield of 100 bushels or more was easily secured.

If the farms of the corn belt were kept clean of weeds there would be a great deal less trouble with insects, is the opinion of Frank I. Mann of Gilman, Ill. There are a number of times during the year when there are no crops in condition for the insects to live on, and these times are tided over for them by the growth of weeds where they do not belong. A few of the insects, such as grubs, root lice and corn root-worm, can be controlled by a crop rotation which introduces a year of clover or some such crop upon the roots of which the insects cannot live. An evidence of the possibilities in insect eradication is the Mann farm at Gilman. For a number of years the men from the state entomological department have been examining the Mann fields every year to see if any injurious insects could be found, and except for grasshoppers they have found none. Mr. Mann attributes this entirely to the systematic rotation of crops, the keeping out of weeds, and the use of strong seed which produces plants with power of pest resistance.

Aim to Get Above the Average

THE actual moneymaking on a farm comes when we are above the average in quality and production. Those who stand on the common level will get a living, but not much more. Farming needs individuality of character and purpose just as running a store or a factory does.

If the usual profit in a flock of hens is $1 each, above the cost of food, the aim should be to increase egg production and the sale of broilers or other kinds of fancy poultry so that there will be a profit of $2 for each hen kept. This is to be accomplished by selecting pullets from the best laying mothers and by breeding up with full-blooded males.

If the cows in a dairy herd are paying an average of $100 a year, make an effort to raise it to $200. Perhaps the quickest way to gain this end is by discarding all animals that fail to give five gallons of milk per day for the greater part of the year. The stock may be gradually improved by selection and breeding. It may be possible also to sell a part of the milk or cream to private customers who will pay double the wholesale rate.

It is not necessary that the farmer should replace all of his grade cows with high-priced, pure-bred Holsteins, Jerseys, Guernseys or Ayrshires. However, for successful and profitable dairying it is absolutely necessary that he realize the remarkable difference in productive capacity of the individual cows in the same herd, though these cows are cared for by the same man and are consuming practically the same amount of feed.

Recently a herd of hogs from the northwest was sold

in one of the central markets for $8.50 per 100 pounds. A
herd of similar size from a so-called corn belt state sold
in the same market on the same day for $7.95. The
northwestern hogs were fed a variety of food, including
barley, a liberal amount of alfalfa, a little ground wheat,
some corn and some sugar beet sirup. The other herd of
hogs was fattened almost exclusively on corn.

Not only did the northwestern hogs bring a higher
price per 100 pounds, but they put on flesh more rapidly
and economically than the others and were in every way
more satisfactory. With the present knowledge of alfalfa
growing no farmer, even in the strictly corn states, can
find a reasonable excuse for not having some of this to
feed his hogs.

Hogs need to run at large in a field where there is forage. This may be clover, alfalfa, rape or artichokes.
In this way they attain growth and put on flesh better
than they will if penned up. If they can have whey or
skimmed milk once a day this will assist the economical
production of meat. The aim must be to bring the hog
up to 200 or 300 pounds at such a moderate cost that
there will be a liberal profit when it is marketed.

With an abundance of hay and corn there ought to be
good profit in fattening beef animals, few or many, according to the size of the farm. It would appear that with
the judicious selection of feeders, with the careful handling of the animals while in the feed lot and with an
even break on other conditions, cattle feeding ought to
be fairly profitable.

Farmers have come to realize the value of maintaining soil fertility and are using manure as liberally as
possible. Land, to be made a source of continuous profit,
must be kept fertile. The proper rotation of crops, combined with the raising of live stock, will contribute largely
in the maintenance of soil fertility.

A few wise farmers in the Chicago district receive

$2.50 to $5 a bushel for all the corn they raise. They understand the selling end of farming as well as the producing end. One is about as important as the other.

These farmers buy 60-cent corn for feeding. They can not afford to use their own product for this purpose. Being careful, systematic men they raise corn of a high type, uniform and prolific, and they are becoming wealthy by this kind of brain work. There is a lesson for all farmers here.

Raise a first-class article, whether grain, vegetables, chickens or pigs, and there will be no difficulty in finding people who want your product if you will but let them know what you have and what you sell it for.

I have often seen men going from store to store with a tin bucket and an old rag sticking out under the cover asking the merchants if they wanted butter, and at every place they would be told that it was not wanted, when in fact those very merchants were getting print butter all the way from Wisconsin or Iowa. They knew the character of the butter in the tin buckets and did not want that sort. As with butter, so it is with all products of the farm. It is quality that makes the article sell.

Conditions are right for money-making by the agricultural class. It simply remains for the farmers themselves to develop methods of selling by which they can take advantage of the improved markets. The rapid growth of cities, and the sharp demand for all kinds of produce are substantial evidence of this improvement.

Co-operation is the first step. Organization may be applied not only in shipping, but in forming neighborhood clubs among city customers to whom regular quantities of produce may be delivered at stated intervals at prices which are reasonable and fair to both sides.

Abroad farmers market and dispose of their produce profitably through agricultural co-operative associations. They improve their methods, widen their markets and reduce their transportation expenses through co-operation. Why can not our farmers do likewise?

When a farmer is located near a good market, the thing for him to do is to sell to private customers. As his business enlarges he can furnish supplies to hotels and restaurants as well as residences. He can obtain any price in reason so long as his goods are choice.

When producers are too far from a good market to drive in frequently the proposed method of co-operation is excellent. A number of them, working together, can agree to ship regularly a given quantity of produce to city consumers and the latter can best handle the business by means of an organization of some sort.

There are many reasons why waterfowl are not more popular for the table than they are, but the chief reason is that they are so poorly fitted for the market. The big duck farms of the east are the only ones to give the proper finishing of ducks for the market the whole attention it deserves. They have educated the market to an appreciation of good waterfowl, and have been rewarded in price for the effort expended.

It pays well to be able to furnish in their season such articles as strawberries, currants, cucumbers, cherries, apples, raspberries, sweet corn, cabbage, honey and other products of the kind. These pay ten times as much as the grain crops. An acre of cherries or apples will net about $150 after paying for the labor of picking and marketing. The others are equally profitable or nearly so.

A farmer raising fruit should make contracts with private customers or grocers as early in the season as he can; that is, as soon as he can tell something about what the yield is to be. He will thus get better returns than by shipping to a large produce market. The same method is best in marketing poultry, eggs and vegetables.

City Men Succeed on Farms

IN many notable cases city men are succeeding as farmers. If they do not know all about raising grain and handling livestock, they are able, as a general rule, to apply business methods to their undertakings.

Successful farm management must include a knowledge of buying and selling. In this particular the city man is apt to be ahead of his rural neighbor. It is essential to know what consumers require, what the usual retail prices are on farm commodities and the facilities available for transporting and selling. The man of city experience understands these things and he goes in for a line of produce like onions, beans, potatoes, ducks, chickens and carnations and asters, on which he gets big profits.

It would not be like a city man to raise wheat at 75 cents a bushel and twenty bushels to the acre when he can get 90 cents a bushel for onions and 250 bushels to the acre. This illustrates the whole idea, and no truth is more striking than the fact that city men are needed in agriculture.

It is difficult to estimate offhand the economic importance of the much-talked-about movement of families from the city to the farm. The "back to the land" exhortation to all intents and purposes is a "go west, young man," motto redressed. So far as migration to the farm interests men with money and intelligence, the whole idea is splendid and can only lead to success.

It is not all a matter of settlement or numerical increase on the land. The country demands introduction of new crops or products, establishment of new enterprises and bringing forth of conveniences and commodities which farming districts lack.

There is also an opportunity for a man with capital to establish himself in a rural community and supply farmers with live stock or other equipment in cases where they are short of means. Money is needed in making the switch from old methods to new. It is also required to aid city residents in getting started on the farm. Investments of this character are safe. The returns enrich both the man with money and the farmer with the stock, who stands sponsor for the returns. There is enough security in the farming business to permit the man with money to unite with the farmer for mutual advantage.

There are other common opportunities, such as establishment of nurseries, production of high-class seeds and manufacture of mill products. The list is in fact long and the opportunities many. The successful occupancy of the land is in fact only the first phase of a greater movement which must follow.

The need of the day is for diversification in agriculture, and this is merely another way of saying that business methods are required on the farm. A more scientific cultivation of the soil is called for and it is equally necessary for any rural community to adapt its products to the market conditions surrounding it. Advantages in selling may be gained by securing private customers and handling all commodities in a tasty, businesslike way.

There are many difficulties in farming, but the advantages of an agricultural life must not be overlooked. In the first place, the farmer, if he is at all successful, has no fear of being displaced. He commands his own time and leads an independent life. In the second place, if he is wise, he may himself produce nearly all the food necessary for his family.

It is best to go in for a variety of products, but not on an extravagant scale. A start is easily made with poultry, vegetables, flowers, bees and pigs. For this sort of farming only a small tract of land is needed, and no large outlay is required for horses, barns, machinery and tools. These facts have to be observed because it is more difficult at the present time to break away from city employment and establish oneself on the land than it was a generation ago.

At that time there was plenty of land to be homesteaded. Especially in the middle west, where most of this land was available, the soil was rich and its fertility needed no attention. It did not take long for the beginner to learn how to grow crops successfully on this rich virgin soil, and the advance in land values made the enterprise distinctly profitable.

When good land was thus available for the taking, thousands of farm homes were successfully established by men having little previous knowledge of the business. At present there is practically no desirable land left for homesteads. Therefore it is a good plan for the city man to begin without investing heavily in buildings, machinery and power.

If he will take a few acres close to a large town, or at least convenient to transportation, he can carry on truck farming with small outlay beyond the first cost of land. One horse and a little light machinery will suffice at the start. Vegetable raising requires patient labor for six months in the year and yields a fine return on time and investment.

Flower farming is as simple as anything else and may be pursued with pleasure and profit the year around, if the farmer will put some of the proceeds of his surplus land into a greenhouse and steam heating plant. A half acre in carnations or roses will yield a regular monthly income amounting to more than fifty acres of corn or wheat. Perhaps, also, it would supply an element of refinement and beauty that would be sufficient to keep the young men and women at home.

The time has come in this country—and it came long ago in other parts of the world—when a tract of ten acres insures comfort and independence.

This is owing to the large markets which exist everywhere and the development of railroads. When the country was sparsely settled, and everybody could own land, it was hard to dispose of produce for enough to pay for handling it. Cash was scarce and markets were indifferent. Today the great cities all around us are calling for farm products at prices which afford large profits.

Last season a Michigan man put in four and three-fourths acres to cabbage. The ground was plowed about the middle of May and with the plowing a good coat of manure was turned under. Then the plot was topped and dressed with muriate of potash, using about 100 pounds to the acre. The seed was drilled in the row and the plants were thinned out when large enough for that work.

The heads were cut the first week in November and about the middle of January ninety-three tons, all from this patch, were sold in Grand Rapids. Twenty-five tons were sold at $23 a ton and the remaining sixty-eight tons brought $25 a ton. This is a total of $2,275 from four and three-fourths acres of land—not all profit, of course, but a good per cent of it is.

The owner had land enough left, supposing his farm to be ten acres, to maintain a herd of swine and a flock of poultry.

Results Which May Be Attained

IT ought to be the aim of every farmer to accomplish these definite results:

Increase profits by enlarging production at a fixed expense.

Diversify crops and all other profits so as to distribute labor evenly throughout the year.

Secure a regular income at all seasons by supplying customers with poultry and dairy products, vegetables, beef, pork, etc.

Shorten the work-day to ten hours, provide a comfortable home, improve the appearance of the premises and try to make life enjoyable.

Let the young people have a little money from the production of fruit, flowers, vegetables and experimental crops. Teach them to plan work for themselves and to love the country.

There are farmers who have delightful homes and who give the young people all reasonable advantages, but they are an exception to the rule. Country life is made dull and distasteful, as a general proposition, by long hours, drudgery and a lack of social interests. This explains the large exodus of young people to town, when they could be happier and more prosperous in the country.

The American farmer, however, has not been doing justice to himself. He has stuck too closely to those products which pay the smallest profits, and he has not sold his goods to the best advantage. By a lack of diversity in production he has continually borne a risk of total failure.

The difference in yield between the land properly

farmed and the land poorly farmed is so great that scientific farming experts are now calling the attention of farmers by communities to the urgency of taking up the study of certain crops and demonstrating the great loss that is being sustained throughout the country in not making closer study in requirements of cultivation for large grain yields. It is rotation and diversity that are lacking—the former to keep up the farm and the latter to keep up the profits.

Every practical rotation must contain crops that use nitrogen and crops that gather it. For example, in the common rotation of corn, wheat and clover, the first two use nitrogen and the third gathers it. In fact, clover is a user and a gatherer of nitrogen. Do not think because a legume adds nitrogen to the soil that it does not use up plant food; in fact, leguminous crops use more potash and phosphorus than most any of the grain crops. A large amount of nitrogen is also used, but it is taken from the air, and in addition an extra amount is stored up in the soil.

Now let the farmer push this diversification far beyond the corn, wheat and clover crops. Cowpeas and oats sown together make splendid fodder and benefit the soil. They can be harvested by midsummer, and a crop of millet grown on the same land by fall. Rye and clover sown together in the fall can be cut for fodder by June 1, and potatoes, corn, rutabagas, millet or cowpeas grown the same season.

While farmers are making $20 to $30 an acre on heavy grain crops, they should not overlook such products as onions, beans, potatoes, sugar beets and fruit, which return a profit of $100 to $200 an acre. These are the things which bring the large profits and place agriculture on a business basis.

Some of the easiest money in this country is made by watching cows and hogs grow up. The man who has enough feed for 200 head of cattle and pigs can make big profits. This system solves the labor question better than anything else, as it gives work to hired help the entire year and avoids rushes even in haying. Cattle and hogs belong in the general scheme of diversified farming with poultry and vegetables.

The system on many farms could be changed so as to raise more live stock and give employment to one or two men all the year around. I do not believe there is much trouble in keeping men where they are well treated, well paid and given steady employment. Farmers have to compete with manufacturers, railroads and other large employers of labor, and they can not expect to pick up good men at any time of the year they happen to need them.

In addition to the ordinary farming, which contemplates a system that is best for the land, it should be the aim of all farmers to so diversify and manage their crops that they can take advantage of the keen market demand which exists for a variety of products other than grain and live stock.

There are large profits in fruit and vegetables, as well as in the furnishing of choice supplies of poultry, honey, butter and a line of commodities which may come under the head of fancy farming. An amateur can safely engage in the production of various articles which pay better than wheat, corn or milk.

Among some of the highly profitable crops which farmers commonly neglect and which may be grown in all parts of the country are grapes, raspberries, strawberries, apples, plums, cherries, pears, tobacco, onions, beans, cabbage, celery and a host more which have an attractive appearance to the person who studies the markets. Alfalfa also sells readily at prices which make it more profitable than grain.

The large profits per acre that can be derived from

tobacco make the growing of this crop a temptation to farmers. It belongs in crop rotation schemes and thus becomes a factor in soil improvement. Tobacco is successfully grown all over the south. It has been crowded out by grain farming and dairying in most of the northern states. The crop pays well, however, in New England and is exceptionally fine there. It is also profitable in parts of Wisconsin, Indiana, Ohio, Illinois and Iowa, although it does not receive any great amount of attention in the central west. Any farmer having clover, sugar beets, potatoes, cabbage, onions and the usual rotative crops ought to give tobacco a trial.

In February, 1912, 2,500,000 bushels of potatoes came here from Ireland and other European countries. During the eight months ended in February, breadstuffs to the value of $10,000,000 were imported by us, against $3,000,000 worth of similar commodities in 1902. Onions, beans and fruits to the value of millions of dollars are brought in every season. This proves that our farmers have been remiss and that their vocation will pay better when they fully supply their home markets with commodities which can be raised anywhere in this country.

In 1870 there were engaged in agricultural pursuits, approximately, 47.36 per cent of the population; in 1910, only 32 per cent. From this, it is apparent, the farmer now is producing to feed two citizens beside himself, whereas forty years ago he labored to feed only one.

Any state could add from $250,000 to $1,000,000 to the revenue of each of its counties annually by an average increase of five bushels per acre in its yield of corn and wheat. If each acre of improved agricultural land in this country could be made to yield only one additional bushel of produce, 12,500 extra trains of fifty cars each would be required to move the aggregate increased yield. Eighty bushels of corn will make more net profit in one year than a fifty-bushel acreage for four years—for about forty bushels yearly is required to come out even on high-priced land. Truths of this sort are what our farmers need to grasp, for the ten-year average yield of wheat in this country is fourteen bushels per acre, while Germany's is twenty-eight bushels, England's thirty-two bushels, and Denmark's more than forty bushels.

Of course farmers who wish to diversify and get a large percentage of retail prices must consider the matter of location. Transportation facilities and the nearness to large markets are two of the first questions. Nature does 90 per cent of the work in producing from the soil—man does all the work in transporting that which is produced to the market where it can be turned quickly into money.

The farmers of Jefferson county, Wisconsin, realize from their cows, in milk product, over two million dollars annually, while from the sale of cows and heifers they receive about $700,000. This combining dairying with dairy stock breeding and raising, makes of the farmer a much better equipped man all around, while it enhances his profits. Most of the milk is handled in creameries, and the skimmed-milk product, with the abundant corn crops, and alfalfa and clover, enables the farmer to turn a fine pork crop every year.

This all-around dairy farming pays well, when intelligently managed, with the added advantage that the farmer is more his own master, and his calling educates him more broadly and more completely.

Dairy farmers must become better stock raisers than they have been, whether they operate east or west, if they want larger profits and a larger share in what they earn. A few men can not control the butter market, or pork market, and the market for cows and heifers, as they do the milk market in large cities.

Succession Crops Feasible

A BRANCH of farming that affords more than ordinary pleasure and profit is that of studying out schemes for succession crops. It is quite feasible to raise two or more crops in one season on ordinary soil. It will be found that this kind of intensive farming is good for the soil. There has to be free use of barnyard fertilizer, and the plowing, disking, harrowing, rolling, and perhaps hoeing, must be in proportion to the amount of production required of the land. Such treatment will build up instead of wearing out a plot of ground. These examples may be varied as circumstances suggest.

Lettuce, radishes, onions, peas, carrots and string beans may be grown and supplied to customers between the 1st of May and the middle of June. The ground can then be prepared in a few days for the succeeding crops, and it will be found that between the 1st of July and the 1st of October a full crop of these products can be grown: Celery, sweet corn, late potatoes, beets, cucumbers, cabbage, lettuce, spinach, onions and turnips.

At first glance it would seem that there are not many vegetables on the list that could be sown successfully as late as midsummer, but those tested form quite an array. Bush beans, carrots, lettuce, beets, corn, parsley, peas, radishes, spinach and turnips all give satisfactory results when sown as late as August. They should be put in as near the 1st of July as possible to make all growth possible before frost. The hardy ones cause no anxiety, as they endure light frosts. The tender sort, such as beans, cucumbers and spinach, may be saved from the cold by a covering of old rugs and similar material.

As the gardener can not duplicate the cool, moist conditions of spring for the germination of August seeds, he must do the next best thing and firm the soil well after sowing. This helps to draw the moisture in the soil where the seedlings can use it. When they have made a start the surface is to be stirred to form a mulch.

Bush beans sown as late as August 10 have been successfully harvested by October 15. In another case an August 1 sowing of peas yielded full-sized pods in less than seven weeks. These were an extra early sort. The crop, however, was not so heavy as from spring-sown seed.

Lettuce planted in early August bore leaves large enough to use before the middle of September and well formed heads from the first week in October until the ground was cleared.

This is only a suggestive outline of the scheme of growing succession crops. There are wide possibilities along that line, and it is feasible to go still further and sow rape as soon as the vegetables are off in September and October. By November 1 this will be in condition for forage. Hogs and sheep can feed from this field of rape for several weeks before winter sets in, and it is again ready for them in the spring.

So far as the effect on the soil is concerned, it is possible to continue the double cropping of vegetables indefinitely. The land will most likely show improvement under such methods of cultivation, but a rotative scheme is advisable on small tracts as well as large ones.

Earning Capacity of Land Requires Study

FARMERS, as well as their financial friends in town, are vitally interested in the earning capacity of land. There is more money to be made in farming today than there has been in the past because of the permanent high prices for produce and an improvement in transportation facilities. Live stock and field products bring nearly twice as much now as they did ten years ago.

But what is the earning capacity of land? A farm of 100 acres can be managed so as to maintain 100 hogs, a dairy of 20 cows, half a dozen brood mares, a large poultry plant, a garden, an orchard, and an apiary. An income of $5,000 on a total expense for wages and family maintenance of $1,500 would be a fair estimate. Out of the $1,500 expense fund the farmer who is operating on business principles will allow himself and family $500 as wages. He must consider that he owes himself as much as he would any other man for a like amount of work, and his wife is entitled to her share in cash.

This would mean intensive, systematic, businesslike farming, but the figures are conservative, and any intelligent person can obtain these results if such a plan is adopted. By doing more with hogs and poultry, the net earnings might be increased considerably. It would pay to still further diversify by the production of beans, onions, and like crops, for which there is always a good cash market.

To gain from fifty acres an income equal to the figures given above one would have to drop the dairy and go in mainly for hogs, poultry, onions, potatoes, strawberries, cabbage, beans, and perhaps cucumbers and sweet corn. Four brood mares could be kept on a fifty-acre place to do the work and raise horses for market. After two seasons there would be three or four horses to sell every year.

It is reasonably certain that any business man who runs a diversified farm as carefully as he conducts a store can clean up a satisfactory income from year to year, keep up his place in proper order, and have a delightful country home. He also will gain considerably in the appreciation of land, and he has always the satisfaction of knowing that his investment is perfectly safe.

Let us consider what two farmers in Illinois are doing to show the earning capacity of land. One of these farmers has 32 acres at Wayne, DuPage County, and operates a dairy of 30 cows, besides carrying a fair variety of poultry, hogs, etc. He also maintains a team of brood mares on the place to do the work.

This man has observed that cows waste a great deal of land. In a drought they scarcely get a living from the grass no matter how much of a range they may have, so he gives them a small field to run in, and feeds them the year around. He puts most of the place into corn and fills a silo especially for summer feeding. He buys never to exceed $200 worth of mill stuff per year, and pays about $300 for wages. His income for milk, pork and poultry is not less than $3,000. Under his system he cleans up $2,000 a year above living and operating expenses.

In the other case referred to, the farmer started in an experimental way on 40 acres. He found that ten good cows would give an income of $100 per month, but that he had to feed them in the midsummer about the same as in the winter. He carried this number for two seasons, with one hired man. He began with equal caution with hogs, raising from 30 to 60 each season. Then he increased the dairy to 20 head, and at this time is operating one of the most diversified little farms that anyone could plan. Two hired hands are employed the year around. The 40-acre farm now has 20 cows, 50 hogs, 400 chickens, 16 hives of bees, 4 horses and a sufficient variety of young stock to keep the place up to the present basis. An acre of land is devoted to strawberries every summer and another to cucumbers. There also have been some interesting experiments with alfalfa, alsike and such forage crops as rape and artichokes. This little farm returns a gross income of nearly $5,000 a year, less than $2,000 of which is expense.

In running a dairy of say 30 cows, two men are needed, but this is a sufficient force for much other work along the line of fancy or intensive farming. I have seen it demonstrated over and over that an acre of strawberries will pay the yearly wages of a hired man, and the picking is done at a time when there is no pressure of other work. Cucumbers are a still surer crop and pay enormously. They are harvested after corn planting, and do not interfere with the regular work of the farm. It is important to have the work so distributed that the men who must be kept for the dairy shall have profitable employment for the entire day. This is gained by having a diversity.

The method of management on a 15-acre farm that raises all the roughage for 30 head of stock, 17 of which are cows in milk, can not fail to be of interest to farmers in all parts of the country. The farm in question is situated in southeastern Pennsylvania, near a city. About 13 acres are in cultivation, the remaining 2 acres being occupied by buildings, yard, etc. This farm came into the possession of a new owner in 1881 with a mortgage of $7,200 upon it. For the first year the farm lacked $46 of paying expenses. During the next six years the mortgage was paid.

Upon assuming management of the farm the owner,

a minister with no previous experience in farming, began to read what agricultural literature was available. One of the first books secured was Quincy's little book on the soiling of cattle. As in many parts of this country the practice of "soiling" is not common, it is permissible to state that it consists in cutting and feeding green feed in summer instead of allowing the animals to run on a pasture.

The system of handling manure is such that none is lost, either liquid or solid. No commercial fertilizers have ever been used, and no manure has been hauled from the city. The crops are all fed, and are thus largely returned to the land in the manure. Of course much valuable fertilizer is added to the farm annually from the rich mill products fed the cows. The roughage is all raised on the farm, but all the grain is bought.

The cows are fed balanced rations every day in the year. Every feed consists of three parts. A portion of it is some succulent material—silage in winter; and rye, timothy and clover, corn, peas and oats, or some other green crop in summer. A second portion consists of dry hay or fodder. This is used to give the manure proper consistency and adds much to the convenience of caring for the cows. A third portion consists of mill products, of which three kinds are used—bran, oil meal, and gluten.

The soiling crops used are as follows: Green rye, beginning about May 1, and continuing about four weeks, or until the rye is ready to cut for hay. Then timothy and clover are fed till peas and oats are ready. When the latter is cut for hay, the silo is opened (about July 4), and silage is fed till early corn is ready. Enough early corn is planted to last till late corn (planted about June 22) is ready. Late corn is then fed till it is time to put it in the silo. From this time forward silage is fed daily till green rye is available in the spring. No abrupt change is ever made in the system of feeding. Even the change from green corn to silage is made gradually.

Every particle of roughage fed on this farm, including hay and all soiling crops, is cut in quarter-inch lengths. Even the bedding is cut in this manner. There are two round silos on the farm, each 10 feet in diameter and 34 feet high. These together hold about 100 tons of silage, and this quantity of corn silage is produced on 4 acres.

We have given the account of a pioneer farmer, starting in with no experience, but going to work in a methodical manner to learn what he could from the experience of others, making a careful study of surrounding conditions, and adjusting himself to those conditions. This farmer, by applying scientific principles and business methods, has blazed a path into a region of great possibilities. The most important lesson to be learned from his achievements is that it is possible to cause land to yield twice or three times as much as the present average from what are considered good methods. The place has returned a gross income of upward of $2,500 a year, with a total expense of about $1,000. It would be feasible to raise poultry also on this place.

Many a farmer fails to get adequate returns from his farm because he stays at home too closely, puts in too many hours a day following the plow, and does not often enough visit good farmers in his neighborhood or other sections of the country where good farming is done. Furthermore, a man physically exhausted from a long, hard day's work is in no condition to follow and get much out of the literature of his business as reported in farm papers, agricultural bulletins, reports, and books, and without the advantage of all the information available from every possible source he will find awkward situations when he comes to replan his farm for profit.

Success in farming calls for the very best effort in a

man along all lines. That best effort is called for in replanning a farm for profit. The farmer who is dissatisfied with his income from the farm needs to think seriously as to whether or not his farm is planned right for the largest returns, remembering that good farming calls for keeping up the productiveness of the farm while getting maximum crops economically from the soil.

There should be a cement cistern in connection with every dairy barn, for holding the liquid manure. The gutters and yard should drain into the cistern. An ordinary pump will do for raising the liquid to a wagon tank, made like an ordinary water sprinkler. It is easy to give the land valuable fertilization by this inexpensive outfit. This liquid may be put on the bare land or on growing crops. It may be hauled to the fields early in the season, or even in the winter. For garden plants, also, it has great value after they have begun to grow, as well as in the preparation of the soil. Few farmers in Europe allow liquid manure to go to waste.

Beef farming is attractive, both from the standpoint of net returns and because it favors permanent agriculture. The practical feeder home-grows most of the roughage and a considerable portion of the grain that he feeds, purchasing such concentrates as cottonseed meal, which has a high protein content and is an efficient producer of market bloom and a fat carcass. In addition to feeding all that the farm produces and deriving the fertilizing value of the resultant manure, fertility is also added to the farm in the form of the purchased feedstuffs.

Learn How to Go Back to the Land

CONTINUED difficulties have caused an influx of city people to the country. Some prosper and are happy. Others find that the "turkeys do not grow on trees and already roasted." Those who have been accustomed to earning five dollars or more a day see the cash supply come slowly, and become discouraged. They do not know the principles of farming, and many mistakes are made.

There are always plenty to advise some great improvement which will require a goodly outlay of labor—these same advisers ever standing ready to do this work at their own price. The principle may be correct, but the labor bill is liable to be excessive.

No farmer would expect to go to the city and launch into a new business without losing money at the start. The sane way is to commence gradually, study conditions and methods thoroughly, and then advance with caution.

Many a city man has gone back to the crowded life discouraged, just because he did not know how to commence. Had he rented a small plot of ground and spent his spare moments in making a garden, there would have been renewed strength in the exercise, and he would have been better prepared in a single season to undertake the larger proposition.

His business principles would enable him to grasp the subject with comparative ease; but he should no longer follow the time-honored sentiment that the man who does not know how to do anything else can farm.

Farming is now a many-sided proposition. No other occupation requires so varied a knowledge. No other develops more fully the best that is in man.

The good and bad years will average up pretty well, after yielding returns more or less remunerative, as determined by the amount of knowledge possessed by the grower and the degree of skill with which this knowledge is brought to bear upon the problems incident to the business.

The factor of market is one that enters largely into the problem of securing adequate returns for our labors, and with such perishable products as small fruits under certain conditions, the problem ofttimes becomes a serious one.

The value of a product at any given time is determined by the law of supply and demand. The consuming class of any prescribed district will use but a certain quantity of any product at a value which will allow the grower exceptional remuneration. The demand at such values will always be within a prescribed limit, as an exceptional value causes any food products to become a luxury.

To illustrate: The strawberries on a certain market are selling freely at 15 cents per box. There is just about an even balance between supply and demand. We will suppose that the supply of such fruit on the market be increased 50 per cent. Will the entire amount then sell at 15 cents? Most assuredly not!

Drop the price to 12½ cents, however, and the increase in consumption will provide a market for the increased supply, for those who have been eating 15-cent berries will eat more freely of this fruit, and some who cannot afford to buy at the higher price will begin to do so at the lower figure.

A still greater increase in the quantity of such fruit placed upon the market will cause a still further decline in values, in order to maintain an even balance between supply and demand.

To be sure, when united in an association, growers may, through this association, often maintain more equable values; but the sphere of such influence must always be within prescribed limits.

The most important factor, perhaps, in demoralizing prices of products, such as small fruits, is the farmer grower who has but a small area devoted to their culture, and who sells the surplus for what can be most readily obtained, by cutting prices to the limit.

If the entire output of such stuff could be handled through an exchange, extreme slumps in values, market conditions extremely annoying to regular growers, might, at times, be avoided, for such extreme lowering of prices is ofttimes entirely unnecessary to make the demand keep pace with supply.

This manner of disposing of or preventing such undesirable conditions is, however, beset with not a few obstacles. To insure the success of such a plan requires exceptional ability on the part of the promoters.

As between the home and distant market, the former is the safer proposition. So between the larger and smaller centers of population, the former usually affords the safer market. In deciding upon a location, then, these points should be deeply considered.

One of the most prominent school officials in the northwest received his start in life as a result of a venture in fruit growing. He was born on a farm in Michigan and the conditions surrounding his boyhood days were hard. The father and his two boys toiled early and late on a farm of 100 acres. They had a poor bit of land, and both crops and prices were disappointing. Debt hung over the family like a pall. They could not sell their place at any reasonable figure. One day the father said:

"Boys, we'll either lose everything we have, or get out of this rut. I know of sixty acres that would be just right for fruit. We can buy it on easy terms, and by selling off some of our stock we can make a fair payment."

They took the place and set out ten acres of fruit trees

the first season. In six years they were out of debt and
the boys were entering college. They have risen to dis-
tinction in professional life. The aged father still owns
the two farms and is in comfortable circumstances, but he
has never made any money from grain raising.

Had it not been for some special lines such as fruit and
poultry, which he was driven to by dire necessity, he
would have lost what he started with and would have
been forced to cast his sons adrift without even a
common-school education. The sons are city men, but
they own farms and conduct them on diversified lines.
They have their land to fall back on in case of reverses
in their other vocations.

This story could be duplicated in ten thousand cases
where farmers failed abjectly until they began to diversify. The special opportunity just now is for a line of
produce which finds a ready market in large cities. The
constant cash demand and the good shipping facilities
give farmers in the older states an advantage over those
who are located farther from the trade centers.

A person of limited means, who is operating a small
tract near a city, should aim to supply a given number of
customers with fresh eggs every week the year through.
If hens are properly cared for, a flock of 200 will yield
a revenue of $25 per month in eggs and $10 in broilers.
Add to this $35 an income of $15 from ducks, making
the poultry department earn a total of $50 per month.
Chickens and ducks are delicacies when eight to ten weeks
old, and help to distribute the profits over the season.

About once a month, through cold weather, there ought
to be dressed pork for private customers. Pigs that
weigh 150 to 200 pounds are desirable for this class of
trade, and command good prices. They can be disposed
of in sections. There is a keen demand for country
sausage, and the small farmer should make it now and
again in winter. Twenty pigs will net $300, or an average

of $25 a month. A farmer, man or woman, who uses a
.little good judgment in conducting a small tract, will
make five acres produce $600 worth of potatoes, onions,.
beans, cabbage and celery. These crops distribute the
summer work nicely and supply a line of produce for
which there is a steady demand.

The items named furnish a living income without half
testing the capacity of a tract of twenty acres. There
could be as much more from strawberries, apples, cherries and honey. There is work for a span of horses, and
if a couple of mares are kept, it is feasible to raise colts,
which is another source of income. If the place amounts
to as much as forty acres, a dairy of ten or twelve cows
may be kept. This yields a substantial profit after allowing $400 a year for wages. By leaving out the dairy, an
ordinary family can do most of the work on a small farm.

I have a yard of bees which worked in a field of buckwheat containing about 10 acres. No other buckwheat
was within reach of them. They brought in over $200
worth of buckwheat honey from this small field.
This is an average of over $20 per acre. The flow of
basswood honey, secured almost entirely from the yield
on an adjoining farm, netted several hundred dollars.
These yields may surprise many, but they are not excessive. I have, during an exceptional year, secured a
yield treble the above from buckwheat, and have harvested a crop of $480 worth of honey from a basswood
grove of less than 10 acres. Honey represents one of the
largest crops, and nine-tenths of it is allowed to go to
waste. It might be harvested at less expense than any
other crop produced. The reason why farmers have not
kept abreast of the times in bee keeping is hard to find.

Avoid the Single Farming Interest

THE unsatisfactory condition of the dairy business shows the folly of depending on one commodity for success. If a farmer will give some of his energy to raising pork, beef, mutton, poultry, fruit and vegetables, he can gradually draw out of the production of milk, and will find his profits steadily growing.

It ought not to be difficult for a farmer owning a herd of cows to push forward a lot of hogs, calves and beef animals. He need not give up live stock raising because one branch of it is unprofitable. A fair proportion of horses, cattle, sheep and swine is advisable in order to keep up soil fertility. The needful thing is to avoid any single farming interest. Diversity is the order of the day, and will bring big profits to the farmer who makes his operations conform to market requirements.

As beef is extremely profitable just now, owing to a general scarcity, this is a safe line of enterprise for farmers, especially those who have dairy herds.

The feed problem is less difficult in this channel than in dairying, and all farmers ought to aim to keep up with the times in providing both early and late fodder crops and silage.

Any who have determined to turn from dairying to beef production, wholly or in part, should get a good Hereford or Shorthorn sire and develop stock suitable to the new programme. These breeds will make beef more cheaply than most of the others. In buying cattle to fatten for market, none will pay better than the breeds named.

There is a great future for the silo in this country. By

51

enabling farmers to keep a much larger number of animals, there will be no excuse for worn-out land. The increased amount of manure, combined with careful rotation of crops, will result in larger producing capacity.

Cattle are not the only animals to which silage can be fed. I have fed it to dairy cows, sheep, hogs, calves and horses. It is a great aid in the production of beef and pork as well as milk.

Raw ground beans are valuable as a feed for fattening cattle, particularly if used with corn or corn silage and some clover or alfalfa hay. The analysis of field beans shows 23.2 per cent protein, 54.9 of starchy material, 5.7 of ash and 1.5 of fat. Compared to cottonseed meal, which is so widely used by feeders, the beans contain about half as much protein and one-sixth as much fat. Soy beans are a good deal richer than field beans in feed value, being closely compared to cottonseed meal. Up to four or five pounds a day per 1,000 pounds live weight should be profitable, and would go best with some corn. About half that amount of soy bean meal would supply the same amount of protein, but would require more corn to balance it up.

Men differ as to the best methods of feeding and best feeds as much as they differ on a great many other subjects. The more we raise on our farms for feed for steers, the better we are off, and I think that fact is fully realized. It is an easy matter to purchase large quantities of expensive feeds, but will the final account justify the act? We should have a variety of feeds, and use them in a way that will be to the best interest all around.

Getting the Most Out of an Acre

THE most intensively cultivated region in Europe is that part of the province of Valencia, Spain, which lies between the mountains and the Mediterranean. It has a rainfall of only about seventeen inches a year, but so fertile is the soil and so skilled are its workers that it produces crops worth an average of $640 an acre. There are districts where 100 acres support 160 families and where single families live on the product of four-tenths of an acre. Farms are rented at about $30 an acre, and the tenant pays 48 cents an hour for pumped water, which flows in a stream of 200 gallons a minute. Almost all farming is done by hand, as minute attention is given to crops and even to individual plants. The average production of the principal crops is as follows, in metric tons of 2,204 pounds: Oranges, 400,000 tons; olives, 65,000; carob beans, 72,000; peanuts, 13,500; melons, 36,000; grapes, 87,000; peppers, 12,000; tomatoes, 27,000; wheat, 62,000; barley, 18,900; corn, 38,000; rice, 200,000.

Denmark contains only some 15,000 square miles. It maintains 2,500,000 persons and exports annually about $150,000,000 worth of butter, bacon and eggs. Danish butter invariably brings the highest price of any offered in the British market, and the quantity of these three exports is maintained equally with its quality, summer and winter.

Dr. Maurice Francis Egan, our Minister to Denmark, says: "Today the Danish farmer buys nothing individually. He uses no seeds till they have been tested by the experts furnished by the co-operative society. He buys his fertilizers, soya beans from Manchuria, cotton and

53

meal from the United States, through the co-operative society. He never kills his own hogs—though there are 500 hogs to every 1,000 persons in Denmark—but sends them to the co-operative bacon factories, which were founded some time in the 80's, when Germany refused the Danish hog because of an outbreak of swine fever. The Danes instantly founded, with the assistance of the Government, large co-operative bacon factories. In order to make dairying possible, the Dane had to regenerate the land exhausted by the lack of scientific treatment.

"Being an educated man, he was an open-minded man, and he induced his Government to furnish scientific experts who could finally answer any question he might ask. As an example, let us take the small farmer, with three cows, three hogs, four head of cattle, and a horse or two. He farms perhaps twelve acres. Now, it is a question with him as to the rotation of his crops; it is a question as to the amount of butter fat that each cow should produce. He has, through the co-operative society, the use of a scientific expert, who visits his farm every eighteen days and answers all these questions, after consultation with him.

"Furthermore, he keeps a duplicate set of books for the farmer, so that the farmer knows exactly the amount of butter fat each cow yields every week, when the cows are expected to calve, the value of the service of every bull in use, and the exact position of the farmer, economically and agriculturally. For this service the farmer pays the expert 30 cents yearly per cow, the Government paying the rest of the expert's salary, the expert being attached to the Royal Danish Co-operative Society."

These little farms of ten or twelve acres in Denmark commonly return the owner $800 to $1,200 profit in addition to family expenses and all costs of operating. It is not unusual for tracts of vegetables and flowers to pay $300 to $500 per acre.

Joseph Gould, an Illinois truck farmer, has for years cleared an average of $150 per acre on his land, in the western part of Cook county. Mr. Gould last season had a profit of $1,800 from ten acres, and his experience attracted general attention.

An acre of celery brought upward of $500, and before the celery plants were put out the same land produced a nice crop of earlier vegetables. The beets, carrots and tomatoes have been below the average in price, or his income would have been larger, for the yield was heavy. Mr. Gould has produced three crops of radishes and lettuce in a single season, and his land is kept in perfect condition. Nearly the entire tract raises two crops of vegetables within five months.

No ground is allowed to be idle; intensive cropping is practiced; early vegetables are carefully looked after, and a home market direct to the consumer for the greater part of the products is made by honest and courteous treatment.

His specialties before celery time are early peas, tomatoes, onions, radishes and lettuce, all of which grow rapidly enough so that the land can be used twice. Sweet corn, squashes, cucumbers, turnips and popcorn are grown every season, and for two years he has experimented with peppers. These thrive finely.

Crop rotation is methodically followed by Mr. Gould, in order to obtain the results noted. This is important for other reasons. It helps to destroy insects and fungous diseases, and provides fresh organic matter which decays quickly in the soil and by its stimulating action liberates from the soil itself more plant food than would otherwise be available. This successful truck farmer studies out the best methods of money-making and helps his neighbors to place their land on a paying basis.

Illinois florists with an investment of $10,000 or less for greenhouses and heating plants are able to clear $5,000 to

$8,000 from the production of flowers. They do not require more than two or three acres of land.

Orcharding is an attractive proposition. With sixty trees to an acre, of either apples or cherries, a nice income is secured from a small tract, with less labor than is required in other lines. A return of $250 to $400 per acre may be expected. Other fruits do equally well or better.

The following figures on production of apples were compiled by Mr. James O. Read, himself an expert horticulturist, while in the capacity of president of the State Board of Horticulture of Montana. While the figures given are based on the productiveness of the McIntosh Red apple, which takes first place in Mr. Read's state, they apply equally well to the popular Jonathan, which still strongly rivals the McIntosh Red and other fine varieties. From his experience as a fruit grower, and from other growers in the same district, Mr. Read places production of apples per tree at three-fourths of a box for the fifth year, one and one-half boxes for the sixth year, three boxes for the seventh year, four boxes for the eighth year, five boxes for the ninth year, and six boxes for the tenth year. On the foregoing basis is compiled the following statement of annual net profits from a standard apple orchard of ten acres, eighty trees to the acre: Fifth year, 600 boxes at $1.10 net, $660; sixth, 1,200 at $1.10, $1,320; seventh, 2,400 at $1.10, $2,640; eighth, 3,200 at $1.10, $3,520; ninth, 4,000 at $1.10, $4,400; tenth, $4,800 at $1.10, $5,280.

Plans to Keep Young People Interested

ONE of the problems that is all the time tugging at the heart of the farmer of this country is the absence from the farm of the young man. There are many neighborhoods in which not one in ten of the male members of the community may be truthfully called a young man. It used to be thought that the time of the young man belonged to his father till he was "one-and-twenty"; but the day of his departure has gradually dropped until now long before he is of age he is away at some other kind of business. With all the drift toward the country that we hear so much about today, it is a drift of men quite well along in years, and not a movement which takes the boys and young men back to nature. The shops, the factories, the stores and the offices are swallowing up sturdy young fellows everywhere.

Some of the best farmers of this country are finding a solution of the young-man question in the plan of settling their sons early on the farm. If these farmers are fortunate enough to be the owners of large farms, the problem is easier of solution; for then they may cut the old homestead up into two or three good-sized farms, build houses on these, and have their children near to them as long as they live.

This is a happy method of working out the problem. As the father and mother grow old, and less able to carry on the farm work themselves, they may have within easy call their boys and girls. Where a spirit of harmony and love exists between the different members of the family this state of affairs may be said to be almost ideal.

In case the old farm cannot be thus parceled out, it is nearly always possible to buy lands not far away upon which the young people may be located. The father may assume the responsibility of the purchase of these farms, giving the children a chance to pay for them on easy terms, and after a long lease of time, if desired, or if his own financial condition will permit, he may buy the lands desired, and give the deed to his children. This has a great point of advantage in the fact that thus the father and mother may, to a large extent, be the administrators of their own estates. This prevents much of the strife that comes up where the matter of settling up the estate is left until after the death of the parents.

The extension of this plan of settling the young people on nearby farms would do more than any other one thing to give us a satisfactory answer to the question: How shall we keep our young people on the farm? Let the children understand that when they are of legal age they shall have a place, either with the parents on the old farm or on a farm near the homestead, and the drift away from the country will receive a decided check.

Young men who have an ambition to conduct a farm on progressive lines ought to have the earnest support of their parents—not only because modern methods pay, but because they will be likely to hold the interest of a studious and energetic boy.

The modern farmer is not simply a corn planter, a wheat grower, a cattle breeder, a sheep feeder, or a poultry raiser, but often all of these and more combined. His farm, therefore, must be planned with reference to all of these operations and the harmonious dovetailing together of the different parts. In planning his farm for profit, the farmer must see all the different problems in a comprehensive way at the outset, omit the features that do not pay, and strengthen those that do.

He will soon perceive that his sons and daughters, if

they are reading people, are keenly interested in every move that indicates progress. They will co-operate in all betterment projects and will in time come to appreciate the advantages of their country life and vocation. It is important for young people to see that they have fine opportunities right at home.

The entertaining stories that are published from day to day about persons who have accomplished astonishing things by moving to some other part of the country do not always serve a good purpose.

It depends mainly on the man himself whether he is going to prosper anywhere or not. The many alluring things which are published to attract farmers are designed first of all to sell the land. They are not issued from philanthropic motives, and the individual will always find that success depends on his own efforts and intelligence, no matter what his environments may be.

It is interesting to learn of old friends who have "made good" in a new locality, and it is pleasant to think of the good times we might have in some other climate or on some other kind of farm; but we must not forget that the lure of the big farm, the fruit ranch, the mild winters, and other far-away things have been fatal to scores where they have drawn one to affluence.

When a man is east, he is apt to think that the west offers him golden opportunities. When he is west, he sees the advantage of the eastern markets and transportation. If he has been drawn south, he may discover that the warm climate takes the tuck out of him, while in the far north it may turn out to be too cold for a comfortable living. The truth is that all sections of this republic are good, and all have special advantages.

A practical farm mother in Wisconsin has solved a problem which had become the most serious of her life. Incidentally, she may have conferred a benefit on the farming community generally.

Her growing children, a son and a daughter, were becoming tired of the old home, and had an ambition to try city life. Having acquired a dislike for the farm, they were planning to go out into the world and do for themselves.

The more animated these young folks became over their new ambition, the more painful the subject became to their parents. Mother love and sense finally found a way to settle the question in a manner pleasing to all.

It was proposed to try some experiments along the line of modern farming and to give the boy and girl an opportunity to own something for themselves and enjoy the profits resulting from their efforts. The mother offered to furnish the capital necessary for raising squabs on a large scale, with the understanding that the son and daughter would care for the birds, and the three share in the proceeds.

The sagacious proposition aroused interest at once, and the project was launched. Every day brought new and interesting developments, and, with some modification of the other labors which had been required of them, the old farm became an attractive place to the young folks.

The squab industry has now been growing on their hands for two years, and is highly profitable. The resourceful mother has brought forward other ideas for stimulating the interest and energy of her children, who are today happy in their country life. All idea of going to live in town has been abandoned. Mother wit has saved the boy and the girl for the farm.

Either individual ownership or profit-sharing is a good thing to institute among the young people in the country. If the working day can be made shorter and the drudgery of the farm lessened, boys and girls will not be so eager to go to the city.

If the average farmer worked about one-half as much land, and diversified his efforts so as to secure an income every month of the year, he would be better off and his family would be happier.

For instance, an acre of ground under greenhouses devoted to flowers would yield better returns than fifty acres of wheat or corn, besides affording a delightful occupation for the family. An acre of strawberries will ordinarily return larger profits than ten acres of grain. The market for truck and fruit grows better yearly. The little things give variety and spice to life on the farm— and they pay better from every point of view.

Many boys and girls might be saved from the follies and misfortunes of city life if their parents would put some thought into new plans for arousing their interest in home affairs. Give them plots of ground for their own use, and encourage them in making experiments with vegetables and fruits. A delightful way is for the young folks to form a partnership if they are old enough to do useful work about the farm. The girls should have charge of poultry and flowers, while the boys manage vegetables and fruit.

Young people who live in a city, and would like to try country life, have an excellent opportunity to gain a valuable experience and earn money during vacation by tilling the soil. No plan could be better than this for the many who are working their way through school. The production of vegetables and flowers is immensely profitable, as there is a constant cash demand in every town, big and little.

The pleasure of such an experiment, if rightly conducted, would be hard to exaggerate. It is nearly always possible to obtain a small tract of land convenient to a car line. One point to be considered is that there is little time to waste in walking. The rent would be $10 to $20 for two acres.

Boys or girls who already live on a farm, and who have an ambition to test their ability in some fancy line of pro-

duction, should get up a profit-sharing scheme. Undoubtedly they would find their parents as willing and eager as
themselves, not merely to develop additional sources of
revenue but to stimulate a love for farming among their
sons and daughters.

For young people who wish to see what they can
accomplish with land, a partnership of two is best. This
is because there is a great deal of work in connection with
raising and marketing flowers and vegetables, and the
enthusiasm is most likely to be kept up when there are
partners to share the labor and planning.

It is best to begin the enterprise by arranging for a
little help from some one who can furnish a team at odd
times. There will be some hauling of vegetables all summer, but perhaps the team would not be required more
than twice a week. It would be quite feasible to rent a
horse and wagon for the season or even to buy them.

If such vegetables as lettuce, radishes, onions, beets and
carrots are planted during May, the first crop can be
taken from the ground in July, and a second crop
put in. Celery, onions, beets and cabbage work nicely
into this scheme. A good crop of potatoes ought to be
secured between June 1 and September 15. The late
vegetables will require some attention after school opens,
and a little help may have to be hired.

I would advise renting the land for two or three seasons, for a lot of preparatory work can be done in
the spring, on Saturdays and at odd times, enabling the
young farmers to raise two crops. A study in double
cropping is advisable, for it means extra profits. An
enterprise of this kind, properly conducted, on a couple
of acres will return an income of several hundred dollars,
besides affording a vast amount of pleasure and valuable
experience.

Make an effort to keep the weeds out of the land and
do not allow the soil to become caked. After the first lot

of quick-growing produce has been taken off, stir up the land with disk or cultivator, and replant. Nearly all successful gardeners make their land produce two crops of vegetables in a season. On a tract of two acres, a plan something like the following should be adopted:

Plant one acre to potatoes, half an acre to lettuce, radishes, beets and carrots, and half an acre to onions. For the second part of the season, put out a quarter of an acre of celery, a quarter of an acre of beets, an acre of late cabbage and half an acre of onions. If the young farmers find the season going too fast for them, they should not attempt two crops that year, but get ready to follow the programme outlined for the next summer.

All of the products named return large profits. Cabbage ought to pay at the rate of $200 an acre; celery, $400; onions, $250; beets and carrots, $100; potatoes, $150. There is no exaggeration in the figures given. Any industrious youth can gain a fine income in this way. The only capital required is for seed, rent of land and such team work as must be done. I will say frankly that there will be mistakes and accidents which will upset some of the calculations, but these will be few after the first season. Hence I advise taking the land for two or more years.

A farmer reports that in a single season seventeen acres of pickles and thirty-one acres of onions and onion sets cashed in far more than the market value of the expensive land on which they grew. Last year he broke the record with $4,600 from ten acres of onions. For five years he has averaged $190 an acre from pickles.

Profit Sharing with Fruit and Vegetables

THE difficulty of keeping young people interested in farm work and rural life has made me an advocate of profit-sharing. After taking part in a number of experiments along this line, I am firmly convinced that the principle is a good one to put in force. It need not be very extensive at first, but when boys and girls are growing up and deciding on a vocation, the profit-sharing system ought to be adopted, and include the whole farm.

While the young folks are putting in about half their time at school, and rendering substantial help through the summer, and perhaps nights and mornings, they are apt to feel the drudgery of farm life, and begin making plans to get away as soon as possible.

This is a critical period, and many parents fail to bring the minds of their sons and daughters back to an enjoyment of their farm home. It is usually the long hours of seemingly thankless toil that cause the boys and girls to dislike agriculture and rush to the cities. I contend that profit-sharing is one of the first steps necessary to remedy this great difficulty in the country. It not only has the element of fairness and justice in it but it may serve to stimulate interest in agricultural pursuits, and so mold the entire career of a young man or woman.

I would begin by allowing the boys and girls to have a share in such things as poultry, bees, live stock and fruit —most particularly fruit. For one thing, this would result in the production of more and better fruit on the average farm. Orchards are shamefully neglected by most people who carry on general farming. The work required to keep trees in proper condition is of a kind that can be put off, and in the pressure of other things during the fall and spring rush, it usually is deferred until the orchard is an unsightly waste. It is much the same with all kinds of small fruits. This, also, is looked upon as a side issue, and therefore neglected.

Apples, cherries, berries and various other fruits can be grown with profit in all parts of this country, with the possible exception of two or three of the most northerly prairie states. Can any one say that apples or cherries pay less than grain, or require more work?

The truth is, they pay far better per acre than any of the ordinary farm crops. It is only through neglect that they fail to return liberal profits, and if each farmer would get up a profit-sharing plan with regard to his fruit, and bring in the entire family, including the hired help, there would be a lot of pleasure in the project, and a nice sum of money for every individual concerned.

In one case that I have in mind, an old orchard of about twenty apple trees was extended until it occupies four acres, and there is an additional acre of strawberries and raspberries near by. This five-acre fruit tract is a joint family enterprise. The head of the house gets his share for furnishing the land and the money required to buy the young trees. He has been investing about $20 a year in young trees, to secure new varieties and increase the acreage. Last year alone he received $300 as his share of the profits on five acres. Two sons and his wife and daughter get a like amount each, there being a revenue of $1,500. It was a favorable fruit season, and the returns may be less on an average. However, there is an abundance of pin money in that family, and the young people are receiving some wholesome training. They are learning to raise fruit in a businesslike way; to care for the trees; to meet market needs, and to handle money that comes to them as a result of their skill and industry.

New Vocation for the City Family

THE city family taking a little farm should be impressed
with the fact that the novelty is pretty sure to wear off
and leave the work irksome and in some cases unsatisfactory. For this reason, every step must be carefully considered. The location is the first thing to be determined.
If city employment is to be continued, it is imperative to
have the farm home within an hour's run. Otherwise, too
much time is wasted in traveling back and forth and too
much money spent for transportation.

A farm located within the range of suburban service
permits city employment, affords good market facilities,
insures school and social advantages, and is quite sure to
advance in value, so that the investment may be profitable
in case circumstances ever compel a change.

It would be well to do with a very small tract—say,
twenty acres—for the sake of the advantages enumerated.
This land is worth, ordinarily, $4,000, and house, barn
and other improvements will make the aggregate $6,000
at the very least. If there are resources in the family, it
would be wise to make the investment about $7,000, in
order that the dwelling might be tasty and comfortable.

The earning power of such a place, devoted to poultry,
vegetables, fruit, etc., is $2,000 a year and upward. This
is a large interest on the $7,000 invested. If the average
salaried man can clear $2,000 in addition to the main part
of the family living, he can afford to give his whole
time to the farm, even if he has to pay interest on the
investment.

With most people getting started on a little farm, it has

to be a straight business proposition. The head of the family must count his or her time worth at least $1,000 and another $1,000 is to be reckoned for investment and improvements, if any progress is to be made. Granting that visible conditions are in line with these suggestions, the owner need not be afraid of a farm enterprise. If he has a little capital, and is known as a man of sense and character, any banker will carry the necessary debt for him, and give him a chance to work out the problem to its logical conclusion. If members of the family have the taste and ability to handle poultry, flowers, vegetables and fruit, there need be no doubt about ultimate success.

A line of work must be chosen which will appeal to the young people. It is a safe proposition that no little farm project will fail if the boys and girls of the family are interested. If they enjoy their work on the land, they will soon come to appreciate the possibilities of this location. Once they see that it can be made to pay better than the ordinary city employment, their interest will be stimulated and they will be contented with country life.

The diversity of products on a twenty-acre tract can be sufficient to give to each member of the family a certain responsibility as well as a share in the profits. Such lines as live stock, poultry, gardening and floriculture appeal strongly to young people, and, fortunately, there are large profits in these features. If bees, squabs, mushrooms or other novelties that possess practical value can be added, so much the better.

If it is desired to have a tract larger than twenty acres, the same investment, or even a smaller one, will do by locating farther from the city. When a place is chosen several miles from a station, a line of products must be handled which will not require quick marketing. It is practicable to raise poultry, hogs, potatoes and fruit when the location is so far out that not more than one trip a week can be made.

Occasionally city people who have saved a little money consult me about getting started on a farm. It is necessary to have some capital, and the more the better, but the situation is alway. hopeful for the family that has prudence and energy sufficient to accumulate $1,000.

To move from the city to the country, with no capital, would appear to be a serious undertaking, and the writer would not advise city people to undertake it. However, if a small capital has been saved up, the move can be made.

A good method of procedure for the man with $1,000 would be to select ten acres close to some suburban station and within an hour's ride of the city. The price would be $1,500 to $2,000. He could get a banker with whom he has had business relations, or a personal friend, to finance the project to the extent of $3,000 or $4,000. It might be best to retain city employment for the first year, while equipping the little farm and getting things started.

Substantial progress can be made in this first year. The family may start a good garden, an orchard, a flock of poultry, keep a few cows and pigs, and grow most of their own table supplies.

If the wife knows how to prepare food and understands how to be frugal, the actual money expense for the farm living may be made very small, while at the same time the standard of living, from the standpoint of food, may be much higher than is possible even with wealthy people in the city.

At first the principal aim should be to produce truck crops for home consumption. As experience is gained, the industry may be enlarged and a market established. Many men have made the transition in this manner; others have started with one or two cows, and have let the business grow from the profits obtained in it; others

have succeeded by beginning in a small way with poultry
or fruit.

The knowledge gained in this way, both as regards the
details of farming and concerning methods of marketing, finally enables the beginner to abandon his city
employment.

Another method that might be almost equally satisfactory would be to buy an equipped farm of forty or fifty
acres, at a price around $5,000, paying $1,000 cash.   In
such circumstances, it would be necessary to give up city
employment, as there would be plenty of work to occupy
the entire family.   Any industrious man getting this kind
of a start will succeed.   The principal care must be to
raise a line of produce for which there is a good cash
demand and which will give the owner something to sell
every week in the year.   An orchard of 200 trees and a
large poultry plant, from which features an additional
$3,000 might be cleaned up, could be added.   Instead
of the orchard, he might prefer to erect two or three
greenhouses, and produce flowers.   The profits then would
be still larger.   Potatoes, onions, beans, strawberries,
celery and asparagus pay nicely.

The degree of success depends largely on the man and
his family.   Any industrious person can secure a fair
income and a comfortable living on ten acres.   He can do
it in various lines, but a diversity is the surest way.

A plan that would distribute the work evenly over the
season, and insure a fair income, would include three
acres of corn, two of pasture, two of fruit, two of
vegetables and one for buildings.   This contemplates a
horse, a cow, chickens, ducks and a few pigs.   Something
is to be gained by using the orchard land for vegetables,
and the fruit trees will be benefited by this regular and
thorough cultivation.

Good Selling Is a Farmer's Need

NINE-TENTHS of the writing on agricultural subjects is devoted to production. The other tenth has to do with selling. It is time to reverse this system of giving information to the farmer. There should be more light on methods of selling produce, and less on the way to raise it.

The farmer needs to be shown how to obtain the largest possible returns on the things he has ready for market. His proportion of what the ultimate consumer pays is altogether too small. That is where he needs advice. A little practical help along this line would be appreciated by men and women who know more about the producing end than the writers who are so prolific with ideas on how to run a farm.

As a rule, farmers make poor bargains. They buy wrong and sell wrong, and are apt to be imposed upon by glib brokers, agents, merchants and other city people with whom they have to do business. The farmer needs a certain kind of coaching. He may be an expert at one end of the business, but after he has raised a nice lot of hogs or chickens, or a crop of potatoes and corn, he is at the mercy of city people who deal in such products. The city man fixes the price on all the farmer has to sell, as well as on all he has to buy.

A berry grower in Cherokee county, Kansas, sold his last season's crop for 90 cents a crate. In one crate he placed this note: "Will the buyer of this crate of berries inform the undersigned, who grew them, how much he paid for them?" In due time a reply came from an ultimate consumer, in Detroit, Michigan, saying he paid $2.40

for the crate. Middlemen got $1.50 for finding a buyer for these berries, while the farmer, who did all the work of growing them, received only 90 cents.

The Kansas Agricultural College, by the establishment of a co-operative buying and selling bureau for all Kansas farm products, will undertake to save the unnecessary middlemen's profits to farmers in that state. This announcement, made by President Waters, before 800 farmers in the co-operation meeting held in connection with the State Farmers' Institute, was greeted with cheers. By resolutions, unanimously passed, the meeting, after considering many plans, with a determination to do something, had just asked the college to establish such a bureau. The announcement by President Waters, promptly granting the request, came as a surprise.

A co-operative bureau at the agricultural college will be the first of that kind in the United States. When developed to its highest efficiency, which may take several years, it will mean a saving of millions of dollars to Kansas farmers annually. It will shorten the distance between the producer and the consumer, thus promoting direct selling. For instance, a farmer with a carload of potatoes to sell need not dispose of them to the local commission man. Instead, he would list his carload with the co-operative bureau. This bureau, in touch with markets all over the United States, would immediately place him in communication with a market for his potatoes. Whereupon the farmer would ship his product direct to the buyer.

That such a bureau would be successful was apparent after the organization of a clearing house for apple growers and apple buyers, a year ago. The college had helped farmers to find good seed and good breeding stock, but the clearing house was the first assistance offered in marketing produce. Upon the announcement, last fall, that the college was again prepared to open a clearing

house for apples, 140 letters from buyers and sellers were
received in one day. Between 300 and 400 cars of apples
were sold through this department of the extension divi-
sion last fall. Since then plans for the organization of
the co-operative bureau have been under way.

An illustration of what women may accomplish in marketing produce is furnished by the experience of a mother
and daughter who own 40 acres near a provincial town in
the central west. The entire responsibility for the management of the place and the care of the family fell to
their lot recently, owing to the protracted illness of the
husband and father.

The following table will show in itself about how the
farm is divided as to crops, fruits, pasturage, and the way
the work is diversified. The figures represent one year's
gross earnings:

Milk from ten cows	$1,400
Three hundred pounds honey, at 20 cents	60
Ten hogs fattened, at eleven months	225
Eggs from 200 hens	240
Fruit and vegetables	160
Surplus poultry sold	75
	$2,160

About $600 may be deducted from this total for wages,
groceries, repairs and mill feed; but their apiary, orchard
and dairy herd are worth several hundred dollars more
than at the beginning of the year.

These women have their horse and carriage, and par-
ticipate in most of the social affairs of the neighborhood.
Their life is not all work, but is strenuous enough even
for these days, when there is a premium set on people
who do things.

They say that if they were farther from town, and
could not have private customers for their produce, they

could make up the loss by raising more hogs and potatoes or such products as do not require too great a proportion of man labor.

By adding a half-acre of cucumbers and an acre of strawberries, they are now able to hire more help for the out-door work, without decreasing the net earnings of the little farm.

These women farmers, one of whom was equally successful as a schoolteacher, use their brains as well as their hands, and their affairs are systematically managed, so that each class of work gets proper attention at the proper time.

I have found that the production of market cream pays well. It is always salable, costs less to ship than the whole milk, and returns more than can be gained by any other method of handling.

The eight-gallon can of milk brings $1 to $1.25 at wholesale, but the cream from the same quantity brings $1.50, besides leaving more than six gallons of warm skimmed milk for calves, pigs and poultry. There is a further saving in hauling and expressage.

If the producer serves private customers only, he gains the profits of both retailer and wholesaler. The increasing demand for cream for family use, ice cream and cooking forms a desirable outlet for dairy products. There is no danger of over-production. Separating machinery is cheap and simple.

The easiest way to increase an income without greatly increasing cost is by raising the margin of profit by producing products of high quality, marketing them at the right time, at the right market, and in a neat and attractive manner.

The expense of marketing poultry products is relatively small, as they contain a high value in small bulk, and can be shipped considerable distances with very little loss. The best trade in the large cities pays the highest premium, and where one can ship a guaranteed amount for the entire year, or during the season, of a product such as broilers, he can safely try for such a market; but where his output is limited, it is a waste of time. There is often a home market which, with a little care, can be developed in a satisfactory manner, and will pay the small producer much better than the larger city markets.

According to the poultryman's location and production, he may choose any of the following methods of disposing of his products:

Selling direct to the consumer.

Selling direct to the retailer.

Selling to the commission merchant.

Selling direct to the consumer offers the greatest returns for the products, as all expenses of commission, etc., are eliminated.   This market is, however, usually limited, unless a parcel post trade is secured in a city or village, in which case he can usually develop a retail patronage which will take his entire output.

The most satisfactory method of selling direct to consumers is to supply hotels, restaurants and clubs, they usually contracting for the entire output, for which they are generally willing to pay a premium, and it is much easier to ship the entire production to one place at certain definite times than to spend much time and labor in dividing the same amount among many small consumers.

In many cases it will be possible to sell one's eggs and dressed poultry direct to some retail grocer, who in turn will be glad to get them and pay a good price, as he can sell them to his high-class trade, and, knowing that they are perfectly fresh, can develop a good business for the poultryman.   It may be necessary to go to some distant city or distributing point to find this market, but it will always pay, when once secured.

Make every customer a friend, and each will bring you another customer.   The endless chain will then be

begun, the possibilities of which no one cares to limit.
To make every customer a friend, it is necessary to treat
him well, to have the stock sold a little better than it has
been described, to give full value and something over on
each order. Sell only first-class stock. Don't let the
temptation of a few immediate dollars lead you to send
out stock that will not be a good advertisement for you.
Every fowl sold is a good advertisement, if the fowl is
good—a bad advertisement, if the fowl is a bad one.
Don't use a cull, even if you sell it for a cull. The buyer
will say to some one that he bought the specimen of you,
and will be sure to forget to add that he bought it as a
cull. Culls are a bad advertisement—trade-killers, not
trade-bringers. They will help to bury you in obscurity,
not to bring you prominence. Be strictly honest. Tell
things as they are. Get a reputation for doing just what
you promise to do, of selling just what you offer to sell.
Be prompt. People like promptness in business. If you
say you will make a shipment of fowls on Monday, ship
them on Monday, so as not to disappoint the customer.
If the shipment is unavoidably delayed, write the customer and tell him the fact and the reason for it.

The most prosperous farmers are those who have had
the good sense to organize in communities, to control the
supply of their products, to market them intelligently, and
place them on sale at a time when the demand is normal
and at fair prices. Slowly the benefits of organization are
becoming recognized; but not until it has been generally
adopted, and its power exercised in its broadest sense, will
the farmers of America come to that prosperity which
their industry and their importance entitle them to.

It requires more business ability, a higher executive
faculty, to run a fruit farm than to run a grain farm. If
you have a hundred bushels of wheat, oats, potatoes or
corn to sell, you take it to the nearest market and accept
whatever you are offered. It is not always so with fruit,

for you can retail the fruit or can more often fix the price
for the fruit than you can for ordinary farm produce.
Business ability is required in learning where is the best
market for fruit of a certain character or kind. It is a
fact that while a certain fruit may be cheap in New
York, it may sell at a profitable price in Boston, Pitts-
burgh, or in Minneapolis, St. Paul, Chicago or St. Louis.

The man who sells fruit should be thoroughly posted on
its value, and should inform the purchaser of the extra
quality of certain varieties.

There are many dishonest commission houses. It is not
safe to send fruit to a commission house which is not
highly recommended to you or with which you have not
had satisfactory experience.

An Associated Press dispatch says: "Unskillful
handling of poultry and eggs costs the people of the
United States $45,000,000 annually, is the conclusion of
the Kansas State board of health, after six months' investigation, in which expert produce men from the department of agriculture were used. The price of eggs
is high, says the report, and competition is keen, but the
producer gains nothing, not because there is a combination to keep the original price to the wholesaler down,
but because of the manner in which eggs and poultry are
handled. Because of the large number of farmers who
are careless in marketing their eggs, the careful farmer
is forced to accept the same price as is paid his less industrious neighbor. In Kansas alone, this loss is estimated
at more than $1,000,000 a year."

Parcels Post Brings Dinner Fresh from Farm

FARMERS living anywhere within fifty miles of a city may send packages of ten pounds to their customers for 32 cents. They do not have to haul them to an express office three or four miles away, but the rural route wagons pick them up and they are delivered in town almost as promptly as are letters or other mailable articles. The new law allows the transportation of any kind of produce, provided it is securely wrapped. Eggs, honey, berries, butter and cream are not excluded, but they must be so packed that they can not damage other mail matter. Such products are to be marked "Perishable."

The system of handling country produce has been both expensive and bad. Fresh eggs, pure cream and dainty things like broilers and sausage have been hard to get at any price. Such articles are only an aggravation when they are stale and handled in promiscuous lots. Under the new plan, a ten-pound Sunday dinner, or such a shipment any day or every day, will go straight from the farmer to the city family, at a cost of 32 cents for postage. This 3 cents a pound added to the price of the products is a trifle compared to the transportation and middlemen's charges under the old system.

The parcels post will prove a boon to city housekeepers in enabling them to deal directly with producers and secure fresh goods for table use. The postoffice department fixes eleven pounds as the maximum for parcels. This is sufficient to carry the main ingredients of a Sunday dinner for a city family, and there is nothing to prevent the forwarding of more than one package. It is not only in the line of economy to thus deal with producers, but the quality of edibles consumed by a household will be improved.

In nearly all discussions of the parcels post scheme the advantages to city housekeepers have been obscured by questions affecting country merchants and express companies. The vital thing with a majority of people is the effect on the cost of living. It is entirely feasible for tens of thousands of families in large cities to establish direct buying connections with producers. On the other hand, the important thing to the farmer is not his ability to get goods from mail-order houses more conveniently, but the establishment of facilities by which he can obtain approximately the retail rate for miscellaneous produce. The new system will enable him to go into mixed and intensive farming, and make daily cash sales to consumers at fair prices.

There has been a constant outcry among farmers against the alleged extortions of middlemen. The unsatisfactory handling of poultry and eggs, fruits, honey, squabs and other delicacies has driven many farmers out of these lines. They have missed the big profits because of bad selling facilities, and in a sense have been forced to confine their operations to one or two staples like grain or milk. With producers in a helpless condition, the large buying companies have controlled the trade, much to the disadvantage of farmers generally.

The widespread movement just now to correct unjust conditions in the milk industry is one indication that American farmers are trying to get out of the rut and do things as business men would do them.

The earning capacity of land is fully twice as much in mixed farming as under a dairy or grain system. There should be a balanced programme of poultry, hogs, cows, vegetables and fruit. These things belong together, and insure an even distribution of labor and a regular cash

income. The consumptive demand is keen and seems to
be growing more urgent year by year. Prices for a
variety of commodities are on such a high level that
liberal profits are assured as soon as selling arrangements
are right.

A factor that should have a marked influence in improving the farmers' chances of finding good markets for
new laid eggs is the parcels post now in experimental
operation. Doubtless it will not be long before enter-
prising manufacturers will follow the lead of German
manufacturers and place upon the market boxes suitable
for carrying even so fragile things as eggs safely through
the mail. When these are obtainable and when the parcel
post service gets in good working order, farmers in
even out-of-the-way places, but with first-class eggs to
sell, can easily work up trade with special customers in
nearby or even in distant towns and cities. The out-
look for such developments has never been better.

The celery growers of Kalamazoo, Mich., in one year
grew 800,000 boxes of celery, each containing six dozen
stalks. The value of this crop is $800,000—one dollar a
box.

Soil Improvement and More Profitable Farming

GRAIN crops in America are altogether too light and uncertain for profitable agriculture. This is largely due to lax methods of cultivation. In nearly all cases where soil impoverishment is the direct cause of unsuccessful farming, it can be shown that fertilization and the rotation of crops have been neglected.

This is true on thousands of farms where the equipment is ample and the work of plowing and seeding is quite thorough. The proof is clear that many landowners do not give attention to soil conservation. It is owing to this that much of the best land is deteriorating. In the newer states of the west, where large farms are the rule, and the soil is still rich, a common fault is improper methods of tillage.

Despite the fertility of soil and the benefits of climate, the wheat yield per acre annually is less than 14 bushels, while England's is 32, Germany's 28, Holland's 34 and France's 20. Oats make an equally distressing showing in comparison; and potatoes yield 85 bushels to the acre in this country, against 200 or more in Great Britain, Belgium and Germany.

The average yield of corn per acre is 28 to 35 bushels, as shown by official statistics; but in all contests, no matter where held, a yield of 100 to 125 bushels is commonly obtained. In many instances of competitive corn-raising, tracts which had formerly produced 25 to 50 bushels per acre have in the hands of experts yielded upward of 100 bushels.

These are powerful arguments in favor of careful and intelligent farming. Landowners ought to perceive that the real profits in grain production only come when crops above the average are raised. Agriculture is a sorrowful spectacle when men with a suitable equipment of animals and machinery secure 10 to 12 bushels of wheat and 20 to 25 bushels of corn to the acre on our rich virgin soils, while in European countries the average is twice or three times as much. It must be remembered that when the average of a crop is 14 bushels a great many farmers fall below this figure and these constitute failures which are both pitiful and unnecessary.

A number of essential principles must be adopted by farmers if they are to raise profitable crops. It is necessary to supply nitrogen for corn and wheat by growing legumes, but before leguminous crops, such as clover and alfalfa, can be grown, nearly every acre of land must be limed to correct the acidity. Fortunately there is an abundance of lime. Crushed lime rock can be purchased in carload quantities at a cost not to exceed $3 per ton laid down at any railroad station.

The physical condition of the soil is injured by loss of organic matter. As the organic matter is destroyed the soils become less mellow, they plow up hard and lumpy, they crust severely after rains and cultivate with greater difficulty. The crusting of the soil, due to the lack of organic matter, is perhaps the most serious physical defect. When soils crust badly it becomes almost impossible to successfully start such crops as alfalfa and grasses, and difficulty is sometimes experienced in securing a good stand of crops like wheat and corn.

The liberation of plant food from the soil is directly dependent upon the supply of organic matter. Organic matter is also the food of a countless number of beneficial bacteria that inhabit every fertile soil. These bacteria are largely responsible for the liberation of plant food

from the soil particles. It therefore follows that as the
supply of organic matter becomes less the number of
beneficial bacteria decreases and less plant food is made
available. Soils deficient in organic matter hold less
moisture than those well supplied with humus. Humus,
or organic matter, is spongy in nature and when incorporated in the earth holds the soil grains apart, giving
large openings into the soil for water to enter, and at the
same time the spongy nature of the organic matter holds
the water within the soil after it has entered. It is estimated that 100 pounds of sand will hold approximately
22 pounds of water, and 100 pounds of clay about 55
pounds of water, but 100 pounds of humus will hold 143
pounds of water. It is therefore evident that the more
humus a soil contains the greater its water holding
capacity.

The organic matter or humus must be supplied either
by plowing under leguminous crops and straw and cornstalks or by using for feed and bedding all the crops
grown on the farm and returning the manure to the land
with the least loss possible.

A rotation suggested is corn with one-half the field
seeded to a legume such as sweet clover or alfalfa, followed the second season with barley or oats, with one-
half the land in cowpeas or soy beans where the winter
catch crop has been plowed under; third year, wheat or
rye, in which clover or meadow grass has been sown;
fourth year, clover, or clover and timothy; fifth year,
wheat and clover, or timothy and clover; sixth year,
clover or mixed grass crop. In succeeding chapters
other combinations suitable to mixed farming are set
forth.

In grain farming most of the coarse products should be
returned to the soil and occasionally a crop of clover
clipped and left on the ground. To avoid clover sickness
it may sometimes be necessary to sow red clover or alsike

for about every third rotation. Where the growth of corn is not too rank, cowpeas or soy beans make a satisfactory catch crop and these may well be used in successive rotations to prevent insect or fungous pests obtaining a foothold through the too continuous use of clover. It should be remembered that the roots of clover contain one-half as much nitrogen as the tops and the roots of cowpeas only about one-tenth as much as the tops. In grain crops about two-thirds of the nitrogen is deposited in the grain and one-third in the stalk and , roots.

On all lands not subject to overflow phosphorus should be applied in considerably larger amounts than are required for the need of the crop actually growing at that time. The fine ground natural rock phosphate can be used successfully and is the most economical form of phosphorus in all crop systems. The first application should be at least one-half ton per acre, and a ton would be better. Subsequently one-half ton applied every four to six years will suffice until the total phosphorus contained in the soil reaches 2,000 pounds per acre. This will require a total application of five to six tons of raw phosphate.

For quick action and in emergencies steamed bone meal or acid phosphate may be used, but this is a much more expensive form than the ground natural rock. Good phosphate direct from the mine in carload lots costs about 3 cents per pound, while steamed bone meal costs 12 cents per pound, and acid phosphate 12 cents.

The loss of phosphorus by leaching is very small unless the land is subject to overflow or excessive drainage, so that erosion losses occur. Phosphorus applied is not removed except in the form of mature crops. Phosphorus and limestone may be applied at any time during the rotation, but the limestone is best applied on plowed land so that it may be worked into the soil during the process of cultivation. Phosphate is best applied either with manure or spread on the land broadcast just before a clover crop or clover stubble is plowed under.

Farmers have been taught that the conditions existing in land that has been newly brought into cultivation from forest conditions are due to the fact that the soil abounds in humus, or organic decay, and that this humus, while containing plant food, has a larger office in the darkening of the soil and thus rendering it more retentive of warmth. It makes the soil mellow and prevents its crusting and baking hard, and above all makes it retentive of moisture so that crops are carried through a dry spell more successfully.

In most of our old soils the long continued and careless cultivation has robbed the soil of this valuable humus and any effort towards its improvement must depend on the bringing back of the conditions that existed in the freshly cleared soil.

The legume crops then not only enable us, through bacterial life that exists with them, to gather the nitrogen that floats as a gas in the air and get it combined in the soil for the use of crops, but they enable us to restore to the soil the humus making materials that were formerly supplied by the forest growth.

With cowpeas and crimson clover the whole face of the country has been changed in many localities where formerly the soil was virtually worn out. There are splendid farms and farmers growing rich on lands formerly thought to be worthless.

The humus restored to the soil through these legumes has enabled farmers to use commercial fertilizers more profitably, because the moisture-retaining nature of the organic decay dissolves the fertilizer that would have been almost useless, and the growing of truck and small fruits for the leading markets has developed in a wonderful way.

The old sandy fields were almost destitute of humus, but the cowpea and the crimson clover have restored it, and hence there has been success attending the efforts of the farmers.

Through growing legumes and feeding them to stock and returning the manure to the ground, we can profitably restore the new soil conditions.

The cowpea will grow on the poorest of soils and over all the south is the most valuable of legumes, and in the north it can be profitably used to get the moisture-retaining humus in the soil and thus help in the restoration of the conditions that formerly existed when clover did flourish and where it now fails.

After a crop of rye or oats is taken off in the early summer there is plenty of time to disk or plow the field and sow soy beans for a late summer crop. It can be used as pasturage or for hay.

Plants in their growth make use of thirteen chemical elements, nine of which they secure directly from the soil. These are called the mineral plant foods; they are phosphorus, potassium, calcium, magnesium, sodium, iron, silicon, chlorin and sulphur.

Soil Conservation Easy to Understand

It is easy to grasp the main essentials of soil improvement, and it is important that considerable study be given to this subject. Many farms now on the market are run down and need a little scientific attention, and thousands of farmers are wishing that they knew how to build up the fertility of their land.

One of the first essentials is a rotative scheme which will tax the land less severely than exclusive grain growing does. A variety of crops not only increases the amount of cultivation, but adds numerous good elements as the stubble or plant growth is plowed under.

Then, as all our lands have become deficient in phosphates, wheat should always have a good application of acid phosphate. This will suffice if the preceding cultivated crop has been planted on a clover sod on which farm manure has been spread. In fact, where there is a good, short rotation and plenty of legume crops are grown and fed, there will never be any need for the purchase of nitrogen in fertilizer.

Rapidly growing crops require an ample supply of potassium in a form available to the plants, that is, soluble in water. Where a good rotation is practiced it has been found that the cultivation of a crop like corn or tobacco during the summer makes the best possible preparation for wheat, oats or barley. After the cultivated crop is off the best preparation is the rapid and frequent use of the disk harrow.

One of the most valuable uses of lime and plaster is to release the insoluble potash in the soil and the accumu-

lation of organic decay with its humic acids will also
have a good effect in rendering the potash available.

The farmer on upland clay soils who practices a good
rotation and maintains and increases the humus-making
material in his soil, will seldom need to buy potash or
nitrogen if he limes his soil once in four or five years, for
the legumes will give him the nitrogen and the lime and
organic decay will help release the potash.

A good fertile soil is one that has a considerable
proportion of organic, that is, vegetable and animal matter in it. The most of this is in a dead and disintegrated
condition, but some of it is in living forms that we call
bacteria. These minute living organisms exist in the
decaying particles and could not live in this soil without
them, and when they are not there the soil is called dead.
Heat and water, when excessive, will kill them, and this
sometimes occurs. They need both heat and moisture,
but only in moderate degrees.

To maintain the needed bacteria there must be a continuous addition of decaying as well as living vegetable
matter for them to live and multiply upon. In other
words, there must be plenty of humus in the soil, for
humus is decaying organic matter. The nitrogen content of the soil is largely dependent upon and often exists
in proportion to the amount of humus there. And nitrogen we know to be one of the most needful elements upon
which all plants, whether large or small, feed.

The legumes contain a larger proportion of nitrogen
than ordinary vegetation. There are some soiling crops
that may be considered as specially valuable. Buckwheat,
rye and the cowhorn turnip are of this character. They
will tame and benefit wild and barren soil and flourish
over a wide range of climate. The rye must be turned
under promptly in springtime before it drains the soil of
moisture.

Lime as an Adjunct in Farming

WITHOUT doubt the judicious use of lime on the fields will greatly increase the aggregate yield of crops. That this liming must be done intelligently is evidenced by the fact that there are some plants that grow better on soils in which there is an abundance of acids than on soils in which the acid has been neutralized by the application of lime.

These plants, however, are in the minority; and, taking the plant creation as a whole, far more is gained by liming than not liming. When, however, the subject is sufficiently studied, it will be found possible to leave some areas unlimed on which to grow the plants that do best in an acid soil.

For the growing of all leguminous plants an acidy soil is objectionable. This is because the minute forms of vegetable life that we call bacteria are destroyed by the acid in the soil, if that acid exists in considerable quantities. These forms of vegetable life are necessary to the development on the roots of the legumes of the little knots or protuberances that we call nodules. In these nodules the bacteria live that take the gas nitrogen and reduce it to a tangible form that can be dissolved in water and thus become plant food.

It is evident that if these vegetable forms of life cannot live in the soils on account of the acid no work of transforming the nitrogen can go on. In that case plants that bear pods will grow well only so long as they are supplied with nitrogen, phosphorus and potassium from the soil or are given their nitrogen in the form of manures. But they do not render any service in securing nitrogen from the great storehouse of the air. But that is one of the main things for which we grow pod-bearing plants.

The man who sows clover on a well-manured field cannot tell whether his clover crop is getting any nitrogen from the air or not and many a farmer is deceived in this way. He grows the clover for a year or two and then turns under the clover sod, believing that he has thus added to the nitrogen in his soil. But as the soil had in it much acid, the bacteria did not exist and the farmer had really been removing nitrogen from his field in the clover and hay crops, leaving the soil with less nitrogen in it than it had before he sowed his clover.

If a man wishes to find whether his soil contains too much acid for leguminous (or pod-bearing) crops, let him sow his clover seed on soil that has not been manured at all or that has not been manured for many years. Better still, let him buy some seed of sweet clover and sow that. If this plant grows well he does not need lime; for it will not grow where there is a large amount of acid in the soil. But many soils will be so acidy that these plants will not grow at all or will make a sickly growth.

In that case lime should be applied. It is safe to apply it at the rate of a ton to the acre, and if in the form of carbonate of lime more can be used without any injury to the crops or the soil. Lime can be applied either in the form of quicklime or in the form of carbonate of lime.

Phosphorus as a Soil Preserver

WHEN the University of Illinois thrashed its wheat on an experiment field in McLean county, agricultural history was made. Upon the plots on which phosphorus was one of the fertilizing ingredients the crop was more than doubled, a record believed to be without precedent. In the plots in which the phosphorus treatment bore a part the average yield was more than fifty-eight and a half bushels an acre, an average gain of thirty-four and a half bushels an acre, which was mainly brought about by phosphorus fertilizer.

In these experiments the standard application of phosphorus in steamed bone meal has been at the rate of twenty-five pounds an acre for each year in the rotation. When raw rock phosphate is used about three times as much is applied, which adds three times as much phosphorus to the soil but at about the same cost for the bone. After two or three rotations the amount of rock phosphate to be applied will be reduced to one-third of the present applications.

"The key to permanent agriculture is phosphorus," said Dr. Hopkins. "To maintain or increase the amount of phosphorus in the soil makes possible the growth of clover and the consequent addition of nitrogen from the inexhaustible supply in the air, and with the addition of decaying organic matter in clover residues and in manure made in large part from clover, hay and pasture and from the larger crops of corn which the clover helps to produce, comes the possibility of liberating from the immense supply in the soil sufficient potassium, when supplemented by that returned in manure and crop residues, for the production of crops for at least thousands of years."

Then he sounds this warning note to American land owners:

"If the supply of phosphorus in the soil is steadily decreased in the future in accordance with the present most common farm practice, then poverty is the only future for the people who till the common prairie lands of Illinois. And this does not refer to the far distant future only, for the turning point is already past on many Illinois lands."

Average barn manure carries 10 to 15 pounds nitrogen, 5 to 9 pounds phosphoric acid and 10 to 15 pounds potash to the ton. This plant food is in a fairly soluble condition, and is readily taken up by the plant. For market gardening purposes it may be balanced and supplemented by suitable fertilizers in case the yield is not up to expectations. In soggy spots slacked lime should be used. Where the crops are light on land that has had barnyard manure and good cultivation it is well to try phosphorus.

Nitrogen is free as air, and potassium is abundant in nearly all of the soils. Both nitrogen and potassium remain in the straw and the stalks, and in the farm manure to a considerable extent.

Phosphorus, on the contrary, is present in nearly all soils in limited amounts and it is being continually removed from the land.

While it is true that some forms of soil bacteria prefer to live in the absence of free oxygen, the large mass of soil organisms can only carry out their life processes in the presence of a plentiful supply of oxygen. Every phase of soil management therefore which affects in any degree the amount of air supplied to the soil is a regulator of the bacterial activities in the soil. Among these important phases of soil management are tillage, including plowing and cultivation, and drainage. It is obvious that plowing to a depth of four inches will not supply the soil with the amount of air which plowing to twice the depth will. It is likewise clear that when a soil is water-logged, or partially so, or, in other words, when its pores are filled wholly or partly by water instead of air, we cannot expect that a sufficient supply of oxygen will be maintained there for crop production, and these facts hold true for bacterial development in soils. Our study therefore of the oxygen needs of soil bacteria serves to emphasize more clearly the necessity for rational methods of tillage and drainage.

No farm should be without its experiment plot, for it has been by experimental work only that anything in agriculture has become known. Knowing the history of a soil, the plot or field experiment, supplemented, in some instances, by chemical and physical analyses, tells the farmer the best plan to follow with the particular soil to restore it to full power. The ratio of straw to grain tells its story to the critical eye. If for several years the straw production is abnormally high and the grain production is low, these facts point to phosphorus being needed. If the leaves of the grain are long, loose, hanging and fluttering and the stems too long for their thickness, the soil probably requires calcium. A bright green to yellowish colored foliage with the tips of the leaves brown or reddish in color, indicates want of nitrogen.

Broad-leaf plants, like burdock and nettles, indicate moisture, while narrow-leaf plants indicate dryness. Nitrogen is abundant where chickweed and red pimperel grow, while lack of nitrogen is indicated by jagged chickweed, field chickweed and vernal whitlow-grass.

Soil that is rich in nitrate of soda is indicated by the presence of goose foot, oraches and burning nettle. Foxgloves, spurry and corn marigolds indicate calcium.

Making the Most of Manure

FARMERS who live near enough to cities or villages to warrant them in buying stable manure are often surprised when they attempt this to find that the available supply has been engaged by gardeners, nurserymen and seedmen, and at higher prices than they can pay. Each of these works land that is much richer than that usually devoted to farm crops. They can afford to buy to make rich soil still more rich, while the farmer whose land is much poorer cannot afford to buy to bring it into condition for cultivation. This only shows that soil fertility tends to increase, while the soil that is already poor, if cultivated, almost inevitably grows still poorer. The use of commercial fertilizers, with which a small amount fertilizes a large surface, to some extent offsets this disadvantage of the poor farmer. It costs a great deal less to drill with a grain crop three to four dollars' worth of mineral fertilizer than to cover the surface with stable manure. Besides, the commercial fertilizer can always be furnished in quantities limited only by the ability of the farmer to buy. The commercial fertilizer is easily applied, and for the single crop it produces results quite as good as would the stable manure. Its defect is that it does not add to soil fertility as the manure must do, and it is on increase of productive power in the soil more than on the gain from single crops that profit in farming must depend.

The man whose land is already rich is the one who can best afford to buy commercial manures. If he buys them he can only save himself from loss by putting a part of

their plant food into a permanent addition to the fertility
of the farm. So far as possible the clover and grass
together with coarse grain and corn-fodder should be
fed on the farm. To do this requires capital, for it implies choice stock which will pay for its feed and leave
the manure pile as profit. It also generally requires that
the farmer on rich land shall grow something that only
rich soil can be made to grow, or whose production is
unusually difficult. Markets are always glutted with
crops that can be grown on poor land and with the least
labor. It is only by growing something that pays better
than the staple easily-grown crops that money can be
made in farming under present conditions.

Valuable lessons are obtained from European methods.
The city of Berlin covers an area of 20,000 acres, and the
sewage farms owned and conducted by the municipality
cover an area twice the size. The sewage disposal problem has nowhere reached the development that is found in
Berlin. The city will ultimately sell this land at great
profit and then turn to some biological method of meeting the problem or secure more land and go on with the
work of land reclamation in connection with the disposal
of the city's accumulations. The prevailing mode of disposing of sewage by pouring it into streams is exceedingly wasteful. It represents so much nitrogen which
has been extracted from the soil, and which ought, by
right, to be returned to the soil. If it could be advan-
tageously used, it would represent a value of about
$200,000,000 a year to England alone. This, however,
is distributed over a quantity of three billion tons. Sewage is so complex in its nature that the recovery of its
chemical constituents would be almost a hopeless task.
That, however, is no reason why some method should
not be devised of utilizing it as a fertilizer. Farmers
have endeavored to use the sludge as a fertilizer; but that
is not always practicable, partly because of the chemical

character of the sludge and partly because of the farmer's distance from the dumping ground.

We are slowly learning to use the millions of tons of corn fodder which used to rot in the furrow, but we have scarcely begun to comprehend what we are wasting by the negligent care of our manure crop or of the inexhaustible store of nitrogen which envelops the earth and which could be put into the soil by sowing leguminous crops like clover, alfalfa and cowpeas more liberally. We are wasting our land by not farming to its last pound of productivity. We are wasting even our weeds, by not carrying a band of sheep on every one hundred acres. We are wasting our time by sowing year after year unselected seed on partially tilled soil, by milking inferior cows which don't pay their board; we are guilty—all guilty more or less—but, fortunately, we know it, we are ashamed of it, but not ashamed to admit it. And we are going to do better.

If any of our young men from the farms are contemplating a professional career, we suggest that before they join the ranks of lawyers or physicians, they consider whether the science of agriculture has not greater attractions. In a few years we prophesy that every progressive farming community will have in its service an experienced soil doctor, whose employment will not only be lucrative to himself, but will pay immense dividends to his employers.

Growing Legumes for Soil Betterment

ALONG the Atlantic coast as far north as New Jersey and south at least to Georgia, crimson clover, frequently called German clover, thrives as a winter annual. Like all the legumes it stores up much nitrogen and greatly enriches the soil in this element. This crop deserves a much wider field of usefulness than has yet been accorded it. In the northern part of its territory it should be sown in July. In the South, September is supposed to be the best time to sow it. It is best adapted to sowing in corn or cotton. In sections where it has not previously been grown it frequently fails, apparently from lack of its proper bacteria. It is therefore well to inoculate the seed when it is sown the first time.

This crop furnishes valuable winter pasture, makes good hay if cut when just coming into full flower, and is valuable as a green feed in spring. It helps to fill the gap in the soiling system between green wheat and early corn. Perhaps its greatest usefulness is in a green manure. It may be plowed under any time in the spring and be followed by corn or potatoes.

In this connection, the practice of a farmer near Hagerstown, Md., is of interest. Ten years ago he began sowing crimson clover in corn at the last plowing, covering the seed with the cultivator, and using 10 pounds of seed to the acre. In the spring the clover was plowed under and another crop of corn planted. Ten consecutive crops of corn have been taken from this field, a crop of crimson clover being plowed under each spring. The yield of corn has increased during that time from about 35 bushels, in the beginning, to about 50 bushels at the present time. Evidently the practice was a good one in this case.

Those who are not familiar with crimson clover should try it on a small scale at first, as there have been many failures with it. The following five-year rotation is a good one on stock farms in middle latitudes, and shows one way of securing the benefits of crimson clover as a green manure: Corn with crimson clover sown at last cultivation, corn, oats, wheat, clover (common red).

The vetches can be made to occupy a somewhat similar place as a green manure, at least in the South.

It seldom pays to turn under a crop of cowpeas in the green state. It is better practice to make hay of them, feed the hay, and put the manure back on the land. As is the case with all legumes, the roots of the cowpea crop add a great deal of nitrogen to the soil, and have a marked effect on fertility. If a heavy green crop of cowpeas is plowed under in the autumn it is best not to plant the land until the following spring. A very good plan for bringing up the fertility of a worn-out field is to sow rye in the fall, plow this under in the spring, harrow thoroughly, let the land lie a month, and then sow cowpeas. Cut the peas for hay and sow rye again. A few seasons of such treatment will restore fertility to the soil. Fortunately, both of these crops will grow on very poor land.

Almost any crop may be used as a green manure, as occasion demands. Those previously mentioned are more generally used for this purpose than others. In plowing up clover sod, many farmers, particularly on fields most in need of manure, wait until the clover is nearly ready to cut for hay before plowing, in order to get the additional nitrogen and humus thus produced. Buckwheat is frequently grown as a green manure. This crop is planted in early summer or late spring and turned under in the autumn. Even corn and sorghum have been used for this purpose. They produce large amounts of humus when thickly planted. Sufficient time should be given after plowing in such rank growth to allow the soil to settle and the resulting acids to wash out of the soil before planting another crop. In southern California, fenugreek and Canadian field peas are used extensively as winter cover crops in orchards. They are then plowed under in spring as green manure.

The quickest way to build up a worn-out soil when barnyard manure is not plentiful is to give it a course of treatment like that just described; then grow only forage crops, buy grain to feed with them, and return all the manure thus produced to the land. Dairy farming permits such a system to be practiced. No other type of farming builds up land so rapidly.

Another type that gives fairly quick results is to grow a succession of pasture crops for hogs, keep the hogs on these pastures and feed them a fourth to a half ration of grain.

There are three general methods of supplying humus to the soil. The first and best is the addition of stable manure. When properly managed it adds large quantities of both plant food and humus. But manure is not always available. When such is the case, the best thing to do is to make it available. Raise more forage, keep more stock, and make more manure. But this takes time and capital, so that other means are sometimes necessary. When stable manure is not to be had, we may plant crops for the purpose of turning them under, thus adding large quantities of humus at comparatively little cost. Plowing under green crops is called green manuring. Under certain conditions this is an excellent practice.

A third method of adding humus is to grow crops like clover and timothy. These crops are usually left down for two years or more. During this time their roots thoroughly penetrate the soil. Old roots decay and new ones grow. When the sod is plowed up, more or less vegetable matter is turned under. This, with the mass of roots in the soil, adds no small amount to the supply of humus. Another advantage from the cultivation of clovers and alfalfa is found in the fact that they are deep-rooted plants, and when their roots decay they leave channels deep into the earth, thus aiding in the absorption of rains and letting in air to sweeten the soil

Properly handled, stable manure is by all means the best remedy for poverty of the soil. Very few farmers handle manure so as to get even as much as half the possible value from it. There is probably no greater waste in the world than in connection with the handling of manure by the American farmer. Five-eighths of the plant food in manure is found in the liquid part of it. This is usually all lost. Not only is this the case, but the solids are piled beside the barn, frequently under the eaves, where rains wash away much of their value. Fermentation in these manure piles also sets free much of the nitrogen to escape into the air.

In order to produce a ton of dry hay on an acre of land it is necessary that the growing grass pump up from that acre approximately 500 tons of water. In order to supply this enormous quantity of water, the soil must not only be in condition to absorb and hold water well, but it must be porous enough to permit water to flow freely from soil grain to soil grain. The presence of large quantities of decaying organic matter (humus) adds enormously to the water-holding capacity of the soil. One ton of humus will absorb 2 tons of water and give it up readily to growing crops. Not only that, but the shrinking of the particles of decaying organic matter and the consequent loosening of soil grains keep the soil open and porous.

Furthermore, humus of good quality is exceedingly

rich in both nitrogen and mineral plant food. The maintenance of fertility may almost be said to consist in keeping the soil well supplied with humus.

The cultivation of leguminous crops is one of the most important and economical means of maintaining a supply of nitrogenous plant food in the soil. Nitrates may, of course, be supplied in commercial fertilizers; but fertilizers containing nitrogen are very expensive, and it usually pays better to supply nitrogen by growing legumes or by the application of stable manure, which is rich in nitrogen when properly handled. In good farm practice both stable manure and leguminous crops are used as sources of nitrogen.

Improper methods of tillage add very greatly to the evil effects that result from lack of humus. In many parts of the country the land is plowed only 3 or 4 inches deep. Below the plowed stratum the soil becomes sour, densely packed, and unfit for plant roots. When such soils are plowed deep and this sour packed subsoil is mixed with the upper portion, the growth of many crops is greatly retarded. This has led many farmers to believe that deep plowing is ruinous. Some farmers have tried to remedy the difficulty by subsoiling. The subsoil plow breaks up the packed layer but does not throw it out on top. But while subsoiling does break up the hard layer into chunks it does not pulverize it or put humus into it. In most cases work done in subsoiling is practically wasted, and it is doubtful if it ever pays. A much better method is to plow a little deeper each year until a depth of 8 or 10 inches is reached. This gives a deep layer of good soil, particularly if the supply of humus is kept up.

When new soil, or that which has lain undisturbed for several years, is broken up, it is always best to plow deep from the beginning, for the deeper layers will be about as fertile as any, except the top inch or two. It is wise, too, never to plow the same depth twice in succession. In general, fall plowing should be from 7 to 9 or 10 inches and spring plowing from 5 to 7 inches deep. There are special cases in which these rules do not apply, but their discussion would take us too far from the purpose of this chapter.

We plow the soil in order to loosen up its texture and get air into it; also to turn under stubble, manure, etc., to make humus. Killing weeds is another object accomplished by plowing. After a soil has been thoroughly pulverized to great depths, so that there is no danger of turning up packed clay, the deeper the plowing the better the crops. But the cost also increases with depth, so that ordinarily it does not pay to plow more than about 10 inches deep.

Some crops prefer rather a loose seed bed. Millet is such a crop. Farmers sometimes plow a second time in order to sow millet on freshly plowed land. Other crops, such as wheat and alfalfa, prefer a fairly compact seed bed; hence, frequent harrowing and rolling after plowing is good practice before seeding to these crops. Nevertheless, it pays to plow the land for them, even if we have to compact it again before seeding. The plowing aerates the soil and helps to set plant food free.

Large Profits in Potatoes

ALL progressive farmers who can bring their plans into the right shape are going ahead with potatoes. Prices continue on a high level and the market demand is so keen that foreign producers are making large shipments to this country. If American farmers are wise they will control this market and reap the big profits which are to be gained from potato culture.

The fact should be kept in mind that the proper kind of cultivation will give a yield of about 200 bushels per acre, whereas the average in this country is under 100 bushels. The yield in parts of Maine as well as in the northwest often runs upwards of 200 bushels, while in Germany it is close to 200. England and Ireland fall a little behind Germany.

For nearly two years now the price per bushel to American farmers has been $1 to $1.50, where they have sold to private customers, and 75 cents to $1.25 when shipping to commission men. It is well to compare this price and yield to wheat figures. In raising the grain farmers are in great luck if they secure twenty bushels per acre and receive $1 a bushel.

Potatoes do not require the richest of soils. They will thrive in a sandy loam. Soggy land is bad for the crop and if any such has to be used it ought to be drained. Regular moisture in light quantities on any ordinary farm will insure a good crop of potatoes.

An irrigated farm has advantages over any other, but where the rainfall is insufficient a dust mulch should be kept around the growing crop for the purpose of conserving such moisture as there is. It is unwise to let potato ground harden and bake in the sun. By giving reasonable attention to the product along the lines indicated success will be attained in almost any section of the United States.

Potatoes do well in rotation with clover, millet, corn, beets, rutabagas, cabbage, etc. It is feasible to dig a crop of early potatoes in June or July and then immediately sow millet, rye or fodder corn on the same ground. It is also a good plan to plant late potatoes on land from which clover, cowpeas, rye or any other early crop has been taken.

There are sixteen states in which the cultivation of sugar beets is already well established in this country. Practically all of these states are large producers of potatoes. More significant still is the fact, recently brought out by an exhaustive inquiry, that the use of sugar beets in rotation with potatoes, corn, wheat and other crops increases the yield of every one of these crops from 25 to 50 per cent. In the case of potatoes the increase was 46.2 per cent.

Early Rose, Triumph, Early Michigan and Early Ohio remain standard early varieties, while some of the best late ones are Burbank, Peerless, Peachblow and Green Mountain. There are many variations in these types, but for all practical purposes the potatoes can be recommended as named above.

It is necessary to be on guard against disease and insect pests. A healthy growth of potatoes can hardly be expected on soggy land or where spraying is neglected. Good seed is of the highest importance, and with this point settled thorough cultivation will insure a crop five years out of six.

The potato scab is a disease that remains in the soil from one year to the next as a fungus and if potatoes are grown in consecutive years on the same soil the disease must necessarily increase.

The potato bug or beetle is destroyed with paris green at the rate of one pound to the acre in twenty-five gallons of water. Arsenate of lead applied at the rate of six pounds to the acre in fifty gallons of water will prove equally efficacious. Scab and blight are controlled by the bordeaux mixture, which is best applied a week or two after the bugs have been disposed of.

Potatoes are so hardy that they are raised to advantage in the most northerly states, and even in Siberia and other cold countries. Seed produced in the north will show good results in southern states, but this is a rule that will not work both ways. Tubers originating in a semi-tropical climate have to be acclimated in the north before returning satisfactory crops.

On any farm in the country some parts are much better adapted to potatoes than others. Sandy soil is not a moisture-retaining soil, and in wet weather there is little danger of tubers rotting in the soil. In dry seasons mulching is highly beneficial, as it tends to hold and conserve the little moisture available. Seeds grown under mulch and those grown with the best cultivation have been compared and the former found to produce 50 per cent better yields. If clover is raised after potatoes grown with a mulch a surprisingly good stand is obtained.

The time to mulch is just as soon as the first crop of weeds has been destroyed by cultivation. A thick layer of leaves or straw is required. This will save the soil from surface washing and will keep down the weeds. It conserves moisture and adds humus.

Plow in plenty of manure in the fall. When the weather becomes favorable in the spring use a disk unless the ground happens to be dry, in which case harrowing is better, as it will tend to conserve the moisture. If the land is not perfectly level the rows should conform to the slope, so that in case of heavy rains the water will run off without washing out the crop. If mulching is thought to be unnecessary the tract must be cultivated two or three times.

The studious farmer tills the soil in an intelligent manner, knowing the reason for and the effect of every operation. He aims to get water into the soil and hold it there for future use. Certainty of crops depends almost absolutely on proper handling of the soil. Without it the soil moisture is not stored in proper quantities and is allowed to escape, and drought gets the crop that otherwise could be saved and made profitable.

A study of the potato question will be a good thing for American farmers, especially those who are just engaging in agriculture. The whole subject of supply and demand, of production and selling, is opened by the existing potato problem.

Here are a couple of good axioms which apply to the situation: Never trust to one crop for success, even when prices are high; do not devote all your land and effort to a single interest, no matter what the rate of profit was in a previous season. One reason is that you may fail to produce a satisfactory crop, and another is that thousands rush to raise a product for which there seems to be an unusual demand. This breaks the market. It would be easy for American farmers to raise so many potatoes that they could not get fifty cents a bushel for them. However, when the market gets too low to afford a profit, this product is excellent food, when boiled, for poultry and hogs.

Growing Sweet Potatoes in the North

WHILE the sweet potato is generally regarded as a southern crop, it is grown with great success in many places in the north. The Island of Muscatine in the Mississippi River is largely given up to sweet potatoes and melons. The former do well in any light, sandy soil, where the season is not too short.

Miss Gertrude Coburn, teacher of domestic science in the University of Iowa, has collected some valuable data regarding the table merit of the different kinds of sweet potatoes grown in the north. Mr. Theodore Williams, of Benson, Neb., and F. D. Wells, a Michigan grower, have been successful in the cultivation of the potato; and the results of the work of these investigators are briefly summarized here.

In Miss Coburn's investigations the soil on which the crop was grown was not rich, having previously grown nursery stock. It was not manured, but thoroughly prepared. Mr. Wells says that the soil best suited to sweet potatoes is a warm, moderately rich sand. If it is too rich there will be excessive growth of top at the expense of the root. Before planting, the surface of the ground should be ridged, and the plants set in the usual way about the first week in June.

The most common way to grow the plants is in a hot-bed. After the first heated period is over, the tubers are placed quite closely together, but not touching, and covered with manure; they are then covered with three inches of soil, the bed covered with glass and watered as often as necessary.

The buds or shoots which develop should be transplanted to the field only when the ground is quite warm. Although plants are generally set in ridges, some growers prefer to set on a level. The ridge system is probably most desirable in the north. The center of the ridges should be about 3½ feet apart, and the plants set 18 inches in the row. Good cultivation is necessary. This should be frequent and shallow to save moisture, and it will also add to the yield.

Southern growers have changed their method somewhat, and now do not believe it is necessary to move the vines to prevent rooting, except under unusual circumstances. Northern experiments show that there is not so much difference between rows in which the vines were undisturbed and those in which the vines were moved twice.

Potash is one of the most important fertilizers for sweet potatoes, although in New Jersey, horse manure at the rate of 10 to 20 tons per acre is used. It should be well rotted. Attention to the vines, says Mr. Wells, does not stop with the end of cultivation. They should be lifted occasionally to prevent their taking root, and this work can be quickly done by the use of a pitchfork. Once a week is often enough.

In the north the black-rot affects sweet potatoes, and this is soon seen on the sprouts. Whenever a plant shows a leaf that is black, it should be dug up and destroyed. Potatoes from affected plants will rot quickly after being dug. As the germs of the disease remain in the soil over winter, the ground should not be used again for this crop.

Money Making From Pork

FARMERS who do not raise a lot of nice pork every year are not living up to their opportunities in money making. At the average price of hogs in the last five years this product pays well.

The present is a good time either for making a start or enlarging operations. Even a very small farm should have a few pigs, as they work nicely in any scheme of diversification.

The sow's rations should be reduced about one-half shortly before farrowing, and it should consist of sloppy feed that will tend to loosen the bowels. An abundant supply of water should be before her. She ought to be separated from other animals a week before farrowing. In extremely cold weather the young pigs are likely to become chilled and may die if they do not receive extra attention. A little care at this time will save the lives of many pigs and pay excellent returns for the slight effort involved. A few bricks should be heated, wrapped in a sack and placed in a basket. Any pigs which appear chilled or are too weak to nurse should be placed in the basket. An hour or so of this treatment should serve to revive the young porker and after he gets to nurse his chances of reaching maturity are increased fourfold.

If sucking pigs are seen to be scouring, give the sow fifteen to twenty drops of laudanum in her feed for a few days. If her feed is reduced this usually checks the scours. If there is no laudanum at hand use powdered charcoal.

As soon as the pigs are old enough to eat I give them a

separate trough where they can eat without being disturbed by the mother. They are given a mixed feed of middlings, corn meal or other ground feed softened with water. They thrive all summer on forage crops and need little grain until a month before marketing time.

Mineral matter such as phosphorus, calcium, sulphur and iron is very necessary to the best development of a pig. It is needed in the body to carry gaseous products, such as oxygen, from the lungs to the tissues of the body; to maintain acidity in the blood and tissues; to aid in the movement of liquids through the body; to aid in the digestion of proteids and fats; and in addition to several minor functions to aid in the formation of muscular and bony tissues. A pig fed on ground corn and water, and provided with plenty of mineral matter will gain twice as much in weight as one fed on ground corn and water alone.

Rape, artichokes, red clover and alfalfa make good forage for hogs. Carrots are excellent food also, either in summer or winter. It is not best to let hogs have the entire run of a large pasture. Confine them within movable fences, giving them access to a part of the field at a time. Such fences are not expensive. They save much waste of grass, secure a large growth of feed from the land and cause the hogs to make rapid gains.

Vermin are a pest and cause heavy losses. Nothing holds back growing pigs more than lice. It is necessary to fight them as long as one remains on the premises. Coal tar dips are a great help in keeping hogs healthy, and where a sprayer is used it is a good plan to spray the litter that the hogs sleep in, and kill the lice there also. Lime is a help if sprinkled over the litter. Black oil poured over the pigs will kill lice effectively. A mixture of lard and kerosene when rubbed in, answers the purpose. Do not use kerosene alone, as it blisters. Good

insect powders can be bought, but they are hardly necessary if the other remedies are used.

Hogs require attention regardless of conditions, age
or sex, but the brood sows require particular attention,
and to the feeder's skill in feeding and managing his
brood sows, provided they have been properly selected,
will be due in large measure his success.

Pasture and forage crops should be provided for the
pregnant sows, because of the cheapness of this method
of feeding and the desirability of keeping the sows in
good form by exercise, fresh air and sunshine. Along
with the pasture and forage crops some grain should be
fed especially as pregnancy advances, for best results,
since the pasture and forage crops provide only about a
maintenance ration. The forage crops that are especially
suited to pregnant brood sows are the clovers, alfalfa,
peas, beans, vetches, rape, etc. The ordinary pasture
grasses also provide a suitable pasture for brood sows.

Keep the sow in fair condition but not excessively fat.
She should receive a nutritious ration at all times, but
care should be taken not to feed a too concentrated
ration close to farrowing time, as the sow is likely to
become constipated. This is a disorder that should be
carefully avoided during pregnancy and especially at the
time of farrowing. To overcome this disorder the greater
part of the grain ration should be given in the form of
a slop all during pregnancy, and toward the close of the
gestation period some laxative feed such as bran, oil meal,
roots, or a small amount of flaxseed meal should be introduced into the ration. It should be remembered that the
digestive tract of the hog is small and that a very bulky
ration cannot be used to best advantage.

It is well to remember that the main demands upon
the brood sow are those for building up new tissue, and
that the kind of feed is important. To build up new
tissue the sow must have protein in her ration. This

may be supplied by feeding any one of a number of nitrogenous feeds. The young sow requires more of this kind of feed in her ration than the old one because she is still growing when her first litter is born. A variety in the feeds is necessary to good results with swine. With brood sows it is particularly true that several feeds combined give better results than any single one.

For a few days previous to farrowing the feed should be limited in quantity and of a sloppy nature, and, as has been previously stated, the tendency to become constipated at this time must be overcome. A box of charcoal, salt and ashes should be kept where the sow can get at it at all times, summer or winter. These materials tend to satisfy the hog's craving for mineral matter and act as a vermifuge and preventive of disease. If brood sows are given free access to the above mixture and are fed a varied ration which contains a sufficient amount of protein, the breeder will not be likely to be troubled with sows eating their pigs at farrowing time.

The quantity of feed for several days after farrowing should be small. The sow should not be offered any feed of any kind until she gets up of her own accord after farrowing and for the first day or two a thin slop will be sufficient to quench her thirst and provide all the nutrition required. Within a week or ten days after farrowing the sow should be getting a good ration of nutritious milk producing food. If skim milk can be had at this time and fed with a ration of equal parts corn meal and shorts, good results should be obtained. About three weeks after farrowing the sow should be getting a full ration and during the whole remaining period during which the sow is giving suck to her pigs she should be fed heavily, for the gain thus produced in the suckling pigs indirectly is made at a low cost for the feed consumed. Generally a sow with a large litter will lose in weight and condition even when given the best of care and feed. These essentials should receive the greatest of attention at all times.

Farmers need to learn the merits of rape, carrots, Canada peas and alfalfa or clover. Hogs can be brought along nicely for the first six months without much corn if they can have a nice patch of forage such as alfalfa or rape. Skimmed milk is a wholesome and cheap addition. They can be finished on peas or corn, as circumstances dictate, and will show a large profit at 8 to 10 months. Animals fed in this way produce extra fine pork and it is possible to have private customers who will take the dressed carcasses, wholly or in part, at fancy prices.

While hogs grow into money fast, the question of economical feeding must not be overlooked. If the feeder does what he should for his hogs on grass he will feed some corn or other grain along each day to furnish the pig more nutrients than he can secure in his grass diet and also to help concentrate his ration.

If this is kept up to the time in the pig's life when he is 6, 7 or 8 months of age he is then a large pig, growthy and strong, but not in any condition to market. He has built up his frame and muscle work large enough so that by feeding six weeks or two months longer he can be finished off on corn into the prime pork the market pays the long price for.

This last period is called the finishing or fattening period, but this does not mean that the pig, which has been allowed to roam over a grass pasture (or, better still, a clover pasture) and been fed perhaps a pound or two pounds of corn or other grain in the evening just to keep him growing fine, should be kept in an 8x10 foot pen and stuffed on corn. He will not do best under these conditions. He wants some good clean soil to eat every day as he had all the rest of his life. He wants a fifty-yard straightaway where he can scamper and shake up his intestines, which are as full as a city boy at grand-mother's on Thanksgiving day.

Now corn alone and a place to scamper in will not be all that is necessary for finishing these hogs. They are still to grow some, their growth requires protein mate-rial, and this protein material must be in excess of that found in the corn. Nothing could be better than the clover field or the alfalfa field, but when these are frosted or covered with snow, the Canadian field peas can be used that should have been thrashed out some weeks before. These should be ground for best results and fed in slop.

If this slop could be made of the fresh separated milk, so much the better. The ration of corn, should you have it ground, and the field peas, which ought to be ground, is very well mixed and makes a good ration when about five parts of corn are fed with one part of pea meal, mixed in a fairly thick slop. Should the feeder not have the pea meal and has only the skim milk, it is well to purchase shorts and make a good slop of the shorts and milk and feed all the pigs will clean up without leaving the trough.

Rape is one of the most satisfactory crops for early hog pasture when clover is not available. It closely resembles cabbage in appearance and manner of growth, except that it does not produce a head. It has large, coarse, succulent leaves, and ordinarily grows from 20 to 30 inches tall. It is a cool weather plant and can be sown early in the spring—as soon as there is no further danger of severe frost. It will endure a pretty severe frost in the fall without injury and may be used for pasture late in the fall, provided the hogs are kept off when it is frozen.

Making a Dairy Farm Pay

THERE is much to be said in favor of dairy farming, no matter what the size of the place may be. It is an excellent system for providing a monthly cash income, and may be managed so as to yield a high rate of profit, particularly if there are good transportation facilities or the farm is located near a large town. Soil fertility is best maintained on a place that has considerable live stock.

A dairy is a good basis for operations in a case where a city family takes land, for it affords an immediate income with which to meet the expense of hired help and the cost of getting started. On any place beyond the dimensions of a garden or orchard it is best to start with an experienced man. Possibly after one season the family may manage the work.

Fifteen to twenty cows are not too many for fifty acres. Ten cows may be kept on thirty to forty acres. The modern plan is to restrict the pasture to a few acres and feed with silage or soiling crops. Summer feeding is necessary to keep up a regular output of milk, and it is best to begin with this fact settled, so time and effort will not be wasted in experiments, nor an undue amount of land given up to pasturage.

A fact in favor of the dairy is that the owner can estimate both income and expense with reasonable certainty. Prices on milk and butter change little, especially where there are private customers. Any one who has a suitable location can command top-notch prices for dairy products which are handled with taste and skill. The demand is continual, is never exceeded by supply, and high prices are willingly paid for choice goods by a large class of customers who place quality above cost.

To get the advantages of dealing with this class of trade, one should be located convenient to transportation. After securing a good equipment, and learning how to produce and sell, it will be easy to find private customers who will pay 25 to 50 per cent more than market quotations for products that they know to be right. If located near a provincial city, the marketing may be done by team.

Good marketing means the difference between success and failure. In Europe, by means of co-operative associations, the middleman is cut out and the farmer and consumer get together. There is no reason why that plan may not succeed in this country.

Selection is more important than breed in starting a dairy. See that the cows come up to requirements in milk production, and are healthy. Then guard against dirt and disease, and feed systematically. Alfalfa, alsike, millet, shredded cornstalks, ground oats or corn, beets, bran and shorts are the best articles of fodder. Corn silage is excellent, winter or summer, and oilcake may be needed for its digestive qualities when stock is not on grass.

No dairy is on the right basis if not earning at the rate of $100 a year for each animal. Considerably more than this will be earned if good selling connections are established. I have personal knowledge of a ten-cow dairy that has advanced steadily from $60 to $125 a month.

Observant farmers know that while the income from milk is large, it does not represent the entire value of a dairy. Hogs fed with skimmed milk and corn gain faster than if fed with corn alone, and skimmed milk is also an aid in poultry raising. Thus the dairy stimulates two other important branches of farming, and many a worn-out and almost worthless farm has been restored to a highly profitable state by the fertilizer returned by the cattle.

The selection of feeds is of prime importance in the profitable management of a herd of dairy cows, and, next to the selection of cows of the proper type and breeding, is the factor of greatest importance in profitable dairying. Feed cows daily one pound of grain for every three pounds of milk produced; from 25 to 40 pounds of corn silage, and what clover or alfalfa hay they will eat.

Do not turn cows out to remain and suffer in cold, stormy weather. Allow them to have water which is not colder than that from a deep well twice or three times daily. It is a good plan to heat their drinking water in the tanks or troughs. Brush cows daily if you can possibly find the time, for it pays better than does grooming of horses. Keep cows in clean, well lighted, properly ventilated stables.

Do not try to save feed by turning to pasture too early. Provide plenty of pure, fresh water, shade and protection against flies during the heat of summer. Supplement poor pastures with corn silage or green soiling crops like rye, peas and oats, green corn fodder, cabbage and other available feed.

Treat cows gently and avoid excitement. Be regular in time of feeding and milking. Weigh the milk of each cow at milking time.

Get your neighbors to share with you in owning a Babcock milk tester, and test the milk of each individual cow. Discard the cow which has failed at the end of the year to pay market price for all the feed she has consumed.

Breed your cows to a pure-bred registered dairy bull, and raise well the heifer calves from the best cows. Breed heifers to drop their first calves at 24 to 30 months of age. Give cows six to eight weeks' rest between lactation periods.

Forage Problem Demands Attention

FARMERS who are after the dollars should settle the question of summer forage at once and for good. With the increased value of land, larger pastures cannot be maintained without loss. Frequent droughts also help to make them unprofitable.

It has come to a point where owners of dairies, beef cattle, horses, or any kind of live stock, frequently lose as much money as a result of light pastures during three months of dry summer weather as they can make in the rest of the year. A total abandonment of pasturage is not recommended, but the grazing fields should be improved and silage and soiling crops made an auxiliary for summer feeding.

One reason why so many pastures become short or fail altogether in summer is that they do not contain enough variety of grasses for forage plants. The ordinary pasture is a timothy meadow which has been run as a meadow for several years. This one grass plant is soon killed out, and nothing remains but chance grasses and weeds, all of doubtful forage value.

For a pasture to be good all through the season, it must contain a variety of grasses and good forage plants. Some of these will come in early in the spring, then become dormant, to again revive and grow for fall and early winter use. While these early grasses are dormant in midsummer, other grasses will be at their best.

The following makes a good mixture on ordinary soils: Orchard grass, redtop, timothy, English and Italian rye grass, red clover and alsike.

It is important to seed or reseed the pasture every

second year, and this may be done at almost any time, preferably in late summer, so that the young plants will have cool weather for starting growth. It is a good plan to harrow the pasture once each year to break up large manure masses and to scratch the surface soil.

By all means, have two or more pastures, so that they can be used in rotation, allowing one to rest and renew growth while the other is in use. Continuous eating and tramping will kill out any pasture. Give each pasture two or three periods of rest during the growing season, and where the area is limited, grow soiling plants for green feeding when the pasture is short and needs rest.

Whether for keeping up the milk supply or pushing the growth of meat animals, it pays to raise cowpeas and oats together, cutting them for use as a green fodder before the oats have ripened. Other crops having special value are millet, vetch and rape. The latter is particularly good for hogs and sheep. A patch of artichokes will also bring these animals along nicely.

Live stock is good property. Every farm should raise and mature for the market all that it can safely handle and maintain in thrifty condition. Cows, sheep and hogs are of special advantage on the small farm. The market value of good breeding animals may be made two or three times that of common, ordinary grade. All kinds of farm stock is in good demand. High prices prevail and an oversupply can not be anticipated for years to come. The average farmer should keep a variety of animals so as to have something for the market all through the year. The dairy and poultry features should be pushed to the limit.

The Siberian alfalfas are found growing in abundance in dry regions, where the mercury freezes in the thermometer, often with no snow on the ground. The summers are so dry and hot that camels find a congenial home. If we could clothe our hillsides and plains with these wild Siberian alfalfas, we would increase their present feeding capacity for stock from four to eight times.

Seeds and plants for these hardy varieties are obtainable in a limited way, and if they prove as vigorous here as they are in their native home under trying conditions, they will soon become a leading feature of our flora, and add immensely to our agricultural wealth. The transplanting of alfalfa plants, although new to us, is something that has been practiced for centuries in parts of India and South America.

The modern idea of a hardy alfalfa is one that will take its place as a wild plant and hold its own with buffalo grass and other wild grasses; one that will cover our steep bluffs and hillsides, now barren; one that will flourish in our gumbo soils in western localities; one that will make our rough land and "sheep quarters" immensely more valuable than at present.

Where the common blue-flowered alfalfa does not suffer from the winter at any time, it is wise to "let well enough alone." But north of this line is a vast region, stretching clear to the Arctic circle, where these Siberian alfalfas will reign supreme in the near future, and they may find a congenial home in the high mountain regions in the Rockies far to the south.

Some people are inclined to shut their eyes and ears to the fact that the common alfalfa is sometimes winter-killed, and blame the farmer for all the failures; such people like to tell only about its successes and to disregard the failures. This is not the best way. The other extreme would be to wait until the seed of perfectly hardy plants is obtained in commercial quantities.

Either view is extreme and unwise. We would plant the best seed obtainable, taking care that it is as free as possible from weed seed. Turkestan alfalfa, which was brought over for the first time in 1898, has made good over a wide area.

Alfalfa is so valuable that even one good crop is a
paying investment. But we must not place all our hopes
upon it as absolutely safe, since even our most enthusiastic growers admit that the plant winter-kills on certain soils and under certain conditions. Some think that
a perfectly hardy alfalfa is not to be expected. But why
not? Does buffalo grass ever winter-kill?

American experimenters have brought alfalfa from
Sweden and Russia and are greatly pleased with the
extremely vigorous, upright habits of growth, quick recovery after cutting, many stems and large leaves, the
abundant seed production, and the fact that the seeds are
tightly retained in the pods instead of shelling prema-
turely. The flowers vary greatly in color from blue to
yellow, ranging into green, dark violet and purple.

This hybrid condition of the plants should be maintained in order to get the greatest amount of forage per
acre. From many successful experiments has come the
belief that the complete solution of the hardy alfalfa
question is in sight.

No movement for the betterment of agriculture is more
general or extensive than that to provide silage for cattle.
The system has been slow in gaining a hold, but it is
coming with a rush now. For a time some of the large
milk dealers objected to silage as feed, but this opposition
was not justified, and has been withdrawn.

Beef cattle are brought along faster and better with
silage for fodder than by any other method. Of course,
in all cases a light percentage of dry feed or roughage is
needed.

The silo has its use on a farm of any size. It brings
system and certainty into the farmer's affairs, and is
profitable from any point of view. A field of corn goes
about twice as far in silage as in the old method of
feeding.

It is generally conceded that silage which is several

months old is better than newer feed. Some feeders prefer silage that is six months to a year old. Silage is
strong in carbohydrates, the principal food requirement
for all animals, but needs protein to balance it. Alfalfa
hay is perhaps the cheapest and best for this purpose.
Throughout the dairy sections it should form a part of
the ration where silage is used. This makes it possible
for the feeder to gain a greater economy in his operations, and at the same time give the animal a wholesome,
balanced ration.

Corn silage may be fed out of doors, in bunks, in the
stall, or in any place where animals can eat it without
waste. In severe weather it is best to feed silage inside,
as some will freeze, and this will be hard for the stock to
masticate, although the feeder need not be alarmed over
feeding freezing ensilage. It will not injure the animals,
but frozen food is not easy for them to consume.

In feeding milch cows, it is a good plan to give the hay
in a rack outside, where the animals will not waste it, and
feed the ensilage in the barn after milking. It may be
given twice a day in rations from ten to fifteen pounds
at a feeding, or twenty to forty pounds per day. Some
large animals will take as high as fifty pounds of silage
per day and make good use of it. Feed the ensilage so
that the animals will eat it up clean, as it spoils when
exposed to the air for several days.

In some of the most carefully managed experiments
ever made, silage has surpassed the usual grain feeding
in bringing on beef cattle. The ease and rapidity with
which gains are made, the greater efficiency of the feed
when given to young animals, the larger number that can
be handled, and the splendid quality of the finished product, are points which strongly appeal to feeders in favor
of silage for making beef.

Even when it comes to the finishing process in the last
month of feeding, it is found that silage is suitable for

the morning and evening rations, while dry corn may be used at noon. The stock will require a certain amount of hay, and should have access to this as desired. Nothing else is needed except the usual allowance of cottonseed or linseed meal.

Sand vetch is also known as hairy vetch. The plant produces many slender branches, 6 feet long, and the leaves and branches are covered with a coat of fine hairs. The seeds are small and black. If the field is not pastured too closely, the seed pods burst open when ripe and reseed the field.

Spring seed should be sown the last of April to the middle of May. If grown for forage, it is well to seed vetch with oats and wheat. The reason for this is that the grain keeps the vetch off the ground. If the seed is drilled, sow one bushel per acre. If broadcasted, 1½ bushels per acre. Seed also one bushel of oats as a nurse crop.

The name implies that it is best grown on a sandy loam soil; however, it grows well on poor soils—and so do cowpeas or clover. All stock relish the green forage and cured hay. Experiments show that it yields between two and three tons of hay per acre.

Soy beans make a rich late summer pasturage, a good soiling crop, a splendid ensilage crop, and a cured hay equal in palatability and feeding value to alfalfa hay. They yield twenty to thirty bushels of seed per acre, worth $2 to $3 per bushel, and can be ground into meal that will take the place of cottonseed meal, oil meal, tankage, gluten or other high-class concentrates, at much less cost.

Owing to their rapid growth, soy beans are an admirable catch crop to follow wheat, oats, crimson clover, potatoes or other early crops. They greatly improve the condition of the soil upon which they grow and enrich its store of nitrogen and humus.

As compared with the valuable and widely popular

cowpeas, soy beans have a wider range of usefulness, are more easily cured for hay, much more easily harvested and thrashed for seed, yield more seed, ripen more evenly, are more nutritious, command a better price, are less sensitive to frost, lose less in handling of the hay, crack less in thrashing, are less likely to be attacked by weevil, and the roots and stubble leave more nitrogen and humus in the soil. Cowpeas have the one superior virtue of making a heavier yield on a poor, sandy soil.

As a main crop, sow soy beans ten days after corn planting time, as a catch crop, as soon as the prior crop is off the land. If drilled in rows to be cultivated, one-third of a bushel will seed an acre; if drilled solid, like wheat, use six pecks.

For hay, cut when the pods are fully formed; for seed, cut when the plants begin to turn yellow, cure as for hay, and thrash. The thrashed forage will be eaten greedily by horses and cattle and they will thrive on it. At present prices soy beans are one of the most profitable crops that can be grown, and they fit admirably into almost any good system of crop rotation.

A still newer crop of great value to live stock owners is called guar. If this fodder crop proves to be all that is claimed for it, some of the others will be relegated to the background. Guar is described as an erect annual reaching a height of three to four feet in an arid country and five to seven feet in the rain belt. As a land improver it ranks with the cowpea, and as a forage plant it is said to equal alfalfa. Just imagine the amount of forage in a crop of alfalfa six feet high! Guar is said to produce enormous quantities of seed—twenty to thirty bushels per acre, even in a dry country, and proportionately larger yields in humid countries. In the cultivation of any of these legumes there is something to be made in producing seed, as well as hay.

Cows Kept at a Loss

E. V. ELLINGTON, in charge of dairy production, Idaho experiment station, discusses herd testing and the dairy industry in that state as follows:

While there are many high producing cows in the Northwest, the average production of cows being milked is low. Figures from the last census show that there are in the state of Idaho approximately 80,000 cows being milked that are classed as dairy cattle.

The value of dairy products produced in the state of Idaho is only $2,000,000. These figures indicate that many cows are being kept at an actual loss to the farmer. Records that the writer has kept on different herds over the state during the past year show that 20 per cent of the cows were not paying for the feed they consumed. For every dollar expended for feedstuffs some animals were only giving returns of 75 and 80 cents.

The dairy cow may be compared to a machine. Raw material is furnished her in the form of alfalfa, oats and barley, and milk is the finished product. Milk production is a question of dollars and cents and if the machine for the manufacture of milk cannot be operated on an economical basis then it should be disposed of.

There is only one means whereby the profitable cow may be detected with certainty from the unprofitable one, and this method consists in weighing and testing the milk and keeping a record of the feed consumed for the entire lactation period.

Keeping daily records of milk is a very simple and inexpensive task. All that is necessary is to have some form of scales and a ruled sheet whereby the milk weights may be recorded daily. It is well to use spring balance scales that will weigh from one-tenth to thirty pounds.

The fat test should be made at least once a month, the testing to be done at regular intervals. Samples from both morning and evening milking should be used. For the small herd a four-bottle Babcock tester is of sufficient size and may be secured at small cost from any creamery supply company and includes full directions for conducting the test. The manipulation of the fat test is very simple, but the directions should be carefully followed.

Guesswork is expensive to the dairyman. No person is able to go into a good sized herd and pick out all the best cows by examination. The highest degree of success cannot be attained unless the dairyman knows accurately the record of each cow. Success in dairying will depend upon the farmer's ability to lower the cost of producing a pound of butter-fat.

With increased cost of every item which goes into the maintenance of a dairy herd, from wrapping paper to hay, and from the fencing around the farm to the labor required in every operation, has come the absolute necessity of getting every part of the dairy on a paying basis or else facing a deficit either in money, which is likely, or in depreciation of the farm land, or in underpaid labor. All of which is primary and fundamental experience with the eastern cow-man.

For this fact remains: Well-tilled land will produce crops sufficient to pay a fair return on labor and investment even if sold in the open market. The feeding of the farm crop to a dairy cow, and the production by that cow of milk, and its further handling on the farm into butter and cheese—provided always that the cow is a satisfactory dairy animal—is proven to be the most profitable way of disposing of products of the farm, under existing conditions of demand and cost of transportation, and at the same time returns the largest possible conservation of fertility to the land itself. What, then, is the answer?

First, the cow must be a satisfactory dairy animal. Second, the manner of the farm management must be such as to get a maximum of the best food possible out of the soil to use as raw material for the cow machine to produce milk from.

Here hinges the question of dairy pre-eminence. The state whose farmers learn best to produce the most valuable and effective feeding materials from their land, and who learn how to build their dairies up with the best possible dairy cows, will lead the world in the excellence, the volume, and the value of its dairy products. Denmark is the shining example of the entire world, and in Denmark the key to the result is the cow-testing associations.

For in dairying, as in fruit culture, the ultimate profit depends upon the profit of each individual, cow, or tree, or vine. The value of a dairy herd is measured not by its best member in her best month, but by the average of all its members for twelve months, and this average is pulled down by its poorest member, as much as it is raised by its best, and there is no way known to know just what each cow is doing but by actual test. Without fear of successful contradiction it can be asserted that the dairy expert does not exist who can tell the best cow in a herd except by the scales and the Babcock tester, nor the value of a cow without an experience covering months.

This is a plea for the organization of cow-testing associations based upon actual experience which has come under the observation of the writer. First of all, why an association—why not individual testing? The only reason is because the average individual will not start and continue the test, and it must be thorough and complete to mean anything.

Importance of Cow Testing Associations

THE difference in dairy profits is not so much a difference in market advantages as in the handling and management of the cows. One farmer keeps cows that turn out a quantity of milk that puts the gross returns well above the cost of keeping the cows, while the other's milking herd is giving a supply the value of which is just running along on or near the same line as the cost of production. In the one herd quite frequently are found some cows that are turning in large profits and cows that are barely paying for their keep. The average profit from such a herd will depend entirely on the proportion of cows in each class.

The University of Nebraska, in a bulletin issued recently, shows clearly through the results of a cow-testing association in a county of Nebraska, that it is the amount of milk produced by the cow that determines her value and the value of dairying as a business. In part, this bulletin reads:

The good cow judge can generally tell the difference between cows of high and low productive capacity, but very few judges, if any, can always tell by type or conformation the cow producing 300 pounds of butter-fat from the one producing only 200 pounds. As a matter of fact, the only accurate way of discovering the unprofitable cow is with the scale and Babcock test. The truthfulness of this statement has been brought out in many instances. The former owner of Jacoba Irene, keeping no records of her production, considered her only an ordinary cow and sold her for an ordinary price.

Her worth was only determined after her owner took steps to have her tested. These figures revealed the remarkable fact that in less than a year she produced 1,111 pounds of butter, or more butter than is being produced by seven average Nebraska cows.

Dairymen need a variety of fodder crops. With summer drouths always possible, it is a good plan to have a field of rye and clover sown in the fall. This, like the first cutting of alfalfa, will be ready quite early. For midsummer emergencies it is well to have soy beans, cowpeas, millet or alfalfa. Cowpeas and oats may be sown together for a late hay crop.

Just west of Omaha, in Douglas County, is located a very prosperous, progressive farming community. Here the price of farm land is already in the neighborhood of $200 per acre. In this locality and in this connection it is of interest to note that the farmer who years ago could not be forced into dairying, has now turned to it and is getting satisfactory results. These farmers fully realize the importance of keeping accurate records of the amount of milk and fat produced by each cow in the herd. They also realized that through a co-operative cow-testing association the expense of obtaining these records would be very materially reduced and the Douglas County Cow-Testing Association was organized. The members of this association entered 21 herds, comprising some 435 cows. The work of the tester consisted in keeping accurate records of the amount of milk and butter-fat produced by every cow in the various herds and also in making careful estimates of the feed consumed by these cows. To do so he had to spend one day each month with every herd belonging to the association. In addition to this work this man was ever ready with suggestions as to how the rations could be improved for economical milk and butter-fat production.

The following table shows the difference between ten

good cows and ten bad ones. An accurate account of feed and milk production was kept:

Ten most profitable cows.		Ten least profitable cows.	
1	.............$123.58	1 (Loss).........$13.73	
2	.... 116.96	2	.... 1.62
3	.... 108.74	3	.... 2.84
4	.... 108.10	4	.... 3.85
5	.... 104.15	5	.... 7.10
6	.... 96.66	6	.... 9.09
7	.... 95.59	7	.... 10.27
8	.... 94.97	8	.... 11.14
9	.... 92.11	9	.... 12.07
10	.... 92.02	10	.... 13.57
Total	........$1,032.88	Total	...........$85.28

From this table the reader will notice that a herd composed of 10 of the best cows would yield a profit of over $1,032. Compare with this the meagre profit of only $85 that would come to the dairyman as a result of a year's work with a herd composed of 10 of the poorest cows, and there is at least one evident reason why the farmer who keeps no record of the amount of milk produced and who thinks it of no importance to test the milk for butter-fat fails to make dairying profitable.

Dairy By-Products Are Important

THE value of the dairy by-products of the country for one year amounts to more than fifty million dollars, according to an estimate made by the Department of Agriculture; and this is a conservative estimate. The item of dairy products is one of vast importance, and is well worthy of careful attention and study.

Skim-milk is by far the most important by-product from the dairy, and the best adapted to varied and profitable uses. Skim-milk, as a human food, is unappreciated by most farmers; but it has been tested under various conditions, by food experts, and has proven a useful portion of an everyday diet for many people. The use of skim-milk ought to be encouraged, and would result in finding city markets for a large amount of this valuable by-product.

A report from one of our leading colleges contains the following:

"Skim-milk has all the protein and half of the full value of the whole milk and is in most localities the most economical source of animal protein. The food elements in skim-milk are equal in physiological value to those of meats and are far less expensive."

As an article to substitute for water, in the preparation of various dishes, as well as for others that are made mainly of milk, there is no waste, but a decided gain in food-value. In making bread, skim-milk will add to the weight and nutritive value of the loaf. Used in place of water, sufficient flour may be saved to pay for the milk, and yet produce a loaf of equal weight, and of more actual food value.

Milk bread is richer in fatty matter, and superior in flesh forming elements, which is scientifically explained as being due to the casein of milk being incorporated with the fibrin of the flour.

The sale of skim-milk to bakers and confectioners should be encouraged, and is capable of being largely increased. Used in this manner, it may be made to net the consumer one dollar a cwt., or more than a large per cent of the farmers and dairymen realize for their whole milk.

As a food for domestic animals skim-milk occupies the most conspicuous position of any food-stuff, especially as a feed for young and growing animals. The facts which seem to have been proven by the various experiments are as follows:

"Skim-milk gives the best returns when fed to very young animals, constituting the larger part of their rations.

"It is next best for animals making rapid growth, but which need other feed than milk, mainly of a carbonaceous nature.

"Except for very young animals skim-milk gives the best returns when used in combination with other foods generally grains.

"No class of live stock will give larger returns for skim-milk than poultry of various kinds."

At the New York Experiment Station chickens were grown successfully on a diet composed mainly of skim-milk, although they were allowed a run of the fields during the time when they were being fed this ration.

It was estimated that at the test, after allowing from 25 cents to 50 cents per hundred for the skim-milk, and some other feed in proportion, the cost of producing one pound of live weight was less than six cents at the time when the birds weighed three pounds.

During this time the milk was fed sweet; but it has

been found equally satisfactory when fed thick and lop-
pered, and the waste is less in the latter form.

If a premium were offered for the most rapid gains in
pig feeding, my opinion would be that some man skilled
in feeding skim-milk with other foods would carry off
the prize. Professor Henry, of Wisconsin, a high au-
thority on feeding domestic animals, says regarding the
value of skim-milk as a food for swine:

"Skim-milk has a value as a feed for stockmen that
is higher than merely serving as a substitute for grain.
All of the constituents of milk are digestible and this
valuable by-product of the creamery is rich in bone and
blood building constituents."

When we consider the use of this food for bone and
muscle building, and also remember its easy digestibility,
and that by adding a variety it makes other food articles
more palatable, and probably assists in their digestion,
we must hold skim-milk as occupying a high place in the
list of feedstuffs available on most farms.

Authorities seem to differ as to the merits of sweet
and sour milk as a feed for swine. My experience con-
vinces me that either is desirable; but the sudden change
from sweet to sour, and from sour to sweet, must be
avoided in feeding any kind of domestic animals.

Calves appear to be the next in favor, as profitable
consumers of skim-milk, and some feeders appear to
think that they can feed their skim-milk to calves, and
derive more profits from it than by feeding it to swine;
but this depends, to a large extent, upon the good qualities
of the animals that are being fed.

In feeding skim-milk to calves one cent's worth of oil-
meal will take the place of a pound of butter fat that
has been removed from the milk, besides, when the milk
is fed warm from the separator, it is better for the calves
than milk that is cold and sour.

A young animal that is fed on skim-milk, with mill

feed or grains, may be made to weigh almost as much as one of similar breeding and fed on whole milk with the same kind of grains, at one year of age.

Calves, for veal, may be started on whole milk, and then gradually changed to skim-milk, and fed for awhile, and then made ready for market by feeding for a week or two on whole milk to put on a smooth finish and improve their sale.

In feeding skim-milk to calves, overfeeding is dangerous, and must be avoided. Calves are more easily made sick by being fed poor milk than pigs. Skim-milk has also been fed to lambs, horses and colts with success.

Cheese may be made from skim-milk, and could be made a profitable outlet for large quantities of the by-product. A product called Dutch cheese, or pot cheese, is also made from skim-milk, and finds a ready sale in many cities or villages. With this, there seems to be no established price; but some claim to be able to make a dollar's worth of this cheese from 100 pounds of skim-milk.

Buttermilk ranks close to skim-milk in feeding value; but its physical condition requires that more care be exercised in feeding it than is required in feeding skim-milk.

As a human food it is excellent, and for cooking it is in demand; but it has been the common practice for many city dealers to sell poor skim-milk for buttermilk, after it has become soured and unfit for use; this has had the effect of decreasing the demand for buttermilk.

Good buttermilk, fresh from the churn, is more valuable for cooking purposes than whole milk.

How to Obtain a Good Stand of Corn

A PERFECT stand of corn is that which produces the greatest possible yield. This is affected by the number of stalks and their arrangement on the surface of the soil.

Of course, a perfect stand for one soil might be only half a stand for another, while a perfect stand for a wet season might be too thick a stand for the same soil in a dry season.

However, no absolute rules can be laid down which will enable the corn grower to decide how far apart he shall make his rows, or how thick the stalks or hills shall stand in the row.

No one can foretell what the season will be. The number of square feet of soil required to support a hill or stalk of corn varies with the soil fertility, cultivation, rainfall, and other seasonal or climatic conditions, the variety of corn, and many other factors.

While it is probably impossible to secure a perfectly even distribution of stalks or hills, recent experiments and experience combine to indicate that each stalk or hill should stand as nearly as possible in the center of a square of soil from which it draws its food.

The size of this square will, of course, be determined by the distance between stalks in the row and between rows.

What this distance should be under the conditions existing in the different corn-growing States may be suggested, if not finally determined, by the tests carried on in the different States.

At the Nebraska Station, corn grown in hills 44 inches

apart, each way, produced the highest yield of grain when planted at the rate of four kernels per hill, but five kernels produced an almost equally high yield of corn and a slightly greater yield of stover.

Two kernels per hill produced the largest ears, and one kernel per hill the greatest number of two-eared plants, tillers, and ears per hundred plants. The percentage of barren plants increased with the number of plants per hill.

These facts sometimes lead seed growers to plant very thinly in the hope of producing very large ears for seed, but the opposite practice is found to result in seed having the greatest producing power, as it may result in the elimination of barren plants, and those that do not produce well under adverse conditions.

Corn grown at three rates, namely, at 1, 3 and 5 plants per hill, for three years, showed an average producing power of 3.6 bushels more for the thickest planting than for the thinnest.

At the Kansas Station, corn was grown in rows, 2, 2½, 3, 3½ and 4 feet apart, and from 4 to 20 inches apart in the row; both listed and surface-planted corn were tested in rows 3½ and 4 feet apart, but all narrower rows were surface planted.

Both listed and surface-planted corn gave the best results when the rows were 4 feet apart, and the stalks 16 inches apart, while in 1891 the best results were obtained when rows were 3½ feet apart, stalks 16 inches apart.

The average results for three years' work at the Missouri Station indicate that the maximum yields from corn planted in hills 45 inches apart each way, was obtained from planting 3 or 4 grains per hill, 4.3 bushels per acre less being secured from planting 2 grains per hill. Lower yields were secured in hills 45 by 22½, or 45 by 15.

On good land the largest yield of 70.4 bushels per acre was secured by leaving 4 stalks per hill, in hills 45 inches apart each way, while on poor land the largest yield of 36 bushels per acre resulted from thinning to 2 stalks per hill.

Four stalks per hill gave a yield of 6.6 bushels less per acre, more than half of which was unmerchantable. One stalk per hill produced almost as large a yield on poor land as did 4, and almost every ear was merchantable.

In all cases the thicker the planting the larger the yield of stover and the greater the proportion of nubbins.

Eighty-five per cent of a stand produced 2½ bushels per acre more grain than did 85 per cent of a stand in which the missing hills were replanted, and 12 bushels more than when the entire plat was planted over. Ninety-four per cent of a perfect stand produced 2.2 bushels per acre more than 85 per cent of a perfect stand.

At the Ohio Station, one grain every 12 inches, or 2 grains every 24 inches, produced better results than three grains every 36 inches, or four grains every 48 inches. One grain every 18 inches proved insufficient to secure a maximum crop, but produced the largest percentage of ears. Four grains every 42 inches proved entirely too thick for best results. The work was continued for three years.

Ten years' test at the Indiana Station showed that in seasonable years the yields of both corn and stover are greater from thick planting, but that in the very dry year of 1894 the yield of corn was less and of stover greater from thick planting.

At the Maine Station, one acre of land fertilized with 10 two-horse loads of stable manure and 750 pounds of commercial fertilizer produced, respectively, 5,246, 5,390, and 4,448 pounds per acre of dry matter when kernels were planted 6, 9, and 12 inches apart, but the ears were larger when the planting was at a distance of 9 and 12 inches.

At the Louisiana Station, stalks 18 inches apart in five-foot rows, produced the largest results, although a closer planting might have proved more profitable during a more favorable season, but is not recommended as a general practice.

At the Alabama Station, on poor and sandy land, to which complete fertilizer was added at the rate of 320 pounds per acre, the yield was largest when the constant area devoted to each plant produced, was a perfect square in shape; that is, when 15 square feet was so planted that the distance in the drill was about equal to the distance between rows.

The highest average yield for two years resulted from single plants three feet, nine inches apart, in rows four feet apart, but plants three feet apart in rows five feet wide, were more cheaply cultivated.

A row of cow-peas should be planted between corn rows on very poor land, in which case the corn rows should be at least five feet apart.

At the Georgia Station, ten years' experiments indicated that land capable of producing 25 to 40 bushels of shelled corn per acre should be so planted as to grow 3,630 plants per acre.

This number may be secured by planting 32 inches apart in 4½-foot rows, 36 inches apart in 4-foot rows, or 42 inches apart in 3½-foot rows.

Soil capable of producing 15 to 25 bushels per acre produces its maximum yield when 16 square feet are allowed per plant, or 2,722 plants per acre.

This number should be secured by planting 38½ inches apart in 5-foot rows, 32 inches apart in 4½-foot rows, or 48 inches apart in 4-foot rows. Soils capable of producing 10 to 15 bushels per acre, give their maximum yield when 18 to 24 square feet per stalk is allowed, or from 2,420 to 1,850 hills to the acre.

Eighteen square feet per stalk may be secured by planting 36 inches apart in 6-foot rows, or 43 inches apart in 5-foot rows, or 4 feet, 3 inches apart each way.

At the Texas Station the highest average yield for five varieties tested, resulted from planting 4 feet by 2½ feet apart, while the planting 3 feet by 2½ feet apart stood second, 5 by 3 third, and 4½ by 3 gave the lowest yields. Golden Beauty and Leaming produced the best yields from close planting, while Thomas, 100-day Bristol and Forsyth Favorite, did best in 4-foot rows, planted 2½ feet apart in the drill.

The increase of 2.2 bushels per acre which the work at the Missouri Station indicated would result from improving the stand from 85 to 94 per cent. A perfect stand would, if secured for each of the 108,771,000 acres devoted to the corn crop in 1909, secure an increase of $142,620,535.20, at the farm value of 59.6 cents per bushel.

As a matter of fact, however, comparatively few fields have even 85 per cent of a perfect stand. In view of the opinion of prominent authorities on this subject, that the average corn field has not over 66 per cent of a perfect stand, while in many cases the percentage is less than 40, it is difficult to compute the loss resulting to the corn-growers of the United States from this cause.

The Culture of Broomcorn

THE principal crops of broomcorn are raised in Kansas, Oklahoma and southern Illinois, although this crop will grow in other sections of the country where soil and climatic conditions are favorable.

It is a profitable crop, as the price per ton for the brush usually ranges from $50 for the lower grades that are damaged by the weather up to $200 and over for the very best. The prices for 1910 ranged from $140 to $190 per ton.

In the Southwest it is becoming more important as a forage crop, and it is used to a considerable extent after the brush has been removed. The seed has but small feeding value.

The two best types of broomcorn grown in the Southwest particularly are the Dwarf and the Standard. The Dwarf is much liked because it grows only from four to six inches high, with a brush of from 12 to 20 inches, however. This type is better suited to the semi-arid regions and to the uplands of the broomcorn section in the Southwest.

The soil should be plowed in the fall or early in the spring, so that it will retain as much moisture as possible. About two weeks before planting, the land should be disked and harrowed, and, if necessary, harrowed a second time before planting. Broomcorn is a good sod-crop.

Broomcorn plants are very tender, and make the most rapid growth in warm weather. They will not stand the cold of early spring like corn. The seed will rot before

germinating, or if the plant germinates the growth will
be retarded by continued cold.

When large areas are planted, the most convenient way
is to divide the field into sections of about ten acres each,
and plant at intervals of about a week. The crop demands
prompt attention, and if this system of planting is followed, there is not so much danger of damage to the
brush from rain, or becoming too ripe.

In case farm hands are scarce, the scarcity is not so
keenly felt, for there is not a very large crop that
demands attention within a period of a few days. A
few hands can take care of comparatively large fields,
and it is much more convenient than to plant the whole
field on a single day.

The method of planting is about the same as for Kaffir
corn. Plant in rows about three feet apart, and four to
five inches apart in the row. The Standard, due to its
large growth, is planted in rows about three and a half
feet apart.

Selecting good seed is very important. Good seed
should give a germination of 90 to 95 per cent, and seed
should not be used that falls much below this standard.
By using seed that gives a germination test above 90 per
cent, one bushel is sufficient quantity to plant twenty
acres; or two quarts of seed will plant an acre.

The soil should be in good condition when seeded;
then the cultivation should begin early and be repeated
frequently to prevent the weeds from getting a start of
the slow-growing plants. A sharp-tooth harrow is sometimes used just as the plants are coming up.

After one good harrowing, the field should receive
about two cultivations of medium depth, then the rest
of the cultivation should be shallow, so as not to injure
the root system.

In this way the soil is finely pulverized, forming a dust
blanket which aids in the conservation of moisture.

Broomcorn is a crop that will not stand in the field without great damage after it is ready to harvest. It should be harvested just as the plants are coming into full bloom, or when the anthers are falling from the head.

The head of the Dwarf is enclosed in a sheaf or "boot." It is more convenient to pull the head than to cut it, after which the boot is removed. The heads are usually pulled and piled in bunches along the row. The brush from three or four rows is piled together, and after drying for two or three days, is gathered and stacked in small ricks.

Because of the greater height of the Standard broomcorn, it is necessary to bend the heads over to make them easy to cut. The stalks are bent at a height of about three feet.

Two adjacent rows are bent diagonally across the intervening space so that the portion of the stalks above the sharp bend is supported in a horizontal position, with the seed-heads of one row extending about two feet beyond the opposite row.

This method is called "tabling." One man can table as fast as two can cut. In cutting, the operator walks along the spaces between the tables, and cuts the heads six or eight inches below the attachment of the straws.

The brush as cut is laid by handfuls upon every second table, making it very convenient for loading on a wagon.

After drying, the brush should still retain the green color. To accomplish this, do not dry it in the sun, as it will be bleached to a light-brown color. By curing in sheds the original green color can be retained to a large extent, and as a result the brush will command a much better price. The average time of drying is about thirty days. It is then threshed and baled.

The Sugar Beet Industry

IN the general scheme of diversified farming the sugar beet may become one of the most profitable features. Sugar is an article of such general consumption that for economic reasons it ought to be produced in this country.

While politicians may wrangle over the economic problems of a tariff, it might be well if we would bear in mind that homely, but wise, answer given by the immortal Lincoln when asked his opinion on the tariff. He said: "If we buy from Europe a ton of rails, we get the rails and Europe gets the money; but if we produce the rails, we have both the rails and the money."

At the present time we have about seventy factories in the United States, of which ten are in California. In 1897 there was produced in the United States 45,000 tons of beet sugar, while there was produced in 1911 560,000 tons. If it were not for the unfortunate agitations that come up over the sugar question, the sugar beet industry would by this time have become much larger than it is.

There is land suitable for beet culture that could be used to produce all the sugar we need in America. The present consumption of sugar amounts to about four million tons, about one-sixth of which is produced in the United States, the balance being imported raw from foreign countries where cheap labor is available, and the cost of refining the sugar in the United States is only about one-half cent per pound. If we imported all the sugar we used, and merely refined it in this country at that refining cost of one-half cent a pound, it would contribute to the American industry only about twenty-three million dollars, whereas to produce the same amount of sugar from American grown beets would contribute close to three hundred million dollars to the American industry.

But there are other and more important reasons why the beet sugar industry should be fostered in the United States, and one of these is on account of the beet's value in crop rotation. In European countries where beet-growing is practiced it is found that they get much larger yields of crops per acre than we do in this country. Take for example barley. Our greatest barley states are California, Minnesota and South Dakota; and from the four million acres of barley we harvest about ninety-two million bushels, while Germany harvests from about the same acreage one hundred and sixty million bushels, or seventy per cent more than we do. The same is true of other crops. Our average yield of wheat per acre is about fourteen bushels against Germany's twenty-eight bushels; our average yield of oats is about twenty-four bushels against Germany's fifty-eight; our average yield of potatoes is ninety-five bushels against Germany's two hundred and five.

Moreover, European economists say that if cane and beet sugar could be produced side by side, the cane sugar at a cost of two cents per pound and the beet sugar at a cost of four cents per pound, it would be cheaper for the nation to raise the beet sugar on account of the indirect agricultural advantages to be obtained through rotating the land with sugar beets.

Good drainage and deep plowing are necessary in the cultivation of sugar beets. Instead of the ordinary furrow four or five inches deep, it is best to make it ten to fourteen inches. The reason is that the root of the plant is fed from the nitrogen of the air and the water from the soil. Very little nutriment is secured from the soil, the larger part of the beet being water and the nitrogen which is caught by the leaves and absorbed by the root. But in the plowing, several methods are employed by industrious raisers. Some use an ordinary breaking plow and follow that with another plowing in its furrow, thus necessitating covering the ground twice. Others use a subsoiler. This is an attachment which is built into an ordinary breaking plow and its function is to break up the subsoil. This leaves the ground loose for the required distance.

The more progressive farmers are now adopting the deep tillage plow. This is a late invention that can be be adjusted to plow from 16 to 24 inches in depth. It takes from a 12 to 16-inch furrow in width and accomplishes its work as fast as the regular plow. By using the subsoiling method of farming the use of about three times as much land is possible and the value of the productive possibilities is enhanced considerably.

The plowing should be done as late in the fall as possible and the land allowed to lie thus all winter. As soon as you can get into the fields in the spring give the land an extra good harrowing, and then cross-harrow it. In fact, put a garden finish on the field and the work of seeding will be materially lightened. Every hour and dollar expended on preparation will be well repaid in the reduced cost of cultivation later in the season. The man who plows deep and gives the field a thorough dressing is sure to get a good crop.

The seeding is done with a special beet drill and the average distance between the rows is 20 inches. This is often varied, however, and some fields have given good yields with the rows only 16 inches apart. Others plant 2 feet apart. It is merely a matter of the productive capacity of the land and the degree of wealth the farmer wants from the crop. The drill seeds the land in much

the same manner that oats or other small grain is drilled
and the rows show up in the same manner as they do.

The small plants are allowed to grow thus for a period
of 10 days or two weeks and then the farm help go
into the field and commence thinning. This is a double
operation. The first is done with a wide hoe, the workmen going along a row and at equal spaces cutting out
the intervening plants, thus leaving a small bunch of
plants at regular intervals along the row. This work is
accomplished as soon as possible so that the small plants
will have plenty of room to grow. The second operation is the thinning of the bunches down to one plant.
The workmen go along to each bunch and pick out all
the plants but the most lively one, and then the most careful attention is given this plant, for if it dies there will
not be time to grow another to maturity in its place. The
beets require as early planting as possible and are seldom harvested before the first frosts.

The cultivation of the beet crop should be given great
care and the attention it needs at the time it needs it.
Beets are cultivated at least once each week by a special
cultivator which handles two rows at each trip across
the field. Shallow cultivation will prove to be the best if
the work is done frequently. It is impossible to cross-
work the field, so it will be necessary to go through the
field about two or three times during the season with the
hoe and cut out all weeds. The elimination of weeds
is necessary to give a proper beet growth.

The beets are harvested as soon as they are ripe by
the use of a lifter. The size of the beets precludes the
possibility of pulling them by hand successfully. It will
be found advisable to clean off the soil to a certain extent
so that no losses may be had through inaccurate tare
weight at the factory. The beets may be left in the field
where thrown out by the lifter until the topping process
can be reached as frost will not have any injurious effect

on the sugar values if not repeated too often. Repeated freezing will ruin the beet as the thawing of the beet releases a part of the sap and sugar that it carries.

The topping is done with an ordinary knife, the operation being to cut off the top of the beet so that all the green sprout is removed. If the topping is not done close enough the weigher will deduct a percentage for tare on account of the fact that the green top does not contain any sugar values. The beet need not be cut square across but just close enough to remove the green sprouts. After the beets are topped they are thrown into convenient piles where they await loading for transportation to the factory. Generally the order is sent to the grower just when the factory desires him to start getting in his beets.

In reference to the yields that may be expected it may be said that the yield will fluctuate in proportion to the care given the crop. One farmer having just as good land as the man across the road may only get a third of the yield owing to his slipshod methods of cultivation. In figures the minimum is close to six tons to the acre and the maximum is about 40 tons. The average may be close to 18 or 20 tons to the acre and at the contract price of say $5 per ton for 16 per cent beets you can figure the profits for yourself. This is not taking into consideration any of the indirect profits which accrue from this crop. Briefly speaking it may be said that time and again it has been shown that when beets re-rotated once each four years with oats, corn and wheat, it increased the yields of the other crops a considerable per cent. Just why, is a story in itself.

Probably the cheapest fertilizer that you can get for beet land is the tops after they have been cut off the beets. Leaving the tops on the ground to rot through the winter and then plowing them under in the spring will be found to give a good coat of fertilizer and one that will be strong enough to nurture the crop. Stable manure is excellent if you have it, but it should be well rotted and evenly spread over the field. The purchase of commercial fertilizers is made to some extent but the cost of the product has led to its being slowly adopted. It will hardly get any lower in price and if you have no fertilizer of any kind it will probably be best if a small amount is used. If any other method of fertilizing is available by all means use that.

The rotation of the crops will be advantageous for it will give the land a rest each season. The necessities of the various plants are different. By rotating corn, wheat and oats after a crop of beets an increase in all the crops will be found. Some farmers find it profitable to rotate a crop of potatoes with the small grains. For the past 100 years the farmers of France have raised sugar beets and rotated their crops in the above manner and they have succeeded in building up the once barren wastes of France into the most productive areas in the world. The reason given for this is the thorough cultivation demanded by beets. And then almost unconsciously the same methods are adopted in the farming of other crops, to the added profit and advantage of the grower.

The pulp resulting from the extraction of the beet sugar possesses great feeding values for stock and in almost all cases it is hauled off by the farmers as soon as it is thrown out at the factory.

Irrigation by Wells Profitable

No feature of western agriculture, except probably dry farming, has had as hard a struggle for recognition and commercial standing as that of irrigation from wells. Ten years ago it was hooted at as a chimera and a plaything. Even today, scores of successful agriculturists in the west contend that it is utterly impracticable and unprofitable except in a few favored instances. Well irrigation has more enthusiastic advocates and more bitter critics than almost any measure affecting the prosperity of the west.

About 15 years ago, J. L. Bristow, now a United States senator from Kansas, sought to interest the farmers of the central west in a movement for well irrigation. Starting in the midst of a cycle of dry years, the movement sprang into immediate favor and assumed considerable proportions. "Pump the underflow!" was Mr. Bristow's slogan. Subsequent wet years rather checked the movement as a country-wide proposition, yet much of the well irrigation in western Kansas and Nebraska and in Colorado of today may be traced back to Bristow's plan to redeem the entire west from the drought tyrant.

Following this movement, the government, a few years later, began experiments which resulted in the institution of a reclamation project at Garden City, Kan., the source of water supply being the underflow of the Arkansas River. This is now the most extensive well irrigation district in the United States. More than 250 wells are drained by electric power generated at a central power plant. The wells are in 28 groups, a pumping station being maintained at each group. The series of stations cover a distance of five miles, the water flowing into a huge concrete conduit, which carries it to the laterals radiating into the fields. About 10,000 acres of land are watered from this plant, mostly devoted to sugar beets and alfalfa. The cost of the water to the farmers is $3 an acre yearly, with some small fees additional, and after a series of years, following the plan of all government projects, the great system will become the property of the landowners.

At the time of the Bristow movement, not 500 acres in the United States were under well irrigation. Now the area so irrigated, including rice irrigation in Louisiana and Texas, is 750,000 acres. In California alone 200,000 are under water from wells, the lift in many places being as much as 200 feet. Critics of the new departure contend that water cannot possibly be lifted more than 20 or 30 feet at any profit. California agriculturists, however, lift water up to 200 feet, carry it for miles in cement ditches, and find the growing of alfalfa, which sells for $15 a ton, profitable. Barley, wheat and all manner of crops are grown with this same expensive water—water which costs from $5 to $10, and even as high as $15 an acre for the year.

In portions of the rice-growing sections of the South, water from wells is now used for flooding, in places, in preference to bayou or creek water. In the rice counties of Arkansas wells furnish the water exclusively for a profitable industry. Rice culture requires many times the amount of water necessary for ordinary irrigation, but the crop is highly remunerative, thus making practicable the heavy cost of pumping.

It is manifest that large works, like the Garden City project, would only be feasible where large bodies of subterranean water exist. Such underflows, however, are not unusual, and in practically every region the ordinary well is available. True, the depth to the water varies and is often great and the supply may not be inexhaustible, but each in its degree will aid in the growth of crops, and is a valuable acquisition to any farm where the supply of moisture is inadequate.

Well irrigation is especially adapted to small tracts of from 20 to 40 acres, but like all enterprises, large operations can usually be conducted more economically than small ones. Given the possibility of securing a good well, it costs approximately $25 an acre to place small tracts under such irrigation. In a section in New Mexico where a strong underflow is encountered at depths varying from 15 to 100 feet, it is calculated that a plant can be installed for $2,000 which will be capable of watering 200 acres. The annual cost of operation will average smaller as the scale of operations increases. There are, however, many advantages for the small farmer, and in the end his profits will doubtless be large.

Power is the most important and the most expensive item to take account of. Where electricity is unavailable, gasoline engines must be resorted to and the high cost of fuel, especially in the remote localities, is a serious obstacle. In this New Mexico locality it costs from $3 to $4 an acre foot to produce water, and under present conditions 2 feet or more are necessary to produce a crop. The endeavor now is to combine the irrigation and dry farming methods, thus reducing the quantity of water necessary. Wind power is used to some extent and is less expensive than any other, but it can only be utilized in connection with large storage tanks or reservoirs. It often happens that the wind ceases to blow just the time when water is most needed.

Advantages of Concrete on Farms

FARMERS of all classes will find it profitable to have concrete buildings, troughs, tanks and walks on their premises.

Persons starting in agriculture should not neglect the opportunity to have substantial and fireproof structures. It is easy to go ahead on this line from the beginning, though hard to change after a start has been made with frame buildings.

Concrete is as cheap as lumber for building purposes, and even cheaper, if sand, gravel and labor are largely furnished on the place. An ordinary farm hand will become expert in the use of concrete with a few days' experience.

Silos, barns and other buildings made of this material are much safer than wood against fire and storm. There is satisfaction in knowing that live stock, machinery and crops are not in danger of being destroyed by the flames. It is a pleasure also to have the snug shelter and tasty appearance that may be obtained from cement construction.

The largest part of concrete is the gravel or crushed stone. This should be clean; that is, free from loam, clay or vegetable matter. The best results are obtained from a mixture of sizes graded from the smallest, which is retained on a one-fourth inch screen, to the larger ones that will pass a one and one-half inch ring. For heavy foundation and abutment work, larger sized pebbles and stones might be used, while for reinforced concrete work pebbles larger than those passing a one inch ring should not be used.

In the selection of sand the greatest care should be used, and critical attention should be given to its quality, for sand contributes from one-third to one-half of the amount of the materials used in making concrete. Sand may be considered as including all grains and small pebbles that will pass through a wire screen with one-fourth inch meshes, while gravel in general is the pebbles and stones retained upon such a screen. The sand should be clean, coarse, and, if possible, free from loam, clay and vegetable matter.

In mixing materials for concrete use two and a half times as much sand as Portland cement, and twice as much gravel or stone as sand—that is, one part cement, two and a half parts sand and five parts gravel or crushed stone. Use just enough water to get the consistency desired. If the sand is very fine the cement should be increased from 10 to 15 per cent. When the mixture does not have a uniform color, but looks streaky, it has not been fully mixed.

If the mixture does not work well and the sand and cement do not fill the voids in the stone, the percentage of stone should be reduced slightly, but the concrete should first be properly mixed. Concrete that is poorly mixed may present features that are entirely eliminated by turning it over once or twice more.

Concrete wet enough to be mushy and run off a shovel when being handled is used for reinforced work, thin walls, or other thin sections. Concrete just wet enough to make it jellylike is used for some reinforced work and also for foundations, floors, etc. It requires ramming with a tamper to remove air bubbles and to fill voids. This concrete is of a medium consistency.

Sometimes bank or creek gravel, which will answer the purpose of sand and gravel combined, can be obtained, and it is frequently used on the farm and in small jobs of concrete work just as it comes from the pit or creek. Occasionally this gravel contains nearly the right proportions of sand and gravel, but in the majority of sand pits and gravel banks there is a great variation in the sizes of the grains and pebbles or gravel and in the quantities of each. This is due to the fact that all the deposits are formed in seams or pockets that make it impossible to secure anything like uniformity. Therefore, to get the best and cheapest concrete, it is advisable to screen the sand and gravel and to remix them in the correct proportions.

Dirty sand makes a weak concrete. Crushed rock is much better than screened gravel because of the rougher edges.

As a test of sand, rub it in the hand and if there is much dirt left on the hand discard that sand.

If, when a large handful of the same is thrown into a pail of water, it leaves the water muddy, discard it.

Following are the four recognized mixtures for concrete:

Rich mixture—One part Portland cement, two parts of clean, coarse sand, four parts of crushed rock. This is used for floors, fence posts, and the like.

Medium mixture—One-half and one and two-fifths parts respectively of cement, sand and crushed rock. This mixture is used for walks and thin walls.

Ordinary mixture—1-3-6 for heavy walls, piers, abutments, etc.

Lean mixture—1-4-8 for footings and in places where volume and not great strength is needed.

When gravel is used, the proportions are one part of cement and from six to nine parts of gravel, according to the amount of sand in the gravel.

To make one cubic yard of concrete the following respective amounts of cement are required: Rich mixture one and one-half barrels; medium mixture one and one-fourth barrels; ordinary mixture one and one-eighth barrels; lean mixture seven-eighths of a barrel.

In construction work such as floors, barns, fence posts, bridges, reinforcements of iron are absolutely necessary. The beginner will need the supervision of an expert in using reinforcements.

Measure exact amounts for each part. Mix thoroughly and not too long before applying the water. Cement will set in 20 or 30 minutes and if disturbed after that loses its strength.

Spread the sand and cement on a mixing board and mix thoroughly, adding enough water when mixed to bring the mixture to the consistency of mortar.

Add the proper quantity of crushed rock and mix all together, after which it is ready for use. In this manner the sand grains are all covered with the finer particles of cement and the crushed rock when added has all the voids filled with temperate mixture. This undoubtedly gives the greatest strength for materials used.

A very common method, however, is to mix all three parts at once while yet dry and then to mix with water until the mixture will pack well, and handle with a shovel.

Get the form walls rigid and do not use lumber that is too dry, as it takes up moisture and changes its shape so as to injure the concrete in setting.

Do not allow concrete work to dry out fast, as cracks will appear. It should be protected from the sun for three or five days and sprinkled with water to insure even setting throughout the concrete.

In two weeks concrete gains strength sufficient for ordinary use, but 60 days should elapse before it is given a full load.

Important Points in Building Silos

IT is a common mistake in building silos to construct them without sufficient depth of foundation. In northern states the frost line may be five feet from the surface, and unless the wall is put down to this depth, the structure is apt to be thrown out of plumb and possibly ruined at the breaking up of winter.

The weight of the silo walls makes little difference, but the damage is most serious where cement or brick has been used. Even with wooden frames there is no reason why the foundation should not be five feet or more in depth. The silo itself may be dug to any reasonable depth in the ground, so far as preservation of fodder is concerned. There is no material damage from water settling at the bottom, most of the liquid being held in the silage. This is merely a question of convenience, and it would seem wise to make the cavity as low as it is necessary to put the walls—that is, three to five feet.

Farmers are turning from wooden silos to those of cement and brick, in order to gain security, many of the lighter structures having been destroyed by wind. They do not gain security, however, unless the foundation is right, and as the average cost is higher with cement or brick, it seems like a foolish risk to have any but the most durable work.

In nearly every case where silo walls are seen to be cracked or out of plumb, it will be found the trouble started with a poor foundation. The necessity of making repairs in a new silo is not only aggravating but it is expensive, if thoroughly done.

There are other features of silo building which deserve consideration in order to prevent early damage. In brick construction there is danger of rushing the work too fast to allow for settling. A small affair like a silo goes up quickly with two or three skillful men on the job, and the walls will settle perceptibly for days after the job is completed. This rapid construction should not be allowed. There is little of this kind of danger in building walls for a large house or store.

The quality of the brick is worth mentioning also. A number of cases are known where brick plants were started up in a convenient place to supply the commodity in a hurry to a few transient customers. When it was too late, it was found that there was considerable lime in the clay, as a result of which the wall cracked in a short time, and much loss followed. It is economy to use brick of a high grade.

Those building wooden silos need to look well to the foundations also. Where it can be done without inconvenience, the silo should be placed south or east of the barn, to lessen the danger from wind. It is possible to anchor one of these lighter structures with three or four iron rods. Such an addition to the expense of construction is not more than $10 or $15, and it may save the silo from destruction in case of a heavy storm. No investment on the farm makes bigger returns than that employed in providing a good silo, but without proper construction money is wasted instead of being gained.

For the past fifteen years, practically all silos built have been round in shape, and this is the only style to be recommended at present. The essential things in silo construction are to have an air-tight wall, smooth on the inside so the silage can settle properly, and a structure sufficiently strong to hold the enormous pressure of the silage, and durable enough so that it will not be necessary to replace it for some time. Successful silos have been built in a variety of ways and of a variety of materials, including wooden staves, concrete, wood plastered with cement, stone, wood, brick, iron and tile. It is not the purpose in this article to give details for construction of silos, but rather to give information regarding the subject in general and the advantages of the first three types mentioned.

The most common silo found in America is that known as the stave silo. This is built on the plan of a stave water tank. It is purchased ready to put together, requiring only that the foundation be made. A foundation is built of concrete. The walls should be about eight inches thick. A stave silo 16x32 feet will cost about $300. The foundation is not included in this estimate. The cost of a concrete block or solid wall silo of the size given is from $300 to $500.

The concrete silo may be built of blocks or with solid walls. The latter is sometimes called monolithic. The kind most to be recommended is the solid wall structure. The advantages of a concrete silo are that when once properly built it is a permanent structure, and is not damaged by fire or wind, or from drying out. It does not preserve the silage any better than does one with a wall of wood. On the other hand, if the concrete wall is properly constructed, so that the air is kept out, the silage will be preserved in perfect condition. The objections that are often raised to the concrete silo, especially by those interested in the sale of the stave silo, are that it will crack and fall down, and, furthermore, that it will not preserve the silage. It is quite true that both these conditions have been met with in many cases. If the structure is properly reinforced, there is not the least danger of it cracking or falling down. If the walls are made of a mixture containing sufficient cement, so that the wall is not too porous, the silage does not spoil. It requires some skill to properly build a concrete silo. A farmer who has had no experience in concrete work should secure the assistance of some one who has had such experience before attempting to build a concrete silo. Cement blocks may be bought in all parts of the country, and they enable a farmer to put up a silo in a few days, at moderate cost.

The two things to be especially regarded in building the concrete silo are to have an abundance of iron for reinforcement and sufficient cement in the mixture to make the walls impervious to air. It is a good plan to go over the inside wall of a concrete silo each year, or at least every second year, before filling with a mixture of cement and water. The mixture should be about the consistency of whitewash. This helps to close up the pores of the wall and to exclude the air. If a concrete silo stands empty during the summer, the walls become very dry. When the moist silage is put in, the walls absorb the moisture from the silage. This may result in white mould forming near the outer edge. This condition, when present, indicates that the concrete has been made too porous. The trouble may be avoided, in case the wall has been made too porous, by applying the cement and water mixture as described. It is also well, where the concrete has been made too porous, to wet the walls with water as the silage is put in, to prevent the absorption of water from the silage.

The forms for building a concrete silo cost about $50. It is desirable for a number of farmers to club together and build the forms. One set of forms may be used for several silos, and in this way the cost of construction can be reduced.

Chance for Big Profits in Novelties

WITH a keen market demand for vegetables and fruit, farmers have a chance to secure far larger profits than they can gain from grain growing or dairying.

Mixed agriculture is the need of the times, with smaller farms and better cultivation. There should be the greatest possible range of production when markets are easily reached. Farmers and their sons and daughters should aim to produce novelties, or at least articles which are not commonly understood by landowners, and for which good prices are paid.

A few gardeners make a large profit from salsify, sometimes called vegetable oyster. This is one of the neglected products for which there is a quick sale. Many prefer it to the oyster, whose flavor it has a hint of, with all the disagreeable features of the bivalve flavor left out.

It can be cooked in many ways. As a soup, served with bread or crackers, it is delicious. Fried, either by itself or in a batter, it is quite as appetizing as the real oyster when cooked in that way.

Boiled, sliced lengthwise when tender, and fried in butter, like the parsnip, it soon becomes a favorite.

Especially is salsify a valuable addition to our somewhat limited list of winter vegetables, because it can be dug in the fall and stored in the cellar, or it can be left in the ground over winter and dug in the spring, when it will be found deliciously fresh and of fine flavor.

The culture of this plant is of the simplest. It likes a rich garden loam, made mellow to the depth of a foot and a half. Sow it in rows for convenience in cultivating,

159

and keep down the weeds. If the seedlings stand too thick in the rows, thin them out so that the plants will be at least two inches apart. Sow early in the season.

Watch the catalogues of reliable seed houses for novelties. The Trophy marked a new era in tomatoes, and was really the first with smooth exterior and solid inside. We had had smooth tomatoes before, but they had big seed hollows inside, and all that we had with solid meat were very rough, like the mammoth Chihuahua.

But the production of the Trophy was a success, because it put this solid tomato inside a smooth skin, and ever since it has been the effort of breeders to keep it there. The best efforts of the breeders should now be devoted to the maintenance of the earliness of the extra early sorts, with increased smoothness. This has been attained in the Earliana, Globe, Success and others.

Then there are the cucumbers, of which every seedsman has his special strain. Of these I have found that there is nothing better than the combination of the White Spine and Long Green, known as the Davis Perfect. It is longer and slimmer than the White Spine, and earlier than the Long Green, and in my opinion deserves its name.

Never follow the fall crop of lettuce with lettuce, for it is sure to be attacked by the wilt. This crop needs a change of soil as often as possible. It is easy to raise lettuce in the winter in a room that has an even and moderate temperature. This is better than midsummer lettuce and sells at fancy figures. Lettuce is raised with least trouble in spring and fall.

When soil can be worked in the spring, lettuce, radishes, onions and peas should be planted in the open garden. All of these can stand considerable frost. It is well to put in some early potatoes. The early vegetables bring big profits.

The Logan berry, a hybrid of the blackberry and rasp-

berry, is getting a start. This fruit is originated by
Judge Logan, of Santa Cruz, Cal. It is proving to be the
easiest and best producing berry that can be grown on the
Pacific coast. It is especially free from disease, is a rank
grower, and yields enormously. It is steadily gaining in
favor with the lady experts of cooking. It is especially
adapted for pie cooking and jam. It is one of the many
twentieth-century agricultural achievements.

Many products now generally overlooked can be turned
into cash. Seven children in one family in Arcola, Ill.,
made $300 one winter peeling broomcorn stalks and sell-
ing the pith to warehouses, there to be shipped to jewelers
and watch factories. It is used by them for cleaning
their wares. It contains no grit nor hard fiber, and will
absorb oil or dirt without danger of scratching. Quite
a number of the women and children around Arcola
make some money on the side this way every winter.

After the crop is harvested, the women and children
gather armfuls of the stalks and pile them up back of
the house to dry. Then, during the evenings or on rainy
days, they peel one joint at a time and take out the clean,
white pith. This is made up into round bundles, holding
two or three pounds each, but nearly as large as a wash-
tub. The price received is 25 cents a pound. There is not
a large or unlimited demand for this material, but it pays
quite a few dollars each winter into the pockets of the
Arcola people.

The dasheen, like the potato, is a native of South
America, but is not a member of the botanical group of
plants to which the potato, tomato, eggplant and pepper
belong. It is closely related to the tanier of the southern
United States and the taro of Hawaii.

It is said that dasheens are even more nourishing than
the potato. In flavor they suggest boiled chestnuts. At the
recent annual banquet of the National Geographical
Society, their edible qualities were thoroughly tested.

They have also received a favorable report of the house committee of a well-known New York club. It is declared that half an acre in Florida yielded 225 bushels of dasheens, which were richer in flavor than baked potatoes.

The woman who does not raise her own strawberries is losing a lot of pleasure, for they grow so rapidly and so luxuriantly, as if they thought to be allowed to live were a grand privilege, and it is rare sport to watch them.

Sauerkraut is easily made on the farm, and pays well. There are two essentials which must be observed in making sauerkraut: First, it must be remembered that if too much salt is used, the kraut will not sour as it should, and the quality will be impaired.

Again, some salt must be used in order to preserve the cabbage till it sours sufficiently to preserve itself. When kraut gets sour, it is like pickles, and there will be no further decay.

To make the best kraut, a slicer should be used, though it may be sliced with a knife, coarse, or fine, as suits your taste.

Use a clean barrel or jar, put in a layer of cabbage, cut fine, then a little salt, using not more than a quart of salt to a 40-gallon barrel of kraut.

If you like the flavor, add a little dill seed or caraway. When the vessel is full, fit a clean board inside, and weight with a clean stone, never a piece of iron.

If your cabbage is early, and going to waste while it is yet warm, make the kraut and keep in a cool cellar.

This early kraut will rot a little on top. Remove this every few days, and wash off the inside of the barrel and weight with warm water, to remove the germs of decay.

Weeds, herbs and roots have a market value that is surprising to persons who do not happen to have information on the subject. Wholesale drug houses quite gener-

ally buy these things, and any local druggist is able to
give the address of a reliable firm to whom such plants
may be sent.   The following prices per pound are quoted:

Cents

Bayberry bark 4
Beeswax, prime yellow...........................29
Black haw bark of root..........................12
Bloodroot 6
Cherry bark, thin.............................. 7
Clover tops (red)............................... 5½
Cohosh root (black)............................. 2½
Culvers or black root.......................... 8½
Elm bark, select slabs.........................12
Ginseng root...........................$3 to $5
Goldenseal root $4
Honey, pure Sp. Needle........................ 7
Ladyslipper 18
May apple root................................ 4¾
Pink root 25
Poke root 4
Prickly ash bark, Northern....................15
Sassafras bark of root........................10½
Senega, Northern 45
Snakeroot button ....
Snakeroot, Texas (Serpentaria).................25
Spikenard root 12
Wahoo bark of root............................30
White pine bark............................... 3½
White poplar bark.............................
Wild ginger 12
Yellow dock root.............................. 3½

Full directions as to how to cure medicinal plants and
prepare them for market will be sent by the purchasers
of herbs to any person seeking the information.

Pin Money in Pickles

PICKLES come only partly by nature—they are born of work and worry. But they fetch in money—if the work and worry are properly expended. Notwithstanding the efforts of the professional pickle growers, there is every season more and more room for the non-professional. If the non-professional is a woman with a knack of seasoning and a dozen or so time-honored and individual family recipes, she may treble her profits by herself putting up the yield of the pickle garden. If she lacks time or strength or skill or facilities for that, she can at least put the pickles in brine or sell them fresh-cut to her neighbors, the handy huckster or her nearest grocer.

In planning a pickle garden, first look over your ground—this literally and metaphorically. The literal side has to do with site and soil; the metaphorical one concerns the possible demand for the supply to be created or the possibilities of creating a new demand for something different. Pickles worth eating are worth also a fair price. Resolve to be satisfied with nothing less. Take account here of individual taste. Hearty laborers relish big salt green cucumbers, but sniff disdain of fancy relishes and unwonted tangs or mixed flavors, such as the mangoes and picalilli, whose appeal to educated palates is irresistible.

If the soil of the pickle garden is thin, it had better be devoted to cucumbers. The long green variety is best; it can be cut at little-finger length, or left until almost full grown, and still be marketable. Have the ground made light and fine.

Keep the hills light and clean, also the whole space between them. Plows can run between the hills until the vines begin to spread. Once they fairly cover the earth, what grass comes up will not hurt them. Rooted in the rich hills, they can easily give odds to anything growing in poor soil. When plowing is no longer possible, a little hoe work and hand-weeding may be in order, but take care neither to bruise the vines nor to throw loose dirt upon the leaves, especially while the dew is on.

Unless there is a ready market close at hand, get the brine barrel ready as soon as the first flowers appear. It must be clean and sweet before the brine goes in—old pork and fish barrels always taint their later contents. Empty whisky barrels or molasses barrels do excellently, but should be well painted outside with red lead, to prevent the ravages of wood worms. Make the brine of soft water and clean salt, strong enough to float an egg. A little brown sugar or molasses improves the keeping quality. Bring it to a boil, and skim clean after everything is dissolved. Pour it into the barrel boiling hot, let stand a day, and skim again before putting in pickles.

The net result is very nearly the same whether the pickles are cut small or at full growth. Decide in the beginning which size it shall be, and stick to the decision. Cut the pickles every morning, while the dew is on— thus they are plump and cool, in the best condition for keeping. Use very sharp shears for clipping, and take care to leave the least bit of stalk to each pickle, but never to wound, bruise or break the vine. If by accident a vine is bruised or torn, cut it off remorselessly, so it shall not decay and set up disease in the whole plant. Be careful of bruising the pickles. In washing, use plenty of water, and drain them well before putting them into the brine. Keep a weighted wooden cover floating on top of the brine, thus insuring that the pickles shall stay covered. Put only one sort and size of pickle into a vessel. If saving various sorts, use brine crocks instead of a barrel, thus making separation easy.

Gherkins, or prickly cucumbers, are grown in the same way, and yield enormously. The vines are hardier than those of the cucumber, will endure more handling, and bear a third more fruit. They need to be carefully watched, as old gherkins are hard and tough. In cutting them, snip about half way the long fruit stalk. Never lift a vine of anything from the ground in cutting. No matter how carefully the lifting is done, the laying down disturbs tendrils and fibers.

String beans make excellent pickles. Plant and tend as though for boiling, pick when the beans are just fairly forming, wash and put in brine. The curious plant known as the Martynia bears seed pods well worth pickling. So does the nasturtium, if given a cool, moist, very rich place to grow. Both make excellent substitutes for capers. They are not, however, very well worth while commercially, unless one puts up pickles one's self for a special trade.

Green peppers are fine for pickling, especially in mangoes. Use the big bullnose sort, and clip the pods with longish stalks just as they are on the point of turning red. Muskmelons, both long and round, can be pickled at all stages, from the size of an egg to the edge of ripeness. When full grown, it is best to cut out a segment and scrape away the seed before putting them in brine. If they are meant for mango-making, tie in the cut piece with a soft string, and pack them well down toward the bottom of the barrel or crock.

Do not plant muskmelons, cucumbers and gherkins side by side in a pickle garden—bees will carry pollen back and forth, tainting each with the blood of the other. With space for all three, keep them apart, planting them at opposite edges of the garden, with beans or cabbage or cauliflower in between. Cauliflower in itself is an excellent pickle. It can be put in brine the same as anything else. Very young corn, with grain unfilled, makes a pickle much relished by not a few epicures.

There is good money in freshly cut cucumbers at 50 cents a peck. This is for the big fellows. Very small ones, adapted to fine work, should be worth three times as much, and the intermediate sizes, a finger length and under, 75 cents to $1 the peck. In brine, pickles are commonly sold in bulk. Barrel prices vary tremendously according to the season, but are seldom low enough to prevent a fair margin of profit.

Too much cannot be said about the opportunity for profit in growing cauliflowers. The market desires snowy white heads, so that protection is universally practiced to accomplish this purpose. Three methods are used: (1) the breaking of half a dozen or more leaves over the top of the cauliflower head. The stems of the leaves are not severed entirely, so that the leaves remain green. (2) Breaking or bending over the leaves as just explained, and pinning with toothpicks or small pins. This is a very satisfactory method for all sections. (3) Bringing the leaves together over the head and tying. This is an excellent plan, but requires more time than securing with the toothpicks. The protection should begin when the heads are about an inch and a half in diameter. Cauliflower is considered a delicacy on most tables, and it pays to exercise special care in the marketing. Although barrels are often used, crates or baskets are better. A package which will not hold more than a dozen or, at most, two dozen heads, certainly has an advantage over the barrels.

The Lowly Onion a Profitable Crop

ONIONS are to be classed among the surest and most profitable of crops. There is a constant demand for them at prices which give a return of $200 to $400 an acre. It is a product that the beginner need not fear to experiment with to the extent of several acres.

Seed onions are of better flavor and keep longer and are more profitable to grow than sets, though some fail to grow them in the home garden because they are more difficult to keep clear of weeds.

The best way to grow onions from seed is by sowing the seed in a bed or cold frame early in the season and transplanting later to the row where they are to grow. A small section of the hotbed will grow 1,000 plants till they are the size of quills, or they can be crowded. By that time the ground will be warm, and all seed will have germinated so that the plants may be set in clean ground that has been worked over to kill all the young weeds.

If one lacks for room in the hotbed, the seed may be sown in a sheltered place—an old brush heap, ash bed, or some place where the soil is good. If there is room to sow the seed in drills six inches apart, they may be worked some to keep them growing before they are transplanted.

When ready to transplant them, wet the ground and pull the plants and then cut off about half the top and slightly tip the roots. Set the plants from two to three inches apart in the row and in rows fifteen inches apart. If very dry, use water when transplanting, and every one will live.

If the soil has been well fertilized with stable manure or poultry droppings, and worked over several times before the onions are transplanted to the rows, there will be but few weeds to contend with, and the plants will not be checked in growth.

Onions should follow potatoes, beans or corn. The land should be well plowed in the autumn, disked and harrowed in the spring, until it is as fine as garden soil.

Always manure heavily before breaking up the land in the fall. On new land, cowpeas are excellent for bringing the land into shape.

Onions should be grown under a system of crop rotation, but the crops used in the rotation must be those that will not exhaust the high fertility necessary to onions.

One of the most important things in onion culture is to mix the fertilizer with the soil. On land that is not thoroughly drained, plow in beds, leaving a double furrow between the beds to carry off surplus water.

The disk harrow puts the land in fine condition after it has been thoroughly plowed in the fall. Never use manure, except that which is well rotted. Bermuda onion growers use as high as twenty tons of sheep and goat manure per acre every three years. Often, in addition to this, they use 1,000 to 2,000 pounds of cottonseed meal, and sometimes a top dressing of nitrate of soda.

Seed is sown as early in the spring as possible, but never before the land is in the best possible condition. Seed may be sown by hand drills in rows from twelve to fourteen inches apart. Where horse culture is employed, the distance should be at least two feet. It requires about four pounds of seed per acre where it is drilled fourteen inches apart.

As soon as the plants are growing well, the cultivator should be started and kept going in order to keep the soil in good condition and to prevent weeds.

A great deal of the art in securing a large yield

depends upon the quality of the seed. It has been found in some districts that home-grown seed from selected bulbs is to be preferred to seed secured from seedsmen or from foreign markets.

Cultivation should be more or less continuous from the time the plants show above ground until the crop matures. Some growers make a practice of cultivating the land once each week. This cultivation should be with either a wheel hoe or the so-called hand cultivator. The onion is a more or less shallow feeder, so that cultivation should only be to a depth of from an inch and a half to two inches. From two to three hand weedings are usually necessary. It is quite possible that a certain amount of thinning would be advisable.

The yields obtained on the soils that are adapted to the cultivation of the onion are from 250 to 450 bushels per acre.

From five to eight acres is all that one farmer should expect to care for during the season.

Many gardeners do not properly estimate the advantage of thinning their crops. If this plan were strictly adhered to, the yield would be increased and the quality greatly improved.

Give More Attention to Fruit

THERE should be a more general production of fruit in the central states. This can be made one of the best features of mixed farming. Market advantages in the middle states, surrounding the larger cities, exceed those of the newer western states and climatic difficulties are much the same in one section as another. Apples, pears, cherries, plums and berries give a larger profit per acre than almost any other farm product.

Experts state that more money can be made per acre from apples and cherries in the central states than in the mountainous sections farther west. The older states are far ahead in market advantages and are practically equal in soil and climate.

Horticulture has been pushed aside by the dairy interest in some of the middle states. This is a mistaken policy which should be changed. The great cash markets and cheap and convenient transportation ought to mean more than they do to those farmers who are devoting their energies to a single interest. They enable land owners to diversify their crops and place their affairs on a business basis.

The stories of orchard possibilities in the lake region are not imaginary. Some of the big successes in horticulture have been achieved around Lake Superior, where climate and soil are thought to be less favorable than in localities farther south.

There are many localities where orchards exist, but where fruit production is not equal to the home consumption. Farmers owe it to themselves, to change this condition and make their orchards a source of pleasure and profit. A little intelligent care will enable them to do so.

It is the tendency of large farmers everywhere who have their minds given up to grain or dairying to overlook such matters as spraying their orchards, pruning, mulching, etc. The small land owner does better with his fruit.

About sixty trees to the acre are sufficient. They should be purchased from the nurseries when one or two years old and placed in even rows on land that has been thoroughly fitted for the purpose. Any fair quality of loam will answer the requirements of an orchard, but, if possible, the owner should select a piece of land that has a clay subsoil, twelve to eighteen inches below the surface. He should avoid gravelly land, because it does not permit tree roots to obtain sufficient hold, and it carries off the water too closely. It is necessary to plow in plenty of barnyard fertilizer and cultivate thoroughly before planting.

It is feasible to use the orchard either for gardening or the growing of common leguminous crops. This makes the land pay something while the trees are maturing, and is good for the soil. The rows of trees should be far enough apart so that a team with plow or harrow may be used.

Therefore it is worth while in localities where horticulture is not flourishing to make a more thorough test of methods for guarding the fruit crop than has been made by farmers generally. Twice in ten years, in some regions, owners of orchards have lost apple and cherry crops by freezing weather late in the spring. This is one crop in five lost through unfavorable climatic conditions, and it would be discouraging but for the facts that four successful crops in five years make fruit highly profitable, and that such losses are, to a great extent, preventable.

The practical farmer will take steps to see that his trees

are not frosted while budding. A cheap oil heater is made for this work. The total expense of providing heaters for an orchard of ten acres would not exceed $300. They would not be used more than two or three nights in the year, and therefore the outlay for oil would be trifling.

Another excellent plan that I have tried is to raise the temperature on a cold night with smudge fires. This is only necessary when a freeze sets in after the trees have shown their blossoms. A little ridge of dry manure or rubbish should be placed around the orchard, or at least on the windward side, with possibly a line or two of it through the center, in case of a sharp frost. The material to be burned is to be almost covered with dirt, in order to make a slow flame. In the evening, if it looks like a frosty night, start the fires and keep the temperature up to the point of safety. This may be a sort of mean job for a night or two, but the result will justify the effort—and it is a job that may not have to be performed more than once in five years. Keep a thermometer in the orchard.

Frost is so apt to come during the budding period, that farmers and orchardists have a keen appreciation of the danger which confronts them, and yet few have any definite method of guarding their interests in this particular. Thousands of neglected and worthless orchards in the middle west, particularly in the lake regions, show that owners have become discouraged through periodical losses. When we consider that an acre of fruit is worth from $200 to $400, the trouble of keeping up a few little fires around the orchard for six or eight hours seems trifling.

Spraying the trees in October and during the budding period in the spring is necessary to keep the orchard free of insect pests, which are ruinous if allowed to work. Pruning is another essential to give the trees uniformity and to prevent them getting too much height or developing abnormal growths.

In many cases it will be found that the old trees have exhausted practically all the available nutritive material contained in the soil, and they need considerable nitrogen in order to produce new wood and to put new vigor into them, and therefore they will stand lots of stable manure. But if they were young, bearing trees in their prime they would need only a light dressing of manure.

While the actual fertilizing material contained in a ton of average stable manure is small, not much above twenty-eight pounds, if lime is not considered, it is a great humus producer. Humus adds lots of moisture, and humus and moisture working together release the nutritive material already in the soil and put it in shape so that those little hungry feed roots can gather it in and send it on its mission of supplying leaf, bud and branch with life and vigor.

If one should want quicker and better results than just stable manure alone will give, phosphate rock, ground bone and potash may be added in the proportion of 100 pounds of phosphate, 200 pounds of ground bone and 100 pounds of potash, but the user will have to be the judge of just how much to apply to the acre, as there are so many different conditions to be taken into consideration that the same quantity will not answer for all.

As cultivation is needed anyway, it is well to raise vegetables in the orchard, thus making the land pay a good acreage profit even if the fruit has a bad season. Weeds are to be kept out of an orchard as zealously as out of a garden. It is also important that we practice a good system of shallow cultivation in young orchards. The trees respond to good tillage just as the corn and other cultivated crops do. Barn-yard manure, cowpeas and clover are three great fall cover crops for a young orchard. Trees ought to stand about thirty feet apart.

Good drainage is important in the apple orchard as elsewhere. The apple does not like "wet feet." For that simple reason it succeeds more often on naturally well-drained rolling land than in low, soggy places.

Just after the leaf buds in the spring and before the blossom buds open the old orchard should be given a good spraying with the regular Bordeaux mixture and paris green, or lime-sulphur and arsenate of lead; another one just after the blossoms drop, and a third some time later if troubled with the coddling moth, which is almost sure to be the case in an old orchard. This fight against the coddling moth must be unrelenting. The worm is migratory, traveling surprising distances in its work of destruction. Spraying should be done in any part of the season when pests are seen. A spraying after the fruit has been gathered in the fall is recommended in orchards where pests are numerous.

Constant cultivation of old orchards has taken from the soil mineral elements that must be supplied by artificial means. This soil was at one time rich in vegetable and mineral matter, and the trees yielded an abundance of fine apples. Soil and climatic change is not an uncommon occurrence, and experiments have been made to introduce the right trees and to improve the soil.

The Northwest requires trees of a very rugged nature, and they can be adapted to the soil by experiments. We need more of this work by farmers and practical orchardists. Too much is left to the experiment stations, the nurserymen, and to scientists. Every orchardist should have his own stock, and each season some test should be made of new varieties, selecting of course, those most naturally adapted to his locality.

To be successful in fruit growing more attention must be given to secure fruit of high quality. If only first-class fruit be offered for sale the demand for it will be enormously increased.

Care and Skill in the Orchard

IF the new order of farming contemplates a larger and more general production of fruit, people must learn how to care for their orchards. There is no profit in neglected trees, but there are returns of $200 to $400 an acre from fruit where a good system of pruning, spraying and cultivation is followed.

The fruit crop depends largely upon the efficiency with which the pruning is done in the fall. The uniform distribution of branches, height of branches, height of trees and the health in general of all parts of them left for bearing fruit—all have their influence. Branches should not be left so long and slender that they will not support a goodly burden of fruit.

As a rule, all water sprouts, those straight shoots running directly up from the main branches, should be removed. Limbs that are seen to be partly dead or decayed should be cut back until one is sure no part of them is left, as it would but invite further decay, and the sustenance drawn by them would be a useless drain on the vitality of the trees.

All tall, thick or topheavy trees demand close and careful pruning. Fruits which are reared high in mid air are not as exempt from the action of the wind as if they were lower down. The top of the high tree itself is apt to be caught in the wind and damaged, perhaps ruined by being broken down.

The low down, uniformly pruned tree also will produce more fruit, and of a quality superior to that of the tall tree, while the ease with which the fruit is picked from the low trees recommends them. After all rotten apples, pruned limbs and other refuse have been cleared up about the orchard, the tree should be given a thorough spraying.

If possible, one should choose a warm day for this operation, so most of the insect pests crawling out to lie in the sunlight will be exposed to the action of the spraying solution. Special attention should be given old knots and rough spots about the trees, as in these places the fruit pests deposit their eggs for next season's crop and at the same time many of these pests themselves are harboring safe retreat till winter is over.

There are several reasons for this fall spraying. It not only destroys the insect pests, but their eggs, also, which have been laid. After the spraying, the trees will be left healthy and clean and free from the pests, while they are developing their next season's crop.

Fall is the best time in which to fertilize the orchard, as a goodly portion of the fertility elements will have penetrated down to the root of trees before the ground freezes up and the work of rejuvenation will have been well begun when the spring opens.

Where the orchard is young it will, of course, have to be plowed after giving it a good coat of manure, straw, cornstalks, etc. This is much more productive of good results the following season than where the orchard is fertilized during the spring.

With the exception of raspberries, which should be attended to early in the spring, all the small fruit bushes should be pruned, sprayed and fertilized during the late fall months. This will include gooseberries, currants, blackberries, grape vines, etc.

All fruit bushes or orchard trees which are where rabbits can reach them should be wrapped in thick paper, gunny sacks, cornstalks, screen wire or the regular tree protector, made of veneer, this protection extending twenty-four inches from the ground.

The pear orchard should be cultivated every year, because it is unsafe to apply the large amount of stable manure to pear trees when in grass that is needed to keep them thrifty. We can keep an apple orchard in grass and top dress it heavily enough to offset this drain on the soil.

In liming the soil of an apple orchard it should be applied at the rate of about one ton per acre at one time, which need not be repeated oftener than once in three or four years. It should be definitely known that the soil needs liming before taking any steps to do it. No great quantity should be put near the trees but the whole of the soil evenly supplied, which would give a very small portion about each newly set tree.

Hardwood ashes are good for trees of all kinds but they contain no nitrogen and in case they are applied, something that contains this element should be added. Nitrate of soda contains it but some kind of coarse manure is better, because there is humus, which loosens the soil as well as furnishes nitrogen. If a mixed fertilizer is used it should be made of about 500 pounds acid phosphate rock, 200 pounds muriate of potash and 100 pounds nitrate of soda for each acre. It may be applied with benefit at any time of year, but about April or May it will be quickly available and be taken up by the tree roots during the growing season.

Common Fruits Return Liberal Profits

PROFITS in common fruit are easily five times as much as in grain farming. Farmers often fail, however, with apples, cherries, plums and the like because they treat them as a side issue and give no real work or intelligent attention to their orchards.

Every farmer should have from two to twenty acres of fruit and the trees should be cared for systematically. If this is done the profit will amount to $200 an acre or more, three seasons out of four.

Plums will grow on any land suitable for the production of ordinary farm crops. It should be sloping or have good drainage. The Japanese sorts do best on light soils. Many are self-sterile, therefore varieties should be planted intermixed. Set the trees close, say eighteen feet apart. They do best under tillage and will be good for twenty years or so. They need more water than many other kinds of fruit. Feed the trees and thin the fruit; also cut out black knot. Spray with lime-sulphur solution and arsenate for most troubles. The best plums for commercial planting are obtainable from all reliable dealers.

The German prune is subject to black knot, but this can be fairly well controlled by cutting out. Italian and German prunes are best of all for cooking. They ship well and will long remain standard commercial plums.

In Europe the plum takes the first place among fruits; here it is considered comparatively unimportant; and its culture is confined within narrow limits. It can be made very profitable.

The cherry is easily grown. It is attacked by few insects. Rabbits seldom molest cherry trees. In preparing the soil, I advise heavy manuring, deep plowing, with thorough cultivation the year before planting. Use two-year-old trees, well branched, and plant 18 feet apart, giving thorough cultivation for three years.

After that, seed to clover and when your orchard comes into bearing, mow all grass and weeds a couple of times during the season. Leave the grass on the ground to form a mulch. It will have a tendency to hold moisture, and also helps to keep the ground loose. The less a cherry orchard is plowed after it comes into bearing the better, as the feeding roots are very near the surface. Roots broken off are not quickly replaced, as the cherry is one of the most backward of fruit trees in putting out new growth where old growth has been broken off.

Cherries can be grown wherever the apple succeeds—north, east, south or west. There is no fear of overproduction, as canning houses stand ready to contract the crop ahead at good prices, while private customers may be secured by all growers who live near a city.

Apples surpass other fruits in money-making, because they are hardier and allow a longer time for handling. An orchardist ought to consider apples the foundation of his enterprise, but he should not neglect pears, plums, cherries and berries.

Spring planting is to be recommended in preference to fall planting. Get the trees out just as soon as the frosts seem to be at an end, placing them thirty feet apart each way. This leaves a great deal of land that may be used for raising vegetables and flowers. This constant cultivation is good for fruit trees, which should have mulching placed around them late in the summer.

The trees should be mulched with straw, grass or leafage of some description. This mulching should not be crowded around the stem, its object being mainly to create moist and cool soil conditions, and to encourage a free root establishment. The mulch material should be occasionally stirred and no weed or grass growth should be permitted to accumulate.

Where mulching material is not available, a frequent earth mulch should be given by constantly stirring the soil within a few feet of the trees. In addition to mulching it will be beneficial to spray young trees with water, particularly on hot or windy days.

Many of our orchard soils are rich chemically in nitrogen, phosphorus and potassium. but oftentimes lack humus. By humus we mean the completely decayed organic matter, which can be obtained by the plowing under of some green manure crop, such as alfalfa, clover, vetch, oats, rye, cowpeas, soy beans, etc. Whatever care and attention are given to young trees will be amply repaid to the grower in after years, owing to the vigor, sturdiness, and other qualities thus imparted to them. The trees begin to bear about six years from planting and at ten years should be in full bearing.

In regard to overproduction, it should be said that this is not a new question. Fifty years ago a pessimistic wail was going up that the apple business would soon be overdone, and would cease to be profitable. At that time, not more than one-tenth as many apples were raised for commercial purposes in the United States as are raised today. One hundred years ago apples were but little raised for commercial purposes; now, trainloads and shiploads move from the orchards to our great centers of trade, and across the ocean to England and other parts of Europe. Asia is calling for our apples. Australia is taking thousands of boxes of our best fruit, and is calling for more. Our highest grade apples cannot be duplicated on the face of the earth, so we have the world for a market for our best fruit.

Northwestern orchardists receive fancy prices for their

fruit, not that it is any better than that produced in other sections, but because they are not afraid to spend money liberally to grade, pack and advertise properly, the product of their orchards.

Senator H. M. Dunlap, of Illinois, tells how he managed several large orchards. He found the best manner of cultivation was with the orchard disc and harrow. With these tools he pulverizes the ground thoroughly. He has a 3-ton truck, run by gasoline motor, for hauling the apples to market, and he uses this power to run a double disc harrow, it is quicker and better than horse power for the purpose. Manure and the legumes are his fertilizers. Work and spray, is his motto. Thorough spraying gives the most perfect fruit. It is the essential thing in controlling insect pests and fungus growth. He uses smudge pots when frost is liable to damage the young fruit in the spring.

Fruits, either fresh or preserved, must not be counted as a luxury, but rather as a necessity, and indeed in these days more and more people are coming to recognize their food value. Available statistics show that fruits constitute a by no means unimportant part of the diet of the American people. They supply to us nearly five per cent of the total food and about four per cent of the total carbohydrates of the food supply of the average family of this country. It has been amply demonstrated that a fruit and nut diet will maintain health and strength of an individual indefinitely.

Fruit Raising Suited to Amateurs

AN amateur who is about to take a farm can not do better than to establish an orchard. Market advantages in a thickly settled state are too important to be disregarded. The keen demand for all kinds of fruit, not only in cities, but in every small town, insures large profits.

It would be wise to devote at least one acre in ten to fruit. Thus on a farm of fifty acres there ought to be a five-acre orchard. It is best to proceed with moderation, for one needs practical experience. The proportion of fruit may be increased as the owner acquires skill. It is equally wise for the established farmer to give some attention to horticulture.

Cherries, apples and pears are among the hardiest of the fruit crops and yield large returns. Late varieties are safest in the north, as losses frequently result from frost after trees have blossomed. Some varieties bud two weeks later than others.

The temperature can be controlled by artificial means. The cost of heating per night depends on several conditions. The cheapest and most reliable fuel is crude oil. I have investigated several methods and have found that the cost of running 100 burners one night is between $2 and $3. At wholesale rates the heaters cost about 32 cents each. They will last for several years. I know of one fruit crop worth $400 per acre which was saved at a cost of $3 per acre.

To be on the safe side, watch the temperature and start the heater when it goes down to 32 degrees. This would not happen more than once or twice in a season. Smudge fires also may be used with good effect around fruit trees on a frosty night and cost nothing but a little work and watchfulness.

Of the sour cherries Montmorency is about ten days later than Richmond, and the fruit is larger. Other good sorts are English Morello, very dark colored, and Late Duke, a good late variety. Slikeman and Downer's Late Red are both worth consideration on account of their lateness; the former is the latest cherry we have; both are of good quality.

Of the early sweet cherries, the black varieties are the highest flavored, and as a table fruit they excel. Black Tartarian is one of the best; Schmidt's Bigarreau is another good sort; Mercer is a good dark red cherry; Rockport Bigarreau and Governor Wood are both light red varieties, with little to choose between them. Coe's Transparent is a large light red; handsome, very meaty, but not quite so luscious as some of the others.

There is no more prolific tree than the plum, and the fruit can be used for many purposes other than as a table fruit. The trees are strong growers and outside of serving as a prey for the San Jose scale, a condition easily relieved by spraying, the trees give no trouble after planting. And moreover, you don't plant only for your children; as the trees bear in three to four years. It is peculiar that the Japanese varieties seem to do better than our own and the European varieties.

In late pears Buerre d'Anjou should be one selection. It is not what might be called a pretty pear, but when ripe, is excellent for the table, having a distinct flavor; the tree is a good bearer, and the pears are extra large. Sheldon ranks high as a table pear; the fruit is of fair size, brownish, of good shape and flavor. Duchess d'Angouleme is a good all-around late pear. Lawrence is the best late pear; it will keep well into the winter; it is a good cropper and the fruit is of a fine quality.

In late varieties of apples the Baldwin ranks high in several essentials. It produces large crops and is a good keeper. Ben Davis, another good keeper, is the prettiest apple we have, according to many judges, and the quality is fairly good on a light soil. Newton Pippin still holds the lead, as a high quality late keeper, but Rhode Island greening is the best keeping green apple to date. Roxbury Rust is the best russet apple, and keeps late. Twenty Ounce is one of the extra large apples which is not lacking in quality.

Yellow Transparent is classified as an excellent apple in Cincinnati, and by some of the dealers in Indianapolis and Louisville it is regarded as very good.

Duchess is regarded as excellent in Buffalo, Chicago, Louisville, Pittsburg, Columbus, Indianapolis, Philadelphia, Toledo and St. Paul.

Wealthy is generally a good apple in reputation. The only market classifying it as poor or fair is Mobile.

Alexander is generally fairly well spoken of; it is regarded as poor by part of the trade in Boston and as a fair apple by part of the trade in Buffalo, Indianapolis, Kansas City, Louisville, Memphis, New Orleans, Norfolk, Richmond and St. Louis.

Maiden Blush is an apple with a good reputation; it is excellent in Baltimore, Chicago, Cincinnati, Columbus, Louisville, New Orleans, Pittsburg, and sells well in other markets.

Pound Sweet is ranked as excellent by some dealers in Boston, Buffalo, Chicago and Detroit.

Tolman Sweet is ranked as excellent in Boston and Detroit and as good by part of the trade in other cities.

Holland Pippin is regarded as very good by Columbus, New York, Philadelphia and Toledo.

York Pippin is regarded as good by Columbus, Memphis, New York, Philadelphia and Toledo.

Snow is a poor apple to send to Kansas City, Louisville, Memphis, Mobile, New Orleans and Norfolk. In fact, it is not appreciated in southern markets; it appears to be in highest esteem in Boston, Buffalo, Chicago, Cincinnati, Detroit and New York.

Apples are not a tender fruit and may freeze slightly, though they should not be allowed to freeze hard. Gather apples in the first cool days of fall, though it is sometimes necessary to gather a little earlier if they are falling badly.

It will be much better to gather a little early and let them lie in the pens than to remain on the trees when they have started to fall. When they are gathered, put in rail pens and cover with boards, and if there are warm days they should be in the shade.

When the weather becomes so cold that they are likely to freeze even when protected with straw, it is time to store them for the winter, although a great many apples are lost by storing them too soon.

There is no doubt about pits being superior to a cellar for apple storage. Select a well drained spot, and scoop out a depression not over a foot deep, put straw in the bottom of this pile, then the apples in a conical heap, cover with more straw or hay, then with dirt. They will keep plump and tender this way when they would shrivel in a cellar, though a few for immediate use should be stored in the cellar, on the floor.

Small Fruits Pay Well

LAND owners who think they haven't time to attend to small fruit ought to make a comparison of profits. It is as easy to raise berries as wheat, oats or corn, and these fruits return a clean profit five times greater than that from grain.

The strawberry should be widely cultivated by farmers, who with plenty of land and dressing seem to have no excuse for not having their tables well supplied with this appetizing berry, besides earning $200 to $300 an acre on such ground as they devote to the product. There are similar profits in other small fruits.

If the soil is not already fertile, it can be made so by the addition of stable manure or commercial fertilizers. To avoid grubs, sod ground should not be used, and to avoid weeds, a hoed crop should precede the strawberries. Cow peas or soy beans make a good preparatory crop.

Fall plowing is desirable, the soil being loosened up in the spring with a cultivator or harrow. Under special conditions strawberries may be set in the fall, but for the amateur grower spring setting is to be recommended.

The single hedge system may be adopted if desired, and rows may be made three feet apart, and the plants set twelve to sixteen inches apart in the rows. Under this system the grower will permit the maturing of two runner plants from the mother or original plant set, and these plants will be layered in line with the mother plant in the row.

This will give the grower three plants for fruiting in the season following instead of one plant, and as there

187·

will be ample room for sunshine and air, there probably
will be an actual increase in the quantity of fruit as compared with the hill system, although it is claimed that
the hill system is the one which will yield the greatest
number of large berries.

Currant and gooseberry bushes, red and black raspberry plants and grape vines, can be planted successfully
any time in the fall before winter sets in, but I always
recommend spring planting.

The most important thing connected with gooseberry
culture is judicious pruning. This work, which cannot
be neglected, is done from late autumn to early winter.
Many of the vigorous-growing shoots and branches are
annually removed, and only a moderate supply of young
growing wood is left. The bush is made to assume a
cup-shaped top, with slightly drooping branches. The
cultivation and manuring are like that for the currant.

In the cultivation of raspberries keep the canes pinched
off as they reach a height of four feet. This is easily
done, and makes them grow outside shoots on which berries will grow the next spring. Cut out all the canes of
raspberries which bear fruit as soon as the crop is
gathered. These canes are useless for further bearing.

The raspberry is a prolific bearer. The first year it
makes canes, and the second year fruit. Private customers can be secured for the fruit, or it may be sold to
grocers.

The currant can be grown to great perfection north
or south, and large yields can be obtained. The hilling
of the bushes should be avoided, and level and shallow
culture practiced.

Gooseberries require an open, airy situation, and clean
culture. The tops must be kept well thinned out to insure good fruit. They should be dressed with well-com-
posted manure, and no weeds should be allowed to grow

in the rows. These precautions are necessary to ward off mildew.

No other fruit can take the place of grapes during their season. They afford an abundant supply of delicious and strengthening food for nearly five months during the year. We should grow grapes and eat freely of them.

Blackberries come late in the summer and furnish excellent fruit for canning, preserving and making delicious pies. There is a good market demand for them.

Late in the fall secure roots of the right variety; place them where they will be protected from the freezing weather, or they may be taken up in the spring, but not allowed to dry out. Prepare the ground as for potatoes, and every third row rake for the berry rows, planting the other two rows with potatoes. Cut the roots into pieces three inches long and plant them one foot apart in the row. Cover level with the ground.

When the canes appear destroy all but one in the hill, which may be done by cutting with a knife or sickle. In this way a stalky cane with plenty of laterals will be obtained. Cut back these laterals to secure a bush form.

The red raspberry differs greatly in character from the black cap raspberry. While the black cap is propagated from tips, the ends of the canes when buried taking root and forming the new plant, the red raspberry propagates from suckers that spring up from the roots of the parent plant. With some varieties, especially the Cuthbert, these suckers are thrown up so freely as to interfere with the productiveness of the parent plants, making it necessary for the plantation to be renewed after it has borne fruit two or three years. Other varieties, like the Loudon and Syracuse, are less inclined to send out sucker plants and therefore remain in fruit much longer than the Cuthbert. But any variety may be kept in fruit for many years if the young suckers, when they first appear are clipped off with a hoe, the same as weeds, but this work must be done each week.

The average red raspberry is not quite so hardy as the black cap raspberry, but the Culbert, Marlboro, Ruby, Herbert and Syracuse have proved fairly hardy.

The fruiting canes of the red raspberry are not so wide spreading and thorny as the black cap, therefore, it is not necessary to plant the red raspberry quite so far apart as the black cap, but it is well to give all small fruits plenty of room. In most instances raspberries, blackberries and currants are planted too closely in the row and between the rows. I favor planting the red raspberry 4 feet apart between the rows and 3½ feet in the rows, so that the plant may be cultivated both ways.

The young canes are usually cropped off to about 3½ feet at the time they appear above the old bushes. The old canes are removed immediately after the fruit is harvested, by means of sharp hooks with long handles, and pulled into the alleys, and later removed with horse and rake, the rake being made for that purpose. Sometimes, if a plantation gets grassy and weedy while the fruit is being picked, we give it a thorough cultivating after the old canes are removed, and sometimes even plow the ground lightly between the rows, following the drainage slope and always throwing the furrow up to the bushes.

The cultivation and growing of red raspberries afford a pleasant and profitable occupation. While the production of profitable crops seems more difficult than in former years, the higher prices paid more than repay our additional efforts, while the demand for this variety of fruit is steadily increasing.

The Cuthbert can be grown on any soil, but a deep, moist, sandy loam will produce the best crops. An abundance of moisture is absolutely necessary in the production of a good crop. Thorough but shallow cultivation is essential, and will aid immensely in conserving moisture, and prevent loss by evaporation during dry weather. Use plenty of well-rotted manure, spread around the bushes in winter if possible. This will invigorate the bush, insuring larger and better fruit the next season, and will aid in the production of strong young plants for future crops.

I would like to say a word about the treatment of anthracnose. It is a disease that can be overcome. We are liable to have years when anthracnose is severe, and then again it disappears. This plan of treatment strikes me as the most favorable, and I think will be found successful in general practice: When you lift the canes in the spring of the year treat with bordeaux mixture; make it double strength, and cover the canes with it soon after they are lifted. When the young growth appears and is about eight inches high, spray again, but use the mixture weak, just half the strength you did before. The theory is this: The spores are thrown off by the canes early in the spring from these infected spots, and when they are covered by a thick bordeaux mixture it prevents these spores being thrown off. You cannot prevent injury to the old canes, but you can prevent injury to the young canes, and if you spray you can make the young canes grow well the first season without any serious damage—but spray the second time when the young canes are about eight inches high.

Currant and gooseberry bushes are often injured by the borer. The egg is laid about June 1st. When hatched, the young borer works its way into the cane, and remains until the following spring, eating out the pith and causing death of cane. As soon as the leaves start, the affected parts are easily discovered, and should be cut out and burned.

Have Early and Late Strawberries

GREAT strides forward have been made in strawberry culture. It is not only possible to grow a profitable crop within twelve months from the date of setting out plants, but there are notable achievements with what is known as the ever-bearing variety.

Successful experiments are being made in extending the strawberry season so that this fruit may be picked both earlier and later than heretofore. The principal point gained is in getting more time for marketing a perishable commodity. Profits already are high, but they will be increased.

While the ever-bearing variety will produce fruit at the same season as the ordinary strawberries and keep on bearing until frost, to get the best results, the blossoms should be kept pinched off until August 1, so as to conserve the energies of the plant for the fall crop.

By planting in the latter part of April, a good crop will be obtained the same year and every year. Picking will begin about the middle of August and continue right along until winter sets in. The blossoms must be pinched off until the supplies of common varieties are pretty well exhausted, and the market demand for fresh stock begins to get keen.

One grower, by that method, gathered nearly 400 quarts from 500 plants set out in the spring. The quality was superb and the size good, but not up to the large June berries, because of the season at which they were borne.

The autumn strawberry is going to give us more money

to the acre because late prices will be highest, and this new variety of berry is both hardy and prolific.

Those who have tested autumn strawberry culture have been able to market the most delicious fruit up to the middle of November in northern regions. These late grown berries are readily taken at 20 to 30 cents a quart, and evidently it will require years to create an oversupply. Ordinary frosts have little effect on them.

All large plant and seed houses are ready to furnish this new strawberry, a fruit which is likely to create something of a furore.

While the autumn strawberries will blossom and yield fruit from June till November, the best results are gained for the producer by raising common stock for early trade and reserving the new product for fall business. It will be found that the late berries command a price about twice as high as that paid for early ones, as the market becomes glutted in June and July.

These autumn strawberries are known to the trade as the ever-bearing variety. They yield fruit as early as any other kind, but the point to be kept in mind is that by holding back the berries of the new variety a heavy yield is insured for the latter part of the season when the common kinds do not yield. The method of pinching off blossoms to retard fruit bearing is quite simple.

Another valuable peculiarity of the new strawberry is that its first fall crop, grown the same season that the plants are set out, will be one of the heaviest it will ever produce. Common strawberries to be a success must be retarded until the second year. The second year's crop of the ever-bearing variety is apt to be as satisfactory as the first, provided cultivation and winter mulching have not been neglected. Each season adds new plants, so that the stock can be kept in a vigorous state. After two or three seasons it may be best to discard old plants.

In getting ready for the new or the common variety it

is advisable to take a piece of land that has borne some such crop as clover, cowpeas or turnips and which has had a lot of well-rotted manure plowed in. A bit of land that has had rather more than ordinary cultivation is best of all. A gentle slope is desirable, or the land may become soggy at a time when the young plants need warm, loose soil. Drained land usually answers the purpose well. Fall plowing is recommended. Then in the spring, before planting, the soil should be stirred up with a disc or harrow, after which a roller ought to be used.

Occasionally a successful grower is found who sets out strawberry plants late in the summer in order to get fruit the next season, but spring planting is preferable. Plant as early as the soil can be worked or as soon as the danger from frost is over. Rows should be three feet apart to permit the use of a horse cultivator, and plants are to be twelve to sixteen inches apart in the rows.

Commence cultivation as soon as the ground is dry enough and let it be thorough, once every week during the summer. As the row begins to widen the farmer should each time narrow down the cultivated space between the rows, and after the row has attained the proper width continue to cultivate to prevent plants forming in the center of the rows.

Do not let the fields become matted, but maintain an open center between the rows. Matting may be allowed in the rows, as this is a natural growth for the strawberry. Better results are obtained by growing in matted rows than under any other method.

The plants must not be allowed to suffer for water in the fruiting season and a mulch will be found to be of great advantage. High cultivation is essential for the best results in all crops, and in growing these strawberries a little extra trouble will pay well.

Pot-grown strawberries are superior to the ordinary ground layers usually sold, as there is no loss of fine roots in taking them up and they can be shipped safely to distant parts and be transplanted at any season, and it scarcely checks their growth.

After the late crop is off, about the middle of November cover the bed to a depth of three inches with hay, straw or leaves. In April, as soon as the plants show an indication of growth, push the covering away so that the plants may come up through. This "mulching" protects the plants from cold in winter and the heat in summer, keeps the fruit clean and prevents the growth of weeds.

For illustration of what the late-bearing strawberry will do the following statement of an eastern expert is quoted:

"In the spring of 1910 I purchased 250 plants each of Americus and Francis, and set them in carefully prepared rich ground about May first. They were set in rows 3½ feet apart, with the plants one foot apart in the row. They occupied just about one twenty-fifth of an acre.

"They were given good care, well fertilized and hoed, and the weeds carefully kept out. The blossoms were kept pinched off until about August 1, and on August 23 we picked four quarts, and they continued to yield berries until November 11, when the last three quarts were gathered.

"During the week of September 12th to the 17th we picked nearly 100 quarts, which were shown at the State Fair in Syracuse, N. Y. The largest single picking was 48 quarts, gathered September 29."

Commercial Handling of Strawberries

THERE are few products that equal the strawberry for profit. It is a sure crop and gives quick returns. The yield is nearly always upwards of $200 an acre and it may run to double this figure.

The best time to set a strawberry bed is the early spring, as soon as the land is in good condition and the plants can be obtained. There is more moisture as a rule at that time, and this, combined with the cool weather of spring gives better growing conditions than fall planting. Plants may also be set in the fall, if extra attention and care are given them.

Strawberries require a rich soil, hence it is well to thoroughly manure the land that is to be used for the crop in the fall, and plow under from four to six inches deep. In the spring, disc, drag and smooth thoroughly. This gives a loose soil in which to set the plants, and a firm sub-soil to hold the moisture, and yet open enough to let the roots through.

Any land that will grow a good crop of corn will grow strawberries. Sod land should never be used, as it is likely to contain grubs and cut-worms, which will eat off the roots of newly set plants.

Plants having a small crown and a large number of white fibrous roots, are best for planting. It is not a good plan to use plants that have borne fruit, as they are weaker. The best plants are obtained from plantations that have not been allowed to fruit. Their roots are white, while the roots of the old plants are brown.

Before planting, all dead leaves should be removed.

196

The roots should be pruned back to about 3 or 4 inches. All flowers should be kept off the plants the first season, as this provides a stronger growth. It is best to get the plants from a nurseryman or strawberry specialist, as they are not as likely to be mixed as when obtained from a neighbor.

The method of planting in common farm use is the matted row system. When the land is in good condition to work, harrow smooth, and mark out rows three feet apart and as long as possible. Then set the plants at 18-inch intervals in the rows and cultivate often enough to keep the weeds out and the soil loose until September. If the plants are then vigorous growers, the runners should be about 6 inches apart. It is desirable to train the runners the long way of the rows, cutting out plants that crowd.

An ordinary planting trowel or spade is used to set the plants. A spade is an easy implement to open the ground with. Strike it into the ground and work it back and forth, draw out the spade, spread the roots of the plant and set it so the crown comes just to the surface of the ground. Firm the soil well about the roots of the plant. This method requires a man to handle the spade and a boy to set the plants.

As soon as possible after setting the plants, cultivation should commence and it should continue at frequent intervals till fall. Keep the weeds down and the top soil loose. If the runners get too thick, cut out part of them, leaving about 6 inches between them. Runners may be encouraged to root by putting an inch or two of soil over each one, near the end.

It requires about 7,000 strawberry plants for an acre, and these will bear 25 to 50 bushels the first season if allowed to do so. The custom is to pinch off all blossoms the first year. A crop of 100 to 200 bushels may be expected the second summer. Clean straw or grass makes the best winter mulch. The rows are covered 2 to 4 inches deep. This winter mulch should be raked from the plants and left between the rows as a protection to the fruits and a safeguard against drouth in the fruiting season.

Winter killing of the strawberry appears to be more often due to alternate freezing and thawing, together with the consequent drying out of the surface soil, than to the low temperature itself. Thus in beds where severe winter injury has occurred, the roots are often found to be killed for a short distance below the crown, while farther down they are alive. In such cases the plants frequently start into growth in spring, but die down in a short time.

The strawberry plant, as well as the bramble plants, can and do endure drouth and ask little aid from man in their season of barrenness, but during the very brief period when their fruits approach and reach maturity they demand more ready moisture than slow maturing field crops. For this reason the fruit grower is at a disadvantage.

Crops that demand highly intensive culture and make high returns for the area planted may render irrigation an economical measure. For example, the new fall-bearing strawberry is generally the victim of the fairly regular heat and drouth of August and September. A method of irrigation that would provide it with a full supply of water might with reasonable assurance be counted on to insure an annual crop. This granted, other conditions affecting success would have consideration.

The center of the most important strawberry industry of New York State is at Oswego. The leading natural advantage of this region for the commercial production of strawberries is the lateness at which the crop matures. When the berry season of New Jersey and southern New York is past, the Oswego berries are in their prime,

Lateness is still further emphasized in the selection of late varieties, as Atlantic, Parker Earle and Gandy. The season opens about June 20 and continues for three weeks.

The question is often asked, What does it cost to grow an acre of strawberries? Growers in the Oswego region have given figures of actual cost as follows: Rent of land two years, $11; plowing and fitting, $6; plants, $15; setting plants, $4; cultivation, $16; straw for winter and fruiting mulch, $15; labor, hoeing, pulling weeds, etc., $10. Total cost, $77.

Many growers raise berries at much less cost, and a few exceed this sum, especially when located near a large town, where rents are high; but it would be safe for one about to engage in strawberry growing to figure close to this total, aside from the cost of fertilizer.

Thorough Cultivation Makes Gardening Pay

WHETHER gardening is conducted for profit or merely for exercise and pleasure, one needs to do the right thing at the right time. It may be taken for granted that a majority of those who take up the work desire both profit and pleasure.

A common source of failure is sourness of the soil, which is found in places almost wholly shaded during the months which intervene between the growing seasons and which also lack a free circulation of air. Wood ashes and slaked lime are good for this and also are a most excellent fertilizer. A peck of ashes well mixed with a wagon load of soil is the gardener's rule, but for small beds, spade the ground deeply and after breaking up the lumps and raking thoroughly, scatter ashes or lime evenly over the surface until it is as white as after a light snowfall; then rake in well. This should be done before planting time, or as soon as the ground can be worked. It is best to have the plowing done in the fall.

Success in the vegetable garden depends largely upon thorough and frequent tillage. The tillage should begin as soon as the plants can be seen, and should be repeated at intervals of about one week throughout the season. Much labor will be saved by substituting a wheel hoe for the hand hoe for stirring the soil close about the plants, while they are small and by using a horse for cultivating between the rows wherever there is sufficient space. If these methods are employed, the most irksome features of vegetable gardening—the weeding and tedious hand tillage—will be eliminated.

As soon as the heavy frosts are over and the ground is tillable we may plant onions, lettuce, spinach, radishes, beets, parsnips, carrots, parsley and peas. The normal season for planting these crops is when the farmer is sowing his oats.

The warm season crops are subject to injury by frost and can not safely be planted until the weather is comparatively warm. The different crops in this group, however, differ in respect to the intensity of heat they require. Thus, sweet corn and string beans are usually planted early in May; lima beans, tomatoes, cucumbers, melons and squashes are planted from one to two weeks later, while sweet potatoes and egg plants should be kept in the hot-bed until the last of May or the first week in June.

Lettuce can be grown successfully on poor soil, but only through the early spring and the late fall, as the ground becomes so hot that it will burn in the head, and then it is ruined for market. On rich land there is always a certain amount of moisture that remains in the soil, and then the evening dews help to keep the ground cool. Keep the land free from weeds. The more frequent the cultivation the larger the yield.

Where garden peas and beans are grown, earliness and tenderness are greatly desired, as well as flavor. These qualities will be found where a good supply of nitrogen and phosphoric plant food are available. A suitable fertilizer for these crops is 600 pounds per acre carrying 4 per cent nitrogen, 8 per cent phosphoric acid and 10 per cent potash.

Tomatoes, corn and potatoes enjoy a medium long season of growth, therefore it is necessary that they have a sufficient supply of the correct food elements to satisfy their requirements throughout their growing season. The market demands a smoothly formed, solid, well-colored tomato, and juicy yet well-filled corn.

Potato growers of the famous Aroostook district of Maine, practice a three-year rotation of corn, clover and potatoes. By this means it is evident that the organic matter of the soil is maintained. When the potatoes are planted it is the custom to apply as high as 1,500 to 2,000 pounds per acre of a fertilizer analyzing 4 per cent nitrogen, 6 per cent phosphoric acid and 10 per cent potash.

Cabbage is an excellent crop for profits and for soil preservation. The large drum-head type is used for the early family trade and for making sauerkraut. It usually produces a heavier tonnage per acre than the Holland or Danish ball type, but sells at a lower price.

The Holland variety produces a head nearly round, and very hard. It is used for winter storage, and is in demand late in the fall. The later it can be stored, the less loss for the buyer, so this should be grown for late delivery.

This may be somewhat of a guide as to what type to grow. In either case see a buyer in the spring, and arrange for marketing, and then, when the time for harvest nears, let him know about what time the crop will be ready and its prospective amount. The average farmer cannot so profitably store his cabbages as he can potatoes.

In setting the plants for a cabbage crop, set in rows—both ways for easy cultivation—and be careful to get the rows even distance and in straight lines.

Use a fine, spike-tooth cultivator. Cultivate as long as you can get through the rows. After the plants are well established in growth, and begin to reach out, do not work very deeply, as the root system of the plants completely fills the soil.

Put on the wide sweeps so you can reach under the leaves and yet not cut many roots. For the last time take off the two back shanks and use only three plate teeth.

Plan your field so you can drive with one wheel in the

ditch and straddle one row of cabbages. This makes it easy to harvest.

Other crops which the farmer can grow profitably in many sections are carrots and rutabagas. Both are excellent stock feed, and all small or imperfect ones can be used on the farm, as well as any surplus.

You should look up the prospective market in the spring, before planting, then use the best varieties and deliver only choice stock, well trimmed and honestly packed.

Horseradish is commonly grown from sets and not from seed. Some claim they have the best success growing it as a second crop after the early cabbage, beets, etc. The crop is dug in the fall, the small roots removed and cut into sets four to six inches long. The top end is cut square and the bottom slanting so as to make no mistake in planting. These are tied in bundles and kept over winter in sand. In the spring after the cabbages are set out, a row of horseradish is set in between the cabbage rows. Small holes are made with a light crowbar or long stick and the sets dropped in and covered two or three inches deep so that they do not come up until July first. Any deep, rich, well drained soil will answer for horseradish.

The humble peanut was grown in this country in 1909, according to recent official figures, to the value of over 18 million dollars. The area under this crop was 870,000 acres, a third greater than in 1899, and the production nearly 20,000,000 bushels. The leader in acreage was North Carolina, followed in the order named by Georgia, Virginia, Florida, Alabama, Texas; others scattered. The average farm value per bushel of peanuts increased from 61 cents in 1899 to 94 cents in 1909.

Practical Study of Gardening

I WISH to call the attention of gardeners and farmers generally to the wisdom of saving the seeds of all extra choice home-grown products. It is the quickest way of securing a variety just adapted in all respects to the soil and climatic conditions, and one knows at planting time just about what to expect from his crop. Melons, especially, vary to such a marked extent, that whenever an especially delicious one is cut, its seeds should be carefully saved, and labeled in some way to indicate their special merit. Squash, pumpkins, tomatoes, peppers, and any other vegetables which are normally picked ripe, should have unusually perfect specimens selected for the seed. Of course it does not pay to save the seed except from unusually good specimens, because even then, many will be produced inferior to the parent stock, and a few, probably, much superior to the parent stock. Vegetables, and such fruits as the melons, usually come fairly true from seed. Other fruits are customarily budded or grafted, and seed selection is useless except for experimentation. Leave the very best of the vegetables to thoroughly ripen. The seeds will be worth much more during the year to come than the single specimen which produced them.

Gardening is profitable to any family that has the advantage of lands. It also may be a source of pleasure as well as profit. For the benefit of beginners, who may be unfamiliar with the quantities of seed needed to plant a garden of a given size, the following tabular statement is inserted. It represents the quantities of seeds which should be purchased for planting gardens suitable to the

needs of the ordinary country home. Any person of
practical ability who wishes to raise vegetables extensively for market can enlarge the quantity of seed or
roots to any extent:

	Farmer's garden.	Suburban garden.
Asparagus	100 roots	50 roots
Beans, green podded	1 pt.	½ pt.
Wax	1 pt.	½ pt.
Lima	1 pt.	½ pt.
Beets	2 oz.	1 oz.
Cabbage, early	1 pkt.	1 pkt.
Second early	1 pkt.	1 pkt.
Late	1 pkt.	1 pkt.
Carrot	1 oz.	1 pkt.
Cauliflower	1 pkt.	1 pkt.
Celery	1 oz.	1 pkt.
Corn, sweet, extra early	1 pt.	½ pt.
Second early	1 pt.	½ pt.
Late	1 pt.	½ pt.
Cucumber	1 oz.	1 oz.
Eggplant	1 doz. pl.	½ doz. pl.
Lettuce, leaf	1 oz.	1 pkt.
Head	1 pkt.	1 pkt.
Muskmelon	1 oz.	½ oz.
Onion seed	2 oz.	1 oz.
Sets, bottom	1 qt.	1 qt.
Sets, top (perennial)	1 qt.	
Parsley	1 pkt.	1 pkt.
Parsnip	1 oz.	1 pkt.
Peas, extra early smooth	1 pt.	
Early dwarf wrinkled	1 qt.	½ pt.
Late wrinkled	1 pt.	½ pt.
Pepper	1 pkt.	1 pkt.
Radish	3 oz.	1 oz.
Rhubarb	1 oz.	
Spinach	1 oz.	1 oz.
Squash, summer	1 oz.	1 pkt.
Winter	1 oz.	
Sweet potatoes	200 plants	
Tomato	2 pkts.	1 pkt.
Turnip	1 oz.	1 pkt.
Watermelon	1 oz.	½ oz.

In growing asparagus the most satisfactory method to
pursue is that of propagating from seed. The plants
should be grown in the seed-bed the first year and trans-

planted to a permanent bed the second spring. As this bed will last for a number of years, great care should be taken to, see that the ground is thoroughly prepared. Upon this rests your success. The land should be deeply plowed and heavily manured with well-rotted stable manure the fall before planting. In planting, the rows should be six feet apart and the plants two feet in the row. Furrow out the rows to a depth of eight inches and plant in the bottom of the furrow. The roots should be covered lightly at first, packing the soil well, however, around them and filling in the furrow as the stalks appear above the surface. It is better not to gather any crops until the second spring after the plants are put out, and then it should not be cropped heavily. The first two years frequent tillage is important, but after that the ground is sufficiently shaded and mulched to give little trouble from weeds. In growing asparagus, occasional applications of salt will stimulate the growth as this is a seashore plant. Among the best varieties are Conover's Colossal and Palmetto.

About the middle of May I plant cucumbers in rich, loose soil, the ground having been laid off in small hills six feet apart, with several holes in each of these hills. The holes need to be three inches deep and each should contain a half-dozen seeds.

After every rain, or in a week at the outside, rake over the surface of the hills, in fact, the whole plot devoted to cucumbers. By that time if the weather has been warm the young plant will be breaking through the ground. After that, continue to cultivate as often as necessary to maintain the soil mulch, and please observe that this is the most important part of the season's operation. Of course if you cultivate properly you will not be troubled with weeds.

Just as soon as the cucumbers appear above the ground, take a shovelful of wood ashes and in the early morning

while the dew is still on the plants, sprinkle them carefully. Repeat this after every rain, or when for any
cause the ashes have been blown or washed off the leaves
of the plant. This will absolutely prevent damage from
the cucumber bug and you ought to have no loss from that
source. The ashes not only do no harm but are a decided
benefit in that they contain valuable fertilizing material
in the shape of potash. Don't use coal ashes. Always
use wood ashes. If you haven't any wood ashes a light
application of air-slaked lime will be of great benefit.

Ordinarily cucumbers are allowed to run along the
ground. I have found that the output from a small tract
is very greatly increased if a trellis is provided and the
vines are trained up on this. This accomplishes a number of purposes. In the first place the vines are off the
ground and are not injured during the process of cultivation or picking the cucumbers. This is exceedingly important. Furthermore, it is then easily possible to see
every cucumber when it attains the proper size for picking. If the vines are on the ground, some which are
overlooked ripen and this to a large extent weakens the
vitality of the plant. This trellis is very easily made,
costs practically nothing, and the only attention that must
be given is that as soon as the vines are 2 feet or so long
they will have to be tied up to the trellis. After that
they will practically take care of themselves.

The most distinctive feature of the garden on the farm
should be the reduction of hand labor to a minimum. In
planting the garden, therefore, it should be laid out in
long rows, sufficiently far apart to permit the use of a
horse and cultivator in tending the crops.

The arrangement of the garden as to length of rows
and time of planting, is not the only labor saving feature
that should characterize the typical farmer's garden.
Field methods should be practiced in preparing the land
for planting, and as much preliminary work done in the

fall as is possible, for the sake of both securing an early garden and reducing the amount of labor in spring. After the land is cleared of refuse from preceding crops, it should be heavily manured, and plowed in the fall. The amount of manure to be applied will depend somewhat upon the fertility of the land, but more largely upon the trueness of the farmer's conception of the plant food requirements of garden crops. The best gardens are possible only where plant food is supplied much more liberally than is considered ample for field crops.

The most tedious labor in the ordinary garden is the hand weeding of the small vegetables. By proper management of the garden a large amount of this labor can be eliminated. One way to avoid excessive labor in hand weeding is to keep weed seeds out of the garden as much as possible, by avoiding the use of manure containing such seeds, and by destroying all weeds in and about the garden before they go to seed, even if they appear after the crops are harvested. But in spite of all that can be done there will always be weed seeds present in garden soil. The way to prevent these from producing weeds that are larger than the vegetable plants and endangering the life of the latter, is to keep them from starting growth before the vegetables have a chance to start. This is done by working the soil immediately before the vegetable seeds are planted, thus killing any weed seedlings that are about to appear above the surface, and giving the vegetables an even start with the weeds that may develop from seeds germinating later. Still another way of reducing the amount of hand weeding is to cultivate very close to the rows with a wheel hoe as soon as the vegetable seedlings appear.

Some crops demand special training or other manipulation to enable them to grow to the best advantage or develop the most desirable product. Common Lima beans and tall growing peas require artificial support in the

form of poles and brush or wire netting respectively.
Except in a region where native timber is abundant it
may be inconvenient or expensive to provide these sup-
ports, to say nothing of the labor of preparing and in-
stalling them.   Therefore, it may be advisable in some
cases to resort to the use of dwarf varieties exclusively.

Other crops demanding special handling are cauliflower, leeks, celery and endive, all of which require
blanching to develop a satisfactory, edible product. In
the case of the cauliflower, the head must be protected
from the sun by tying the leaves or otherwise securing
them over the top.   Endive likewise is blanched by tying
up the outer leaves so that the inner portion of the plant
will be protected from the sun.   With both these crops,
the blanching plants must be closely watched, so that they
may be used when they have reached the right stage of
development.   Leeks and celery are usually blanched by
hilling up with earth, though an early crop of celery is
sometimes blanched by means of boards placed edgewise
along the row.   When earth is used, care must be exercised to avoid getting dirt down in the "hearts" of the
plants, and repeated bankings are necessary.   This is a
somewhat laborious process unless a person is equipped
with special tools, and at best there is much labor and
expense involved in the production of a good crop of
celery.

The labor of growing some crops is enhanced by the
necessity of transplanting.   The crops usually transplanted are cabbage, cauliflower, celery, eggplant, pepper,
sweet potato and tomato; and an early crop of any of
these sorts cannot be secured without it, for the seed must
be started in hot-beds long before the weather is suitable
for planting these crops in the open.   The making and
care of hot-beds in which plants are usually started en-
tails considerable labor, as well as the process of transplanting.   Late crops of cabbage and tomatoes are some-

times grown from seed sown where the crop is to mature, and late cauliflower and celery may be started in carefully prepared seed beds in the open, thus obviating the labor involved in the care of a hot-bed.

There is a tendency for some gardeners to leave the plants of carrots, onions, and similar vegetables too thick, or to defer the thinning too long, with the intention of making use of the thinnings. Usually this is a serious error, except in the case of beets, which can be used quite young for greens. The crowded seedlings do not reach edible size as soon as they would if not crowded; and the removal of part of the crowded plants when they are wanted for the table is likely to seriously disturb and impair the growth of those which remain. A better plan is to make at least a preliminary thinning as early as possible, leaving the plants perhaps twice as thick as they are eventually to stand; and then to pull out every other plant after they reach edible size. This method of thinning is especially adapted to beets, carrots, lettuce and onions. The other root crops, like parsnips and salsify, should be thinned to the full distance at the first thinning.

Celery is an exceedingly profitable crop and one can make it pay either by starting with seed or procuring plants. The latter may be set out in July or August after some other crop has been raised on the ground.

The best location for celery is a moist, cool spot, of rich loamy soil protected from the wind. Enrich the soil heavily with well-rotted stable manure. Give deep plowing and cultivate thoroughly, in order to have the ground mellow at the time of transplanting.

Setting plants in furrows, in trenches and on the level surface are methods employed by various growers. Good results have been attained in the following way: Mark off rows four feet apart and furrow with stirring plow, turning the ridges in the same direction. Set the plants six inches apart in the side of the furrow next the ridge and a little above the bottom. In subsequent cultivation keep the furrows open and use them as ditches for water in case of drought.

Thorough cultivation should be the rule from the start. Permit no weeds to grow. The ground should be cultivated after each application of water.

When the plants have attained the proper size for use, the leaves are brought into an upright position by boards placed on either side of the row, so that they slope toward the plants at the top, or else by dirt drawn against the plants and packed firmly around them. The object of this is to cause the leaves to take an upright position and exclude the light from the heart of the plant, so that the latter growth is white or "bleached." The process of bleaching requires from two to four weeks, depending upon the variety and time of year.

After the bleaching process is carried as far as desired, the plants may be dug. For early celery this may be done in September, but the late crop should not be taken up until there is danger from freezing. The plants are usually lifted with a spade or potato fork, and the decayed outer leaves removed. They are then ready for storing.

Beets, carrots, turnips, rutabagas and Irish potatoes can be stored in outdoor pits, but they must be covered sufficiently to prevent freezing. One of the best ways of handling these crops is to place them in a conical pile and cover first with six or eight inches of hay or straw, then with earth to a similar depth.

Celery may be stored in various ways, but one of the most satisfactory methods for home use is to dig the plants with the roots on, and plant them in moist earth placed on the cellar floor, or in boxes to be placed in the cellar. In either case, the cellar must be cool, the ventilation good, and the earth surrounding the roots kept moist by repeated applications of water. In applying the water,

212   PRACTICAL STUDY OF GARDENING

care must be taken to wet only the roots and not the tops
of the plants. If the cellar is kept dark, all new growth
made during the winter will be thoroughly blanched.

Cabbage intended for late winter use will keep better
in an outdoor pit than in a cellar. The same is true of
parsnips, salsify, horseradish and some of the other root
crops. Except where the ground is especially well
drained, the pits are usually made entirely above ground.
For storing cabbage in this manner, the plants are pulled
with the roots and leaves on, and placed upside down in
regular order on a level piece of ground.

Onions intended for winter use should be cured as soon
as possible after harvesting, by being kept in a dry place
where the air can circulate freely about them. Some
growers spread their onions in a thin layer on the floor
of the corn crib; others place them in shallow, slatted
trays stacked under an open shed, or exposed to the sun
during the day and placed under cover at night. The
bulbs may also be spread thinly on the floor of a barn loft
or the attic of a house. No matter where they are placed,
they must be kept dry and have a free circulation of air
about them.

Tomatoes, cabbage, sweet potatoes and other vegetables and garden plants and especially those which are
started under glass and transplanted, are subject to
serious injury by cutworms. They appear sometimes in
great numbers in spring and early summer and frequently
do severe damage before their ravages are noticed. The
method of attack is to cut off the young plants at about
the surface of the ground, and as these insects are of
large size and voracious feeders they are capable of destroying many plants in a single night, frequently more
than they can devour. During the past two years these
insects, working generally throughout the United States,
destroyed hundreds of thousands of dollars' worth of
crops. By the timely application of remedies, however,

it was found that these insects could be readily controlled, large areas being successfully treated. The usual method of control is by the use of poisoned baits.

Take a bushel of dry bran, add one pound of arsenic or Paris green, and mix it thoroughly into a mash with eight gallons of water, in which has been stirred half a gallon of molasses. After the mash has stood several hours, scatter it in lumps of about the size of a marble over the fields where injury is beginning to appear and about the bases of the plants set out. Apply late in the day so as to place the poison about the plants over night, which is the time when the cut worms are active. Apply a second time if necessary. Where garden maggots or other small insects have appeared, treat the soil with tobacco or kerosene emulsion.

Cucumbers and squash have the same enemies, but the beetle will leave the cucumber for the squash, which induces some growers to plant a few squash-vines near cucumbers in order to trap the beetles.

Late blight of potatoes causes extremely heavy damage some years, the extent depending largely upon weather conditions. It is most likely to appear during damp, sultry weather in August and September. Where the disease has been prevalent in recent seasons the only safe method is to spray thoroughly throughout the summer so as to ward off possible attacks. The disease is caused by a parasitic fungus which attacks the stems and under portions of the leaves, spreading in favorable weather with extreme rapidity and sometimes wilting an entire field in the course of 48 hours. It can scarcely be checked by spraying, but its appearance can be prevented by this method.

Commercial Value of Garden Flowers

NEARLY all the common, hardy flowers have great commercial value. It is possible for farm families to greatly increase their income by raising such a variety of flowers as can be grown on an acre or less.

The aster is a favorite in the markets and is a money-maker for those who have taste and skill in gardening. The evolution of the aster in the past five years has been something wonderful.

Persistent effort on the part of growers induced the plain, unpretentious little China Aster of our grandmothers' day to bestir itself with most gratifying results.

The magnificent chrysanthemum-like blooms of the present day bear little resemblance to their Chinese ancestors. To become familiar with the possibilities of this old friend in its new development, it is only necessary to look at the displays in florists' windows during August and September.

This will suggest, too, many commercial possibilities of aster culture. Last year an acquaintance of mine marketed nearly $300 worth of asters, grown on the rear of a city lot.

There is nothing difficult or complicated about aster culture. The plants are usually free from bothersome insects, and if given half a chance they attend strictly to business, and flower within two months after they have been transplanted to the garden.

It is not best to raise them two successive years in the same soil, and one should have well rooted plants ready to set out by the first of July, earlier if blossoms are desired before September.

Procure seed of the large variety from some reliable seed house. Plant in April in boxes of sifted earth. You will find cigar boxes just right for this purpose, as they will be light to handle, and are just right for standing upon a window-sill, if one has to grow them in the living room.

Make four drills about a quarter of an inch deep, the length of the box. Put about eight seeds to the inch in the drill, and cover with earth. Pat down and keep moist. The boxes may be placed near the heat, where the earth will be kept warm, if the top is kept well moistened.

It is a good plan to keep covered with wet moss, or if moss cannot be had, place a cloth over the box to prevent evaporation. If the seed is fresh, and the earth kept warm, the plants will appear by the fourth day.

The box will then be uncovered and placed in a strong light, or the little plants will grow long, weak stems. Aster-plants cannot be given too much sunlight. As often as the weather will permit, place the boxes of young plants outside in the sunlight, but sheltered from the strong wind.

When the plants have their fourth leaf, they should be transplanted. Place them an inch apart in flats—boxes containing earth two inches in depth. As soon as they are well established in these new quarters, give an abundance of water, and their growth will amaze you.

They should be kept outside all of the time after being placed in the flats. Watch out for frosty nights, however, for aster-plants will not stand even a little frost. Meanwhile, during the time that the plants are growing in the flats, we must be preparing the plot in the garden. Any rich soil is suitable for asters. Of course the richer, the better.

Spade or plow them deep in April. Keep working it occasionally until time to place the plants in it. If at transplanting time the soil seems at all hard, spade again.

You will find that all of this preliminary working of the land will make the subsequent cultivation easy. Nearly all the weed growth has been destroyed.

The plants will only need attention after every rain, when it will be necessary to break the crust to prevent too rapid evaporation. In case of drought, keep the top soil well stirred.

If you water at all, give a thorough wetting, and proceed after it the same as after a rain. This plan is better than a daily sprinkling. The plants should be about ten inches apart in the row, and the rows can be as close together as will permit of proper cultivation—twelve to fifteen inches.

If you are growing your asters for the market, or for large blooms and long stems, rather than for a mass of blossoms, you should remove all but six branches from each plant. Remove them as soon as they appear.

Six flowers are all that one plant can mature and give you large, long-stemmed blossoms. If you are working for still larger flowers, let each plant bear only three.

You will find that on these remaining flower-stalks there will be a bud form at the base of every leaf. These must be carefully removed. This disbudding operation is really about all the work there is to aster cultivation, after the plants have been transplanted into their permanent quarters.

As a cut flower the aster has very few rivals. Its keeping qualities are not surpassed even by the chrysanthemum. Its range of color is nearly, if not quite, equal to that flower. For three seasons now I have found a ready market for choice, long-stemmed asters, at fifty cents a dozen. The demand seems unlimited.

While asters are easier to manage than other flowers,

it will be found that dahlias, gladioli and nasturtiums fit naturally into the gardening scheme and give great pleasure.

Dahlias can be raised from seed, or from small plants supplied by dealers, but neither of these methods is as satisfactory as starting them from dormant tubers. Do not plant an undivided bunch of tubers. Best results are obtained from placing one, never more than two, tubers in a hill. If two are used they are not separated.

Plant them two and a half or three feet apart each way. Place the tubers about four inches in the earth. Let only one sprout or plant grow from a hill. Some tubers will send up several, but they must be removed as soon as they become visible above the surface of the ground. Stake early and tie plants to the stake with strips of cloth. It is imperative that they be kept well tied to their support. While the plants are self-supporting, they are full of sap and very brittle. A wind storm will ruin dahlias if they are not tied securely to their stakes.

From each tuber planted in the spring you should in the fall have a clump of from three to five with which to start your next season's plants.

Keep top soil loose around your plants, but do not cultivate deeply after they have commenced to make rapid growth. Dahlias throw out a network of threadlike roots quite near the surface, and in cultivating great care should be taken not to injure these roots. In midsummer supply a top-mulch of barn-yard manure if you can procure it; if not, use lawn clippings. Make this dressing as thick as you can, up to eight inches. Your dahlias will need no further care other than to keep them properly tied to stakes and the blossoms well cut.

Gladioli have been termed the poor man's orchids. Anybody can grow them and in almost any soil, although they have a special liking for rich loam. Many of the newer sorts are wonderfully beautiful, and one of the advantages of the gladiolus is the fact that the blossoms will last for two weeks or more when cut, if the cutting is done just before the first flower on the stalk opens. Then, day after day, the other blossoms will unfold, until the stalk is full of glorious color.

The bulbs should be planted four inches deep, and care should be taken to have them go in the ground right side up. If the soil is kept stirred, less water will be necessary, and the plants will respond with extra fine flowers. If one desires a long blooming season of gladioli, plantings should be made every two weeks from April to June. They may be planted in rows eighteen inches apart and six inches in the row. One particular advantage of the gladiolus is the fact that it is seldom attacked by insect pests or plant diseases. These flowers also have commercial possibilities. One has only to study florists' windows during the summer and fall to be convinced of this fact.

Pansies prefer a partly shaded location and salvia thrives best in full sunshine. A late mulch benefits salvia.

Keep your pansy blossoms picked. Let no seeds form. In early winter cover with a layer of leaves and place a few branches on top to prevent the wind from blowing the leaves away. Remove the covering early in the spring and you will probably find buds already showing color, and it will not be long until you have plenty of these charming blossoms. Start mignonette and nasturtiums in the plot where they are to grow. Both varieties are rapid growers.

The beautiful lily-of-the-valley succeeds outside, in almost any location, but prefers shade and plenty of moisture. When it is once planted and becomes established, the crowns keep increasing, the large ones flowering each year without any attention beyond the application of a top-dressing of manure or rich soil in the fall.

Lilies-of-the-valley may be propagated by seeds, which ripen freely if allowed, and should be sown in the spring outside. The usual method of propagation, however, is by the numerous crowns which form at the joints of creeping roots, or underground stems. If the crowns are allowed to grow undisturbed, they become too thickly crowded, and do not produce such fine flowers as when more space is afforded.

Select and prepare a piece of ground in a border, with either an east or west aspect. It should be manured and well trenched. The crowns should be lifted in the fall, or at any time before growth commences in the spring, and placed together, according to their size.

In planting, a shallow trench should be cut out, the crowns placed upright in it about two inches apart, so that their points are just below the surface, and the soil filled in. Other trenches may then be prepared and planted in a similar way, leaving a space of about nine inches between them. Hoe occasionally to keep the surface open and clean, and watering in dry weather, until the leaves dry away, will be all that is necessary afterward. Crowns thus treated may be lifted for forcing the following winter, if required, but they are much stronger if allowed to stay until the second year. The crowns to be used for early forcing should be placed rather thickly in pots or boxes, and a little light soil shaken among the roots; but not over the tops. They should be covered with moss.

Another plan is to insert them similarly in propagation frames, and pot up as they come into flower. The roots do not grow during this period, consequently it is immaterial which method is adopted. Plunge in a bottom heat of about 85 degrees, and if possible maintain a surface temperature of 10 degrees less. This will encourage the production of leaves and flowers and at the same time—conditions not readily obtained with the earlier supplies. If pots or boxes are used, empty ones of similar size may be inverted over them to keep the crown dark. This is considered beneficial in assisting to start them into growth.

It is important that the soil be placed as lightly as possible around the roots, in order that the heat may pass through readily. Water of the same temperature should be given to keep the whole well moistened. The very earliest batch sometimes fails; but if the crowns are good, and proper attention is given in forcing, each of the later ones may be relied upon to produce flowers.

Grown in pots, and forced into flower early in the spring, the lily-of-the-valley constitutes an invaluable subject for decoration. The natural flowering season is May. By obtaining a plentiful supply of crowns, and forcing carefully, the season may commence in January, and a succession of flowers be secured thenceforth until June.

Making and Care of Hotbeds and Cold Frames

THE cold frame and hotbed are worthy of much wider attention than they now enjoy. With their aid the autumn season can be prolonged and the spring season hastened. They will yield herbs and salads in variety in early spring and hasten the starting of summer crops. To the flower lover they are a real necessity for the carrying of many things through the winter, and few people indeed have ever fully developed the possibilities of pleasure possessed by an ordinary glass-covered frame.

The function of a cold frame is to ward off cold winds, to keep the ground clear of snow, and in the spring to increase the feeble heat of the slanting sunbeams, and thus foster plant growth.

The construction is simple. The back board is usually twelve inches and the front eight inches wide. The two are connected by a tapered board twelve inches wide at one end and eight inches at the other. Standard sash are 3x6 feet, and it takes a box of 6x8 inch glass to glaze three sash. The frame work can be readily made by a local carpenter or any one handy with tools; and when complete the frame is set in a sheltered, well-drained position, usually near the house.

A cold frame is simply a frame having sash, but no other means of heating. Fill the frame with soil 6 inches deep in front and 8 or 9 inches at the back; make shallow drills, 3 inches or 4 inches apart, across the face of the soil in the frame, and in these sow the seeds, covering them thinly and tamping them gently; then water moderately through a fine hose. Now put on the sash, and keep all snug and warm until the seedlings appear, when the sashes should be tilted up during the day to admit fresh air freely and make the plants sturdy. As the seedlings wax in strength, remove the sash both day and night, in fine weather, but replace it as a protection against wet, muggy or cold weather. As soon as the plants are big enough, transplant them into the open garden.

In sowing in a cold frame, carefully observe that the kinds of plants are of somewhat the same nature, strength and time of germinating. When this is not the case, or there is any uncertainty about it, better sow in pots, pans or flats, and set these close together in the frame; as the seedlings appear in the pots or flats, remove these to the lightest, sunniest place in the frame, and the ungerminated ones keep by themselves. Afterwards as regards transplanting, treat as directed above in the manner of seed sown in the frame.

A hotbed is a cold frame placed upon a quantity of fermenting manure. The hotbed is usually made ready in February or March. In the preparation of the manure it is best to collect the requisite amount from the horse stable, and make it into a compact heap, watering it if dry. In a few days active fermentation will be in progress, when the heap should be turned, watering again if necessary, shaking out the lumps. The aim is to induce an active and uniform fermentation of the whole mass, and to have it continue for some time after the soil is placed on it.

Select a well-drained spot, and make the pile of manure eight or nine feet wide by whatever length is necessary, with a depth of fifteen to eighteen inches; or a foot of soil may be dug out and filled in with manure, well tramped down. Place the frame on it. Then put three or four inches of good soil uniformly over the surface.

Some manure or soil can be thrown up against the outer boards, which will help to hold the heat; put on the sash and keep tight for three or four days. There should be a thermometer kept in the hotbed, and when the temperature falls to 70 degrees seed may be sown with safety. The temperature in a hotbed should not be allowed to go above 70 degrees in the day, nor below 50 at night. Seeds may be sown in it in the same way as specified in the case of a cold frame, but it is safer for the amateur to sow in pots, pans or flats than to sow in the earth-bed of the hotbed. While a hotbed is new it is well to always keep a chink of ventilation to allow the discharge of "steam" or ammonia; if not, a damp mould will spread over the seed-pots or the seedlings will rot off. Keep the sprouted seeds by themselves, and the pots of unsprouted ones by themselves; give increased light and ventilation to the former. As regards hardening off and transplanting, treat as for cold frames. A hotbed should be covered overhead with straw mats or carpet at night in cold weather to conserve the heat, but this covering should be removed in the daytime.

With a hotbed the amateur can start almost any kind of vegetables or flower seed. By sowing such vegetables as eggplant, pepper, tomatoes, etc., and such flower seeds as heliotrope, scarlet sage, vinca, verbenas, etc., along in March, it is possible to have nice stocky plants ready to set out as soon as the weather conditions are favorable, insuring early returns from the vegetables and a long season of bloom from the flowers.

I know of no better way of getting the youngsters interested in agricultural matters than that of teaching them how to make and care for the hotbed.

The preparation of the manure is not such a particular job as is generally supposed, but the simple principle involved is not generally known.

The yeast fungus, when once introduced into a manure heap suitable to its development, spreads rapidly, and soon has the whole mass in a state of heat.

If the manure is very hot, the soil should be put on at once, but if not, the sash should be placed over the manure for a few days, until the manure is well heated, then the soil put on.

The bed should be watched, and as soon as the seed of weeds which are in the soil begin to come up all over the bed, it is time to plant the garden seed.

Planting the seed is one of the most fascinating parts of the work. To put the tiny seed into the mellow earth, and in a few days see the little plants shove their heads up to the light of day is well worth while.

The bed should be marked off into perfectly straight rows that run toward the rear from the front of the frame, the depth of the rows to correspond with the varieties of the seeds planted.

The seeds of eggplant, tomatoes and peppers are thin, and require more moisture than the seed of cabbage and other vegetables that have the thick or round seed, and should be planted deeper.

The main object is to plant just deep enough, so that the seed will not dry out after they germinate, and before they are well up and started. The soil should not get very dry any time after the seeds are planted, or even after the plants are up and growing.

War on Field and Garden Pests

IT takes a lot of vigorous effort to make a successful war on field and garden pests, which annually wipe out a large part of farm profits.

The cutworm seems to have been about as destructive as ever in recent years, and some orchardists and gardeners have felt like giving up in despair. Fungous diseases and other destructive agencies also have gained ground.

The war against them should go on, however, and land owners need to study methods. There is a great deal at stake, and this is no time for discouragement. Plant diseases and insects may be increased by continuously planting one crop upon the same field. Every crop has its peculiar insect enemies, and it is natural to assume that these enemies will be more numerous the second, third or fourth year the same crop is grown.

The cutworm has not only a wide distribution, but it is a promiscuous feeder as well. Scarcely any crop of field, garden or orchard is not subject to attack. It may clean vegetable and truck gardens absolutely. It not only takes potatoes, sweet potatoes, lettuce, beets, carrots, etc., but all the ornamentals fall before its voracious appetite. When very numerous it destroys, or at least damages, alfalfa. Apple, pear, peach, currant, blackberry, raspberry, gooseberry, grape and all fruit trees are victims of this gourmand.

Spraying with paris green, one pound to 100 gallons of water, to which five pounds of freshly slaked lime has been added, will often save vegetables. Spraying alfalfa or other succulent vegetation with this same mixture, or with two pounds of lead arsenate to fifty gallons of water, has often been used with marked success.

A poison bran mash has been used by many gardeners. A pound of paris green to forty pounds of bran should be sweetened either by use of cheap sugar or molasses and sufficient water added to make a stiff mash. Place in small bunches near the plants likely to be attacked.

Spray orchard trees late in the summer, after the fruit has been gathered, while the days are still warm. They also need spraying just after the blossoms have fallen in the spring. In bad seasons a third spraying is necessary. Use both an insect poison and a fungus poison, applying both at once. Use lead arsenate or paris green for the insects and bordeaux mixture or lime sulphur wash for the diseases. Better buy the lead arsenate and lime sulphur already prepared unless you have had experience in making these mixtures.

The codling moth, principal cause of wormy apples, is responsible for an annual loss in the United States of $12,000,000 in fruit and an expenditure of $3,000,000 to $4,000,000 for sprays and labor for spraying. However, spraying with arsenical sprays saves 90 to 95 per cent of the crop.

Spraying machines are as much a part of modern orchard and garden tools as pruning shears and cultivators. There is not an orchard, garden or farm that would not be better for their use. Indeed, in some cases, it is almost a question of abandoning the cultivation of certain crops or the use of spraying machines for their protection. It is quite feasible for neighbors to co-operate in the purchase of an outfit.

He who does not spray from this time on will be left behind in the race for success in the market and his supply of fruits will be deficient in both quantity and quality.

There are those who have taken advantage of the aids to practical horticulture, and their fruits are known in the markets as being clean, smooth and sound. Anyone knows how poor a chance for sale wormy, knotty or scabby fruit has beside that which is nearly perfect.

Many experts declare they cannot raise fruit successfully unless they spray at the end of the blossoming period and again after the fruit has gained some size. The cutworm is particularly destructive and hard to fight. These insects eat the buds and young foliage only during the night. During the day they hide at the base of the tree, going down a few inches into the soil.

The best treatment for this pest is to scatter poisoned bait close to the tree. This is made by mixing one pound of paris green to twenty pounds of bran, then adding one or two quarts of molasses. Work up with enough water to make a stiff mash. Do not let chickens have access to this poisoned bran. As a supplement to this treatment spray the trees with bordeaux mixture. The same scheme of treatment will answer for the garden cutworms. The bordeaux mixture will help to protect plants. When cutworms attack corn or other crops the poisoned bran scattered in the fields will prove effective.

For successful coping with the codling moth it is essential that all fallen and diseased fruit should be gathered and destroyed. Where bandages are used these should be removed and thoroughly cleaned or destroyed. The poison used with best results in killing codling moths is arsenate of lead. Bordeaux mixture or a lime-sulphur wash is added as a fungicide.

The potato beetle is one of the worst insect enemies of potatoes. They come in small numbers, first laying clusters of orange-colored eggs on the under side of the leaves. Then is the time to begin to destroy them, before they have had time to do much injury. The eggs hatch in about a week, hence if the plants are promptly sprayed with poison the young will be killed and the pest reduced or destroyed altogether.

Paris green at the rate of one pound to the acre in twenty-five to forty gallons of water is a common remedy. It is also used in connection with bordeaux mixture, the latter killing the blight. Lime should be used with the paris green. Perhaps a better insecticide for potatoes is arsenate of lead, applied at the rate of five or six pounds to the acre in about fifty gallons of water or bordeaux mixture.

The cottony maple scale is one of the best-known insects because it heavily infests several common shade trees, and because the cottony masses beneath the body of the adult female in summer make it a conspicuous object. These large white masses are a deposit of waxy threads within which are the minute, oval, pale yellowish eggs. The soft maple is the tree most generally infested by this insect. The boxelder is also subject to injury, and next to this, perhaps, the linden or basswood.

· Among the other trees and woody plants often more or less injured are the elm, honey locust, black locust, walnut, sumac, willow, poplar, beech, hawthorn, bittersweet, grapevine and Virginia creeper. The common kerosene emulsion, made by mixing kerosene with one-third of its volume of strong soapsuds, is a satisfactory spray and should be applied twice in the summer. Where caterpillars are usually numerous apply arsenate of lead freely.

The government has shown that insect pests cause a loss of about ten per cent on nearly all crops. The annual damage is placed at $420,000,000. The cinch bug wheat pest sometimes costs us $20,000,000 a year.

The boll weevil costs the cotton planters $20,000,000 a year.

The tree-insect pests cost the nation $100,000,000 a year.

The grasshoppers, cutworms, army worms, wireworms, leaf-hoppers and other insects cost the nation, annually, more millions than can be counted separately; but the total for all insect pests is $420,000,000. Now, have we not paid this price about long enough?

The value of the birds destroyed as "game" and for "food" is not a fraction of the value they would save to the national wealth, if permitted to live. Regarding the slaughter of our birds, the increase of insect pests, and the losses they inflict upon us, the great mass of the American people are sound asleep. The situation is illogical, absurd and intolerable.

In preparing the lime-sulphur mixture this plan may be followed: Sulphur, 15 pounds; unslaked lime, 20 pounds; use an iron kettle, thirty to sixty gallons, and some sort of a tank equally large that will hold hot water. In the iron kettle heat to boiling five gallons of water. Add the lime broken into small pieces, but not pulverized. Add immediately the sulphur, stirring it in as the lime slakes. Add hot water as necessary to keep from boiling over. Boil constantly from the time the lime is put in until the mixture is done. Boil for an hour or more until properly cooked, when it will be of a dark amber color. Color does not change when mixture has sufficiently cooked. Add hot water until you have forty-five gallons, keep stirred and strain through a fine strainer into the barrel or tank. Spray onto trees immediately. Apply when the leaves are off, during winter or in early spring. Never let the mixture stand over night or until cold before applying it; it will not do the work when allowed to stand. Remember to keep it boiling all the time while cooking. Where desirable, steam may be used for cooking this mixture, but the mixture must be constantly stirred during cooking process.

230 WAR ON FIELD AND GARDEN PESTS

For the arsenate of lead mixture use the following: Lead arsenate, 6 pounds; water, 120 gallons. This mixture stays in suspension better than paris green, but is more expensive and has little advantage over paris green except where rains are frequent it is less likely to burn the foliage. Arsenate of lead will adhere to the foliage longer and therefore should be more valuable for the late sprays or for leaf-eating insects.

After five years of experimenting with different spray material in apple orchards, the New Hampshire station is just out with suggestive conclusions. The work was conducted on different farms in different parts of the state, and the sprays were used primarily as fungicides. Prof. Charles Brooks, author of the bulletins, reaches conclusions a bit contrary to the general spraying verdict. While lime-sulphur is advocated as the best all-around spray, Prof. Brooks says: "No fungicide has been found that holds diseases in check as well as bordeaux. When showers follow soon after an application of bordeaux, the leaves are likely to be spotted and the fruit somewhat rusted. However, the injury to fruit is seldom great enough to be of importance when apples are sold in barrels. If extra fancy fruit is wanted for sale in boxes, the use of bordeaux under New Hampshire conditions seems questionable."

Second thought will indicate that Prof. Brooks is not so far from the general advice given on spraying. People want fancy fruit, hence they substitute lime-sulphur. It is largely to avoid spray injury that lime-sulphur has replaced bordeaux. No one ever questioned the high value of bordeaux as a fungicide. The trouble is it does too well, reaching the fruit as well as fungus. In New Hampshire experience, no commercial bordeaux has been found as satisfactory as home-made. "The best formula of bordeaux for the apple orchard is 3-3-50, that is, three pounds each of copper sulphate and lime to 50 gallons of water."

Regarding lime-sulphur, Prof. Brooks says: "It proved a satisfactory substitute for bordeaux in most cases. It caused little or no injury, and in some seasons controlled the diseases as well as bordeaux. In 1910, two sprayings of lime-sulphur were entirely inadequate to hold scab in check. When diseases are serious and the season a rainy one, more applications of lime-sulphur will be required than of bordeaux. As a poison for insects, arsenate of lead is the only thing that has proved satisfactory for use with lime-sulphur. The iron sulphide mixture gave good results the one season it was used, and is apparently worth further trial. The Baldwin is apparently more susceptible to spray injury than the McIntosh.

"The number of sprayings required will vary with the season and the diseases and general care of the orchard. The removal of all cankers will greatly decrease the leaf spot, and the destruction of the fallen leaves is of value in controlling both scab and leaf spot. The application of a strong fungicide before the leaves are out, and one of a regular strength just before the flower buds open, will decrease the number of sprayings needed later."

Enemies of the Corn Crop

THE corn root-worm has ruined thousands of acres of corn during the last thirty years, and yet it is one of the easiest species to control, when once the farmer becomes acquainted with its habits. Like most insects of this class, it is useless to attempt to hold it in check by the application of poisons; it covers too much territory, and, during the period when it does its injury, it is concealed beneath the surface of the soil. As one becomes better acquainted with its life history, therefore, the more evident it becomes that the application of good common sense in the farming operations is the only remedy needed.

This insect is closely related to the striped cucumber beetle, belonging to the same genus, is about the same size and shape, but the color is a light green. The adult beetles may be found feeding upon the silk and pollen of the corn during the last of July and through August until the corn plants approach maturity, when they lay eggs on the base of the stalks, just below the surface of the soil, and pass the winter in the egg state. The eggs hatch in late spring or early summer, and at first eat the smaller roots, but, as the plants develop the larvæ bore out the larger roots, causing the plants to dwindle and die, or to become so dwarfed as to amount to nothing. The full grown larvæ are white, chunked invididuals, about one-tenth of an inch long, and nearly as thick. They pupate in small oval cells in the ground and the beetles appear soon after.

As the larvæ do not feed upon anything but the corn roots, it is evident that if a regular rotation of crops is practiced, so that corn is grown on the same soil only once in three or four years, there will be no chance for the insects to increase. The trouble invariably comes from planting corn after corn, except on river bottoms, which are overflowed several times during each year. I have seen corn grown on the bottom lands along the Wabash river near LaFayette, every year for the past twenty-eight years, and I have never known a crop to be injured by this insect. But on the upland, black prairie and muck soils, where corn is the principal crop that can be successfully grown, this insect is sure to give trouble. On such land oats and grass should rotate with corn.

The corn root-aphis is a different proposition, as it belongs to the suckling class or true bugs, but like the other, it does its work on the roots under ground, and so is difficult to reach. These lice are usually attended by ants, as the latter are very fond of the "honey dew" which is given out by the lice through two little tubes, which are situated on the back of the adult insect. The ants even gather up the aphis eggs and store them in their nests where they are cared for during the winter. During April and May, as soon as the smart-weed and fox-tail grass make their appearance, these eggs begin to hatch and the ants carry their young wards and colonize them on the roots of these plants. As soon as the young corn plants are well started, the second brood of lice begins to appear and the ants transfer them to the corn roots where they continue to increase with great rapidity, and to suck the life out of the corn plants.

It is evident from the above, that the land seldom becomes infested with these lice until the second or possibly the third corn crop. If, therefore, a three or four-year rotation is practiced in which corn appears only once, there will be but little, if any, damage done by the aphis.

Then, too, the proper fertilization of the soil is of great importance, as it enables the corn to make a crop in spite of the lice. A heavy dressing of stable manure is generally preferable for this purpose. A dressing of kainit drilled in the row, at the rate of 100 pounds per acre at the time of planting has been found to almost completely protect the plants from the attacks of the lice. This material is used quite largely in some sections.

As the ants protect the eggs in their nests during winter, it is a good plan to plow the field which is intended for corn the second or third year, as late in the fall as possible, and as deeply as possible, in order to break up the ants' nests. This will also assist in destroying the weeds which serve as a starter for the lice in the spring. By dipping the seed corn in a solution of wood alcohol and oil of lemon before planting, the number of lice and ants may be greatly reduced, but this will prove true only when the weather conditions are just right. If heavy rains follow the planting, the material is washed off and so loses its force. With our present knowledge, therefore, rotation, late fall plowing, early and thorough cultivation, and the use of kainit are recommended.

Wealth in Honey Under Skillful Management

IT has been asserted that a thousand dollars can be cleaned up easier in the production of honey than in almost any other line of farm activity. Whether such a statement is literally true or not, it is certain that bee-keeping belongs in the line of mixed farming, and is worthy of general attention.

A few persons develop a large business in bee culture, and grow wealthy from the sale of honey, whereas the majority who start apiaries fail to realize enough from them to pay for the time and trouble involved.

There is a seeming inconsistency here, which is explained by the fact that the losers have been neglectful of vital points, while the winners have given skilled care to such questions as food supply, disease, protection from cold, and marketing the product. It is a business that calls for much reading and watchfulness.

It pays to winter the apiary in dry, snug quarters, and the shed or house ought to be ready by November 1. It is a common mistake to place the colonies in a cellar at the approach of winter. They are pretty sure to suffer from dampness or a lack of ventilation. The ordinary granary will answer the purpose, if space can be spared. It is essential to keep the hives free from wind. An even temperature is necessary, or moisture may accumulate from the alternate freezing and thawing.

Moths are usually prevalent in the hives after rainy weather of the fall, and many dead bees can be picked out of the combs when it comes time to prepare for winter. One diseased swarm will have a bad effect on the entire

235

apiary. If there are any colonies affected with moths or foul brood, they should be kept separate from the others.

It is best to take out all the honey where there are indications of disease and give the bees a clean hive, with a fresh supply of food. Wash and fumigate the old boxes before they are used again. It is important to have clean, well-made hives, with joints so tight that worms cannot secrete themselves out of reach of the bees.

Owners of apiaries who are not satisfied with the appearance of their swarms in spring will be wise to introduce a new lot of Italian queens bought from reliable dealers. This, with clean hives, will be apt to bring success again.

A vigorous swarm will gather 100 pounds of honey in a season, in addition to its own food supply, provided the distance to travel does not exceed a quarter of a mile. This product is worth $14 to $20, according to whether the producer sells at retail or wholesale. Call it $15 for the sake of the illustration. One hundred colonies would earn $1,500. Letting the food supply be governed by chance, a colony will produce thirty-five to seventy pounds in a good season. One hundred colonies will earn about $750. Owners need to provide a patch of buckwheat or alsike near the apiary. This will insure honey-making in bad seasons and save the bees a great deal of travel.

It is easy to handle bees when you know how. Undoubtedly a beekeeper often gets stung; it would be useless to deny it, and it is scarcely consoling to a novice to tell him he will get used to being stung; but after a time a beekeeper really does become inoculated, after which, although the momentary pain may be sharp, there are no disagreeable after-effects, such as swelling, etc.

The fear of stings prevents many from liking the work, and yet, when properly protected with a bee-veil, and working only in the warm part of the day, and never when cloudy, rainy or cold, and with the use of a good smoker, one need rarely be stung.

In many cases the sting of a bee is attended with much pain and swelling, while in others there are no ill effects produced whatever, and there is no doubt but that the system may become inured to the poison so that no bad effects are produced.

It is much easier to prevent the anger of bees than to stop it after it has begun. If you mismanage a colony of bees and arouse their anger, it is quite likely that this disposition will remain with them for a few days.

A bee away from home, or laden with honey, never volunteers an attack.

Thus, in order to render bees harmless, it is only necessary to cause them to fill themselves with honey, and this is done by frightening them with smoke. When smoke is driven into a hive through the entrance, the bees at once begin filling themselves with honey.

But with them, as with human beings, it is the most experienced which are slowest to take fright, so when the old bees are all at home, it is more difficult, and takes more time to compel them all to fill themselves.

For this reason it is much safer to handle bees during the warmest part of the day, or at a time when the greater part of the old bees are in the field.

The bees which compose a swarm are usually filled with honey for the journey which they expect to take, and they are harmless unless crushed, or very much irritated by the anger of others, and the smell of the poison.

An expert may open a hive without smoke and without danger, and may handle the combs and return them to the hive without getting a single sting, by being quiet, steady and fearless. It is a fact that the fearless apiarist may often be entirely unharmed, while others a rod away may be stung.

When you wish to open a hive of bees, arm yourself with a smoker, cover your head with a veil, and step boldly to the front of the hive; send the smoke through the opening for half a minute, then stop, and repeat the operation after another half-minute, or until they make a steady hum, which will show that they have given up the desire to fight. Then open the hive, smoke gently, and you may lift the combs, one after another.

I do not like the plan of building a repository in the side of a hill any better than I like a cellar under the dwelling. With either plan there are bad results, and a frame building, high and dry, is in every way preferable. Outdoor wintering is not generally successful, but some experts use chaff hives with sawdust cushions over the top of the brood chamber.

In case of outdoor wintering, it is well to have all hives facing southward, so the sun can shine on the entrances and keep them free from ice. After a heavy fall of snow, always sweep in front of the hives, leaving the snow banked around the other three sides, as it will do no harm there, but will help to keep off the prevailing winds.

Bees will take an occasional flight during warm days in winter, and sometimes many are seen lying about dead on the snow, but such are generally the old ones that are easily chilled and fail to get back to their hives. Such losses are not serious.

With too small an entrance, in a damp climate, there will be moldy combs, and more than the proper amount of dead bees. The trouble becomes aggravated in the course of the winter by the clogging of the entrance with dead bees. Let the full entrance be given as in summer, and see that the dead bees are cleaned from it every few weeks.

During heavy storms in winter, it frequently happens that hives are entirely buried in snow. While the snow is light and porous, air will penetrate it and reach the entrances of the hives; but should the snow become crusty or ice form at the front, the bees would be in danger of suffocating.

Some people are of the opinion that if we have a cold, steady winter, in which the bees remain confined to their hives for several months, there is less danger of winter losses, because fewer of the bees wander away and get lost. There would be a point in this, if it were not for the danger of the overloading of their bowels with fetid matter, which they cannot discharge in the hive without greatly endangering the life or health of the colony.

Diarrhœa is often brought about during the winter season. It is no doubt caused by fermented or extremely thin honey. It has been found that bees located near cider mills or cane mills will contract the trouble from feeding too much on the apple pomace or cane juice.

Cold weather, dampness or a sudden change of temperature has been known to bring on the disease. As soon as the outbreak is noticed, the bees should be kept as warm as possible, and the hive should be well wrapped. During the cider season the pomace should be removed and fed to the hogs, where the bees cannot partake of it.

During the winter the bees are huddled close together in a compact cluster, the interior of which is at a normal temperature, while the space outside of it may be even below freezing.

As the season advances, and the weather gets warmer, the cluster expands itself, brood rearing begins, and honey is brought in, but all the work done is only inside the cluster, as the temperature is too low outside of it to admit of anything being done.

At no time of the year does skillful treatment and care of the bees yield a greater reward than during the spring months. A great mistake is often made in taking the bees out of winter quarters too early in the spring, as the weather is unsettled at this time, and a cold snap of a few days will be apt to cause the colony to dwindle to almost nothing, if it does not entirely succumb.

I would advise setting them out about the time soft maple and elm trees begin to bloom. If there are only a few hives, they can all be set out at once. Select a pleasant day, so the bees can enjoy a cleansing flight. Bees often become badly mixed up if a great number of hives are set out at one time, some of the hives getting too many bees, and some not enough.

If the bees are disposed to dysentery before setting out time has actually arrived, they may, with profit, be set out some pleasant day for a flight, and then placed back toward evening, when they will be able to endure a much longer period of confinement.

As soon as the warm weather approaches, go over the entire apiary and examine each hive, to ascertain the condition of the bees. You may find a few colonies where the queen is absent. This is quickly noticed by the disconcerted action of the bees themselves; and then, looking further, it may be noticed that no brood is present. Such hives place under other hives, with free access between them. The queenless bees will readily unite with the colony over them.

Care and Marketing of Extracted Honey

THE care and marketing of extracted honey require considerable special knowledge. There is a continual demand for this commodity, and apiarists should take advantage of it. Imperfect combs may be used up in this way, provided the quality of the honey is good. An almost unlimited retail trade can be worked up for extracted as well as comb honey. Extracting is strongly recommended in working colonies for large returns, for much work is saved the bees and more honey is obtained. Much that would otherwise be used in the production of wax for building the combs is carried up into the super, thus adding considerably to the surplus. Honey, unlike many other commodities, will keep good almost indefinitely, if properly taken and stored. Fermentation and the consequent spoiling of honey should be avoided by making sure that all honey, when taken from the hive, is ripe. If it is allowed to remain in the hive until there is no doubt of its ripeness, there need be little fear of fermentation. This is said to be caused in some instances by the presence in the honey of pollen grains, but if the brood nests are properly managed, it is seldom that pollen will be found at all in the supers.

When the heat in the brood chamber, generated by the bees, has extracted the superfluous water from the honey by evaporation, the sealing of the cells takes place, because the honey is then in a condition which the beekeeper terms ripeness.

On removing the super, it should be placed in a warm room, and if the work of extracting can be carried on at once, while the honey is warm, it will be an advantage, as it will flow more freely than if allowed to get cold by standing a day or so in a cold room.

The cappings, or cell covers, should be shaved off with a sharp knife, warmed by standing it in a pitcher of hot water, and if cut from the bottom with a sawlike motion, while the top of the frame is held forward, the cappings will remain in a sheet and fall into the pan held below.

When the uncapped combs are put into the cages of the extractor, they should be so placed that the bottom bars go around first, for thus the honey is more easily thrown out as it leaves the cells in the direction of the pitch given them by the bees when they are building their combs.

It is always advisable to return combs wet with honey in the evening, so that the excitement they cause may be over by the morning. Returning such combs at unsuitable times, and placing scraps of comb about for the bees to clean, are undoubtedly the cause of much robbing.

Before putting honey into kegs, place the kegs in a dry place, driving up the hoops occasionally. Through tin and glass no moisture can pass.. The wood can be made a little like glass by paraffining it. Have your kegs hot by standing in the sun or otherwise; pour two or three pounds of hot paraffin into the keg, bung tight, roll the keg over and over, tipping it on each end, then knock out the bung and pour out the paraffin.

If you have been lively about it, you will get most of your paraffin back, but a thin coating will be all over the inside surface.

About the worst thing you can do is to have the wood of the keg soaked so the hoops are very tight before putting in the honey. The honey will suck all the moisture out of the staves, loosen the hoops, then ferment, and perhaps burst the keg.

There are other things besides bees and hives needed

in producing extracted honey. A honey house becomes a necessity, even when the apiary is very small, though of course if one has only a half-dozen colonies or so, a small room may be used in lieu of a house specially built for the business, particularly when comb or section honey is produced.

Extracted honey production needs a larger equipment of tools and appliances than does comb, and needs more care and labor in getting it into proper shape for market. So far as the handling of the product is concerned, there is more labor in the extracted, but in the preliminary work or management of the bees, the comb takes both greater skill as an apiarist and more labor.

Our attention in the future should be given more to the practical management of bees, to reduce the labor and expense to the minimum. The more the work is simplified, the more we shall feel we are advancing. Better results are obtained from working for both comb and extracted honey, and it will be observed that there is a steady demand for each kind.

Management the Key to Poultry Success

POULTRY dealers are learning to make money. Success is measured by the dollar standard in all commercial enterprises. Ducks and chickens are fed and housed, not for their beauty, but for their earning capacity.

This fact will not be disputed, and it is clearly proven by the developments in the poultry industry. Capital is being invested quite freely and thousands of new plants, large and small, are being put on a business basis, so that they will return reasonable profits. No branch of business shows greater progress.

One of the most successful poultry raisers in Illinois has only five acres of land. He keeps from 600 to 2,000 chickens, and raises wheat and corn enough for them on about three acres. He buys the refuse from a hotel, paying merely a nominal price. It may not be very profitable to feed chickens exclusively on corn worth 75 cents a bushel, but by providing a variety of cheaper food, the question of feeding becomes less serious.

In order to get a good supply of eggs in the winter, conditions for the hens must be made as nearly like summer as possible.

To do this, one thing necessary is plenty of green food for the hens to eat. There are various ways of supplying this.

If there is a field of winter wheat, rye or alfalfa, where they can help themselves, the green-food problem is solved, when there is no snow on the ground and the weather is warm enough so that the hens can be out.

During cold and stormy weather, when they are shut

up in the houses, clover or alfalfa, cut into short lengths, is a good green food. The hens will eat them dry, but relish them much better if steamed. To steam, cut into short pieces and pack in a tub or bucket, pour as much boiling water over them as they will absorb, and cover tightly for thirty minutes before feeding. It may be fed either by itself or mixed with a mash.

Sprouted oats are a good green food. To prepare them, soak the oats in warm water for twenty-four hours, then spread in shallow boxes and keep in a warm place. Keep them moist by sprinkling with warm water, and they will soon sprout.

When the sprouts are about two inches long, cut the oats out in chunks and feed to the hens. They will eat with relish both the sprouts and the oats.

Another way of furnishing green food is to feed vegetables. Turnips, beets and mangles should be cut in halves and fed raw. Potatoes may be fed either raw or cooked and a little bran mixed with them.

Cabbage heads should be hung up where the hens can pick them. Giving the hens regularly any one of these green foods will make a noticeable gain in the production of eggs, but of course the hens will relish a variety of green foods, as well as of grains.

About thirty years ago, when poultry farming was young, as a business, a cry arose that it would not be long before there would be such a surplus of stock that prices would go tumbling; but notwithstanding that, there are ten successful plants today to every one thirty years ago, and the demand is not half reached! With the increase of supply came the increase of demand, and today we are no nearer meeting the demand than we ever were.

However, there is a change in the market which must not be lost sight of. Almost anything in the poultry line sells, but the choice prices are alone given to the "fancy goods."

The word "fancy" implies more than appearance. It means also quality. Poultry and egg buyers are becoming particular, but they are willing to pay for their goods. If they want the brown eggs, they will not take white; and if they prefer the white, the brown ones offer no temptation. The market today demands choice, plump, fresh stock. Have you got it? If so, the market is waiting for you.

We have today quite a number of breeds, and all, to a certain extent, are practical. But they will not any one of them fill all the purposes; therefore, it is necessary for a man to select only such breeds as will best serve his customers.

Of the entire list of breeds, none will meet the demands of Americans so satisfactorily as do the American varieties, and in this class the most popular are the Wyandottes, the Plymouth Rocks, with the Rhode Island Reds closely following; also our American strains of Light Brahmas and Leghorns.

The Brahmas belong to the Asiatic class as a breed, but the Light Brahma, as bred by our people, is so different from that bred in England that one would hardly suppose them to be of the same family. This is also true of the Leghorns, which belong to the Mediterranean class.

It will cost the farmer no more money to raise thoroughbred poultry than it will to grow scrubs. The pure breeds will not only bring more money in the wholesale market but it is a fact that poorly graded poultry lose more heavily in shrinkage than do those that are of pure blood. Commission men say that there is a marked improvement in the quality of the poultry that now comes to the city markets, and say that this improvement has been influenced by buyers who collect poultry from farmers and ship it to market.

The shippers can pay a higher price for a better quality

of poultry and then make more money, for the reason
that they get better returns.

Juiciness in broilers is due to pure food and rapid
maturity. As a broiler cannot be secured on free range,
and as it can attain the required weight in a given time
only by a systematic feeding of pure foods, it carries with
it a reputation and demand on account of its juiciness,
tenderness and purity.

At the Ontario Agricultural College, in a test with
different rations for fattening poultry, a mixture of 2
parts corn meal, 2 parts ground buckwheat and 1 part
ground oats, with an equal weight of skim milk, gave a
pound of gain for less than 3½ cents a pound. Four
parts corn meal, 2 parts each buckwheat and ground oats,
with an equal weight of milk, made the cost a trifle over
4½ cents per pound; while ground oats alone, with equal
weight of milk, made the cost nearly 5 cents per pound.
A very good fattening ration consists of 100 pounds of
corn meal, 100 pounds of wheat middlings and 4 pounds
of animal meal, with an equal weight of skimmed milk.

If the fowls are confined in small pens and kept quiet,
they will fatten much quicker. Give all they will eat
three times a day, with plenty of pure water to drink.
Separate the cockerels early from the pullets. In half an
hour after feeding, remove the drinking and feeding vessels. Two weeks before marketing them, feed with corn
and corn meal. Keep before them a box of sharp grit.
There are two kinds of broilers or fries; the smaller are
known as squab broilers, weighing from three-fourths
to one pound each. The demand for these is not great.
The average broiler weighs from 2 to 3 pounds, and sells
for from 20 cents to 50 cents per pound, according to the
season of the year and the purchaser. During June and
July the price falls rapidly, and at the end of July in
the open market frequently falls to 12 or 15 cents per
pound. In preparing fries for the market, when nearly

large enough, put them in a pen, having a shady run; give them fresh water twice a day and all the fattening food they can eat. Muscle and bone-making food for this class is not required; therefore, feed corn in various forms—cooked corn, mashed corn, ground corn, whole corn, warm potatoes and bread crumbs, and any kind of milk. A little sugar and fat meat will help along the fattening process, and this should be concluded as fast as possible, for during these days the chicks will eat considerable, and unless they put on flesh rapidly, there will be no profit in raising them.

There is already a fair demand for guinea fowls, especially in New York and other cities in the eastern part of the United States, and this condition will soon obtain in all leading markets if present indications count for anything. As the demand for guinea meat increases, as a substitute for game or other birds and fowls, guineas ought to become a source of considerable profit to poultry raisers generally. Very young birds for broilers bring good prices early in the season, while the older fowls are readily salable throughout the autumn and winter. In recent years the varieties have been improved. The birds are good rangers, and do well with comparatively little care—even when young are hardy and healthy.

The first thing to do in taking up poultry as a business is to find some breed adapted to the locality, then stock up with that breed and study it. Personality enters into the success of the poultry industry to a large extent. A man must be good-natured for one thing, and willing to give his time and patience to detail work. For these reasons a man who takes up this business for pleasure often succeeds much better than the man who goes into it for purely the money it brings him. Success in this business comes slowly. It must be built up. It requires patience, but when success does come, everything after that is easy and the profits are good.

Winter Egg Production

DURING the months of October, November and December of each year there is a scarcity of fresh eggs, and the prices, in consequence, go up. This scarcity is due to the molting period for old hens, the lack of early hatched pullets, and the general failure to so feed and manage chickens as to secure winter eggs.

The utmost care should be taken to select early pullets. Those hatched in March and April may be depended on for a liberal egg supply from the time they are seven months old. The hatching should have winter egg production in view, and therefore it is important to select the eggs of fowls that are prolific layers and which have good constitutions.

The great thing is to get the eggs during the months of November, December and January, and this can be done with early pullets. The older hens will not do much for a couple of months after molting, but will help out the supply after the turn of the year. The demand for strictly fresh eggs is so keen that prices remain high all winter.

A poultry house should be so constructed that it can be opened during the day, that the warm sun and fresh air may disinfect it. An open front is the approved modern idea. It gives fresh air without draughts. The opening should have bars to keep out animals. The place needs to be large enough so that the scratching floor is apart from the nests and roosts.

A common mistake with beginners is in having too many varieties. In their enthusiasm they cannot content themselves with a single breed. They read what breeders of every variety have to say, taking in every word, and forgetting that these breeders have axes to grind. But the beginner is not long in seeing his mistake. He sooner or later cuts down to a single variety.

Some, too, grow tired of the variety they have chosen, and are continually changing. That class of poultrymen hardly ever get beyond the hobby stage of the industry. Select a single variety, and stick to that.

Inbreeding is another bugbear. There is nothing that will so quickly ruin stock as this. The house must be dry and free from lice; the warmer the house the better, but there must be no draughts.

Regular feeding is also an important point. Fowls soon learn to know when their feeding hour arrives, and will be in a more or less anxious state until they are fed. Have a bill of fare, and stick to it. But see that that bill of fare is composed of a variety. To endeavor to keep a flock on a grain diet will soon breed all sorts of trouble.

Ground bone, sunflower and millet seed, culled potatoes, scrap meat, stale bread soaked in whey or skimmed milk, cabbage leaves, and all table leavings, are good food for fowls and help to form the needed variety. For a regular grain diet, wheat and corn are favored. If oats are fed, they should be chopped. A daily mash composed of bran, middlings, ground oats, linseed meal and boiled potatoes is excellent. It is best when moistened with milk, but it should not be sloppy. Grit and charcoal are needed at all times. Crushed oyster shells or bits of old mortar help to supply the lime that hens need.

Some kind of green food is necessary for a large production of eggs, though it is not essential in fattening. If it is not easy to furnish a variety, a little alfalfa or clover hay will do nicely. Beets, turnips, carrots, potatoes and cabbage are easily supplied on any farm, and they are a valuable food, either boiled or raw. Give all the clean water the fowls will drink. It should be kept in vessels that they cannot upset.

At night, feed corn and wheat, sometimes one, sometimes both, enough to fill their crops. Now, this is the way I feed, but I do not guarantee it to produce eggs unless combined with some details of more or less importance, and all directed by an intelligent interest that is quick to note and to provide for special conditions.

The morning feed should be given early, for fowls are early risers, and should not be kept waiting for their breakfasts. It should not be necessary to say that the warm mash should not be thrown in a dirty or muddy place, but on planks or a firm, hard spot. Shallow troughs are better yet. Perhaps it is best to give the mash in the morning, while through the day the hens should be compelled to take exercise by hunting for grain in a litter of straw or hay. If they can be allowed the run of a barn through the day, it will help to keep them active.

Hens dread the snow, and will not walk through it unless forced. Therefore, on snowy days, sweep a path from their house to the barn or shed where they can take their exercise. If you don't see to their daily exercise, the hens will stand around in their house, shivering and miserable, and the eggs will shrink.

This is one of those details that good judgment should approve. It is impossible to enumerate them all. Elaborate directions are thrown away unless there be a critical and judicious eye to administer them.

The amount of brain and muscle work used in the management will give a proportionate profit, and of the two, brain work counts first in this, as in all work.

Egg Type in Hens

MANY poultrymen claim there is an egg type in fowls, and that they can pick out the good layers as well as the poor ones in a flock. This claim is based on the theory that certain peculiarities of form or shape, such as long body, wedge shape, broad rear, small head, etc., indicate good laying qualities.

A statement in the last United States census report of 1900 reads: "It has been discovered that there are 600 embryo eggs in the ovary of a hen. It has been further ascertained that two-thirds of this number can be secured in the first two years of the hen's life, provided suitable measures are employed." Concerning these statements, Prof. James Dryden writes:

"One of our hens has already exceeded this limit, having laid 568 eggs the first three years, and to July 31 of the fourth year she had laid a total of 670 eggs, and was still laying, having till November 1 to complete that year. A Brown Leghorn hen has also exceeded the 600 limit, having laid up to the same date 628 eggs, with prospects of many more.

"As to the other statement, that two-thirds of 600 eggs may be secured in the first two years, or 400 eggs, in our experience only one hen has reached it, having laid 442 eggs in the first two years. Furthermore, no records have been reported from other stations of 400 eggs in two years. Three Barred Plymouth Rock hens of like age, and fed in the same pen, laid 145, 144 and 212 eggs, respectively, the same year, and 40, 116 and 181 the second year, one lacking seven eggs of making 400 the

252

first two years. This one has the wedge shape, is medium long in body, rather long in neck, with small head. She laid a small egg.

"In view of the great variation in layers, the question as to whether there is an egg type becomes very important. If the good layers can be picked out of a flock by reason of some characteristic shape or form, the question of improvement becomes a simple matter. With a view to testing the theory held by many that there is such an egg type, Prof. Dryden sent a number of photographs of good and poor layers to poultry breeders and judges, whom he asked to pick out good and poor layers in a certain group, and give their reasons for the selection. Some of these gentlemen had expressed publicly their belief in the egg type theory. It may be, as some of the gentlemen protested, hard to decide the question from photographs, but a side-view photograph should show if the hen has a long body and a wedge shape, the two points most relied upon by those who say they can pick out the good layers. It must be conceded, however, that the photograph does not offer the same opportunity for a critical study as the hen herself would. The replies received did not seem to offer much support to the theory. They showed a varied collection of guesses."

Common-sense management means success and liberal cash returns; indifferent methods of work result in failure. Fowls must be kept healthy; feed bills must not be allowed to equal the income, and there should be a constant weeding out of old and poor stock. Every summer and fall it is necessary to select the most vigorous and promising pullets for winter egg production, and these fowls need to be fed and managed with that end in view. They are not to have the same feeding and housing as birds that are being fitted for the poultry market. Unless owners are able and willing to give thorough attention to these details and bring their flocks up to proper condition, there is no profit in poultry.

If a landowner has wheat, barley or rye, these grains may be substituted for corn and oats, but when it can be done without great expense or trouble, ground corn and oats should be the staples for fattening as well as for egg production. Do not feed whole oats at any time. After the fowls that are to be marketed are placed in the fattening pens, it is essential to feed them regularly and abundantly three times a day. Clean water and grit should be constantly supplied. To the diet of grain and vegetables it is well to add a little scrap meat, with some fat.

A greater variety of food is required for egg production. In addition to the grain rations mentioned, it is well to give such articles as millet seed and sunflower seed, with a regular supply of meat scraps and ground bone. Clover, cabbage and boiled vegetables of all kinds are valuable. Hens make use of old mortar and oyster shells and it is not difficult to supply such articles. Where a good deal of the food has to be purchased, it is feasible to procure stale bread at city bakeries. This is sold at a low figure. Table refuse obtained from hotels and restaurants make a good diet in itself, but is improved by the addition of grain. Laying hens need exercise, and should be let out on every dry day, but never when it is wet. Their housing must be managed with intelligence and care. It is ruinous to have fowls on damp floors or in drafty rooms. Filth is equally dangerous.

Many flocks of hens are totally ruined by lice and disease. To keep them free of vermin, it is necessary to have dusting corners to which they can have access at any time, winter or summer. By using insect powders on the birds and washing roosts and walls with kerosene, lice can be conquered. Afterward the hens will not be troubled with them if there is plenty of dust at hand. Ordinary loose road dirt should be spread under the roosts once or twice a week. This will help to make valuable compost.

Losses in the poultry yard are heavy enough in many cases to wipe out all possible profits. Chicken raisers who mean business will give intelligent care to their stock at all ages and in all seasons. The most common mistake is that of allowing young birds to run about on wet ground.

Perhaps the reader has noticed that deaths are most frequent immediately after rain storms. Nearly all such fatalities are due to young chickens becoming chilled on wet ground. They are as sensitive as children, and are attacked with a variety of ailments in much the same way, if not kept dry and comfortable.

In rainy weather see that the young flocks are kept in snug pens or houses where the floors can not become damp. Some warming foods are desirable. This kind of care is good for matured fowls, also. While houses need to be clean and warm, they must be ventilated. Do not allow drafts to hit the fowls. Ventilators should not be over the roosts. It is safest to have them low in the walls and some distance from the roosts.

For real success and money-making from the flock, it is necessary to keep a close watch; to provide all comforts; to prevent disease by never allowing filth to accumulate; to keep the fowls busy, hence happy; to not overcrowd, and to give an everyday careful oversight. The comforts mean the right rations in plentiful supply, good housing, grit, charcoal and clean water.

To the man who wishes to enter the poultry business at a small expense, I would advise stocking with a dozen hens of some good breed. It is well not to try to do much until the beginner has learned how to make a small flock pay. I find it profitable to market eggs where they must be guaranteed fresh, working up a good trade for the produce at a fair price.

Preservation of Eggs Until Prices Advance

In the production of eggs for market, farmers should aim to have them to sell in fall and winter, when prices are high. Extensive experiments with the use of water glass (sodium silicate) prove that spring and summer eggs may be kept in perfect order for months, with little trouble or expense.

The fiscal supervisor of the State of New York, Charles Dennis McCarthy, has been following this plan in providing eggs for various public institutions, and has saved a great deal of money. The eggs are purchased in the spring, when prices are low, and stored until winter, so that the state institutions avoid paying high prices. A year ago it was suggested to all institutions reporting to the fiscal supervisor to preserve eggs for use in the months when the market price is the highest—December, January and February—and a statement was enclosed to each institution, relating to preservation of eggs in water glass, furnished the department by the New York State College of Agriculture. A number of institutions acted upon the suggestion of the department and preserved a considerable number of eggs in liquid glass, which proved successful beyond expectation.

Water glass provides an excellent means of preserving the surplus spring and summer eggs for fall and winter use. These eggs do not take the place of fresh laid ones for table use, but are satisfactory for all cooking purposes.

Dilute the commercial "N" grade of water glass with nine times its amount of clear water. Keep this solution in tight earthen or wooden jars. Only fresh, clean eggs should be used. The level of the liquid should always be kept above that of the eggs by adding water as needed.

For twelve dozen eggs, it requires a four-gallon jar, one and one-half pints of water glass and fourteen pints of water.

In considering how to handle poultry for profit, does it not become plain that the overproduction of eggs in spring and summer is a serious mistake? Eggs become so cheap at times that farmers cannot afford to haul them to market. There is a good profit in poultry, however, the year round, especially in broilers about 2 months old.

Instead of allowing the overproduction of eggs to drive the market down to 8 or 10 cents a dozen, why not keep a big incubator running, hatching out chickens? A broiler will bring 40 to 60 cents, three-fourths of this being net profit. Such farming is worth while. An ordinary sized poultry yard will clean up $1,000 a year if it receives a reasonable amount of attention, and only an acre or two of land is needed for the enterprise. It takes a great many acres to net $1,000 in regular farming.

The selection of eggs for incubation is important. Do not use eggs for this purpose which have rough shells, or are unusually large or small. Hold the eggs before a strong light and look through them. If they have a matted appearance, they are not fit to produce strong chicks, and as a rule they are not fertile.

Soft-shelled eggs will not produce strong chicks, because in growing the chicks the lime from the shell produces the bones and muscles. If the shell is weak, the chick will be weak also. Soiled or washed eggs should never be used for hatching.

Eggs should be kept in a temperature of about 45 degrees, if possible, and should never be kept where the wind can blow on them, or where the sun shines strongly.

If the draft is too strong, the eggs will dry down. If eggs are dried down before hatching, the chicks will be dried down, small and weak.

Eggs for incubation should not be laid longer than a week. The older the egg, the lower the vitality of the chick. Usually the cellar is the best place for keeping eggs, for here the temperature is more even, and it is not too dry.

The first two or three days after the setting of the incubator are vital. The heat should never get higher than 102 degrees; a little below will do no harm. For the first two days the eggs should not be turned, but thereafter turn every morning and evening until the eighteenth day, when they should not be touched until all fertile eggs are hatched.

Have both ventilation and moisture in hatching rooms. The cellar is usually about right where there is a floor, and if there is an outside entrance it should not remain open.

Chicks hatched where there is moisture are stronger than dried-down, non-moisture ones. Do not allow strong sunlight or too much draft in the hatching room.

The last few days, do not handle the eggs, and keep the temperature not higher than 105 degrees, nor below 103.

Sometimes the chicks, after they are dried off, open their mouths and seem to want air; then open some ventilator or open the incubator door a little.

In gathering eggs for incubation, give the hens enough good, clean food and exercise and clean quarters. They should have free range, if possible. Meat scraps, lime, milk, ground bone, oyster shells, wheat and bran mash are excellent for laying hens. Plenty of fresh, clean drinking water should be within reach. Green or cooked vegetables are also good for the health of the hen, and make healthy chicks.

Favorite Breeds of Ducks

LESS disappointment will be experienced, perhaps, in raising ducks than any other line of poultry. Ducks grow into money fast, and this is the main consideration. They are less subject to disease than chickens, and make less trouble than either turkeys or geese.

If possible, give them the range of a patch of clover, but if they have to be confined to a yard, let them have a swimming hole and a variety of greed food. Pekin ducks are in great favor, and are good layers, beginning in midwinter, and furnishing twelve to fifteen dozen eggs.

The Indian Runner will lay at four and a half to five months old, if fed for that purpose. Some have been known to reach 250 eggs a year, but the general run is about 200. They are non-sitters, will lay ten months in the year, and are profitable because of their wonderful laying qualities. It does not require any more to feed them than it does to feed a flock of hens of the same number.

Hatching by incubator is the best method, and the business ought to be in progress by March 1. With this kind of planning, young Pekins can be furnished to customers from the middle of June till fall, and possibly the year round. The young ducks should be fed both for growth and quality. For one day after hatching no food is to be given. Then light ‘rations of moistened bran and corn meal will do nicely. Heavy feeding is to be avoided at first. When spring opens and they begin to get free exercise, they should have all the food that they will clean up. They also require a clean swimming hole or pond.

Fatten them on clean, wholesome food, such as shorts, boiled potatoes, ground corn or oats. Ducks are in great demand when from two to four months old, if they have been carefully fed. They are as profitable at this age as later, for they are heavy feeders, and in fattening at the age of eight or ten months they eat a lot of grain. Not only is this the case, but at two or three months they command from 25 to 35 cents a pound, against 18 to 20 when full grown.

In fattening more mature ducks, whole corn or wheat may be fed to some extent. Boiled potatoes, carrots, beets and various other vegetables are excellent. Bran or shorts moistened with skimmed milk also makes an economical food. Articles of this kind save high-priced grain and answer the purpose nicely in fitting poultry for the market.

For the flock that is to be kept for breeding purposes, more green food is necessary. Alfalfa, either whole or ground, and corn silage, are recommended, with one ration a day of wheat or corn. Always feed soft food in long troughs, and have plenty of them, to avoid crowding; and when the meal is over, stand the troughs on end against the wall to keep them clean for the next meal.

While ducks are the healthiest of domestic fowl, especially if allowed considerable freedom in summer, they require clean and comfortable pens in winter, with a reasonable amount of room. It is bad policy to allow ducks or other fowl to be disturbed by live stock. The laying quarters at least should be free from noise and all other disturbances.

The opportunity is at hand for money-making from ducks, as farmers are able to send dressed fowls to city customers by mail, so that the usual trouble and expense of marketing are eliminated. Fresh fowls may go daily or weekly to town people, without the necessity of driving to an express office. The postal wagons on all rural routes will collect such packages, and Uncle Sam does all the work of transporting and delivering. To make good profits, therefore, from poultry, there should be incubators going all the time, hatching either chickens or ducks, which will sell readily for meat at from two to six months of age. Such poultry meat is a great delicacy, and commands liberal prices.

Pekin ducks at two months are worth rather more than chickens of the same age. Either class of birds will sell at 40 cents to 75 cents apiece, according to weight. Ducks eat more than chickens, and gain in weight proportionately. Ten to 15 cents is ample to allow for feeding a fowl up to two months of age. This allows a large profit. Birds fattened at six or seven months have consumed 15 to 25 cents' worth of food, according to the advantages of raising or buying it. They are then worth $1 to $1.50 each. There is more profit in meat than in eggs.

In order to succeed with ducks, it is necessary to have eggs from strong, vigorous stock, and they must be fresh —not over one week old. Other duck eggs may be different, but the Pekin's eggs are worthless for hatching purposes when ten days old.

Duck eggs, as a rule, require four weeks to hatch. They may be hatched with either incubators or hens. Only large hens are suitable. If an incubator is used, keep the temperature as near 103 degrees as possible, turning the eggs regularly twice a day. They should be allowed time to cool a little once each day until the twenty-sixth day, or two days before they are due to hatch.

When ducks begin to pip the shells, the temperature may be allowed to rise to 104 or 105, but be careful not to let it go higher. Protect the ventilators from cold drafts, but don't shut out all the air.

Don't bother the eggs while they are hatching, unless it it is absolutely necessary, because it lowers the temperature every time the inner door is moved. Of course, in the mild weather it is safe enough, but even then the door should be kept closed as much as possible. If the little ducks do not come out shortly after they pip the shells, do not become alarmed. They do not come out as soon as chicks, as they require more time after breaking the shell. In this respect they are more like goslings.

Sometimes they will break the shells twenty-four hours before they are ready to come out. But they seldom need any help. A duck egg presents a queer appearance at a certain stage of incubation, for when held before a bright light the shells appear to be nearly half empty.

Don't throw the eggs away. They may all contain live ducklings. When the fowls hatch, they should not be taken from the incubator until they are thoroughly dried off and able to hold up their heads. Then they should be placed in a brooder or some place where they will be comfortable. If placed in a brooder, see that they have fresh air. Fresh air, however, is not essentially cold air.

Have the brooder floor covered with some clean litter. Cut straw or hay is best. Don't use sawdust; the young ducks will sometimes eat it. However, it is not necessary to keep ducklings in a brooder except at night, after they get a start. Even while they are very small, they seem to prefer sunshine in the daytime to the brooder heat. The Pekin ducklings soon outgrow the brooder. A number of duck houses should be provided, with dry floors and good ventilation.

Green food is essential from the start. If there is plenty of grass in the yard, that will do, although they like it best when added to their grain food. Use green clover, green rye, cabbage, dandelions, onion tops, etc. Green oats are also good for this purpose. All should be cut small enough for growing ducks to eat with ease.

Disease Injuring Turkey Raising Industry

THE turkey-raising industry has been almost destroyed by disease. Not only in New England but everywhere in this country the commercial production of the turkey has been reduced to small proportions.

That dread disease known as blackhead is the cause, and as it is rapidly spreading throughout the country, it is a matter of serious concern, not only to professional breeders but to farmers as well. For some years previous to 1893 the poultrymen in New England complained that their young poults died in large numbers, and very few birds lived to be older than five or six months. Samuel Cushman, the poultryman at the Rhode Island Agricultural Station, gave the symptoms, described the conditions of the diseased organs, and suggested the communicable character of the ailment. He was the first man to call it blackhead in literature, a name used by the farmers for the reason that the heads of the turkeys became dark-colored. Other names for the disorder were "liver trouble," "spotted liver" and "cholera." A close observer is pretty sure to detect the ailment.

Prof. Leon J. Cole and Philip B. Hadley, of the Rhode Island Station, assisted by William F. Kirkpatrick, have made an exhaustive study of the disease, and their findings have recently been published. The main features of the results of their investigation are as follows: Black-head, in whatever species of bird, presents three symptoms which are invariable: First, diarrhœa at some stages of the disease; second, a condition of increasing languor or stupor and a disposition of the bird to keep away from the flock; third, loss of appetite and more or less prolonged emaciation.

The first course which the disease may follow is seen in young birds, in what is commonly known as "white diarrhœa," frequently causing great mortality among poults from five days to three weeks old, although deaths may continue much beyond this period. In these cases, death is sometimes preceded by a period of a day or two of stupor, in which the bird remains by itself and refuses food. This acute form is more likely to attack the younger birds, and frequently causes the death of 90 per cent, and occasionally the entire flock will be wiped out.

If the disease does not show until after the birds are three weeks old, it is likely to remain latent in them or change into a slowly progressive form which may not cause death for several months. In the typical chronic form, the birds often hold their own against the disease for a year or more, during which time emaciation gradually increases. In these birds, the disease is ultimately fatal in the majority of cases.

One of the most important features of this disease is that turkeys having a chronic form of the disease are especially susceptible to the effects of unfavorable conditions. Quick fattening of a flock of turkeys for the market, especially if the young birds are fed much corn, often brings about a marked increase in the mortality.

The organism which causes blackhead is a minute parasite belonging to the lowest group of animal life, and is called a cocidium, and is akin to the parasites of hydrophobia and malaria. The infection of the bird begins in taking up, along with food and water, some of the parasites described. These may undergo a partial development before being taken into the body of the bird, and after entering the alimentary tract, where they liberate the original infecting elements. These are able to impart infection to other birds, which take up particles along with their food. The same organism has been found in guinea fowls, ducks, pheasants, quail, grouse, pigeons and sparrows.

The chief danger lies in the fact that where domestic poultry is kept, the ground is contaminated and rendered unsuitable for the raising of turkeys. For this reason it is never safe to allow turkeys and other poultry to use the same yard. The investigators say that it cannot be doubted that the common English sparrow has disseminated this disease throughout the country, and it is still carrying it from one locality to another.

Poultrymen and farmers are advised not to waste their money on so-called remedies and cures for blackhead, but to follow the preventive measures indicated below:

Protect the yards and flocks which may be infected with blackhead, by careful examination of all new stock, whether turkeys, fowls, geese or other domestic birds.

Keep the turkeys on ground which is as fresh as can be obtained. Change the range at least every year or two, and, above all, keep them isolated from other poultry.

In fattening birds for market, begin to increase the rations gradually. If birds show a loss of weight in successive weighings, there is no use to attempt to fatten them. Overfeeding does not cause blackhead, but it does frequently cause the sudden death of birds in which blackhead is present.

When birds have died of blackhead, their bodies must be promptly burned or buried very deep, in order to prevent rats or other rodents from eating them and thus spreading the disease. In the early stages of acute cases of the disease, if the bird is isolated from the flock and placed in a dry, well ventilated location, free from drafts, and fed sparingly on soft, light food, with little corn, it will have a beneficial effect.

Parasites Cause Heavy Poultry Losses

VERMIN are exceedingly destructive to poultry, and in many cases cause such heavy losses that the business becomes a failure. An unrelenting war against parasites is a necessary part of a farm program.

Lice and other parasites increase very quickly in the warm weather, and we should get a start of them by exterminating the parent stock that has survived the winter. In this way, the work will be much easier, and more pleasantly done. The necessity for their extermination will be more plainly seen if we understand just how they affect the poultry.

There are a great many different kinds of lice that attack the fowls, but we can consider them all under three classes, as they attack in the three different ways. These three classes are body lice, head lice and mites. The body lice are on all parts of the fowls' bodies, but more especially in the soft, fluffy feathers. They usually remain on the fowl, and they increase very rapidly. It has been estimated that within eight weeks one of the lice will have 125,000 descendants. You will see from this how much easier it is for one to destroy these pests before they get well started in the spring.

Body lice are not blood-suckers, but live on the roots of the feathers and scales of the skin, causing irritation. In getting rid of them, nothing equals a good insect powder. Hold the fowl by the legs, head down, and dust the powder into the feathers near the roots, rubbing it well into the feathers and skin with the hand.

Head lice are true blood-suckers. With their long bills,

266

they puncture the skin and the blood vessels beneath. They are a constant drain on the health and strength of the adult fowls, fastening themselves on their heads and sucking the blood from a position over the brain. As the chicks are hatched, these lice leave the old hen and fasten on the chicks. If you pick up a droopy chick and examine its head, you are almost sure to find these lice fast by their bills, busily sucking the blood. You must look close, or you will mistake them for pinfeathers. They cause such extreme weakness that often the bodily organs are unable to perform their functions properly, and people think the chicks are dying of cholera or other diseases, when it is really the head lice that are killing them. To destroy these, rub some sweet oil or lard well into the feathers and skin on the heads of the chicks, and of the older fowls also.

Mites are even worse than these others. They hide during the day in the cracks and crevices of the hen houses, especially about the roosts, and attack the fowls at night, after they have gone to roost. Mites are very small, and if you see them, you are likely to mistake them for dust, for they have that appearance. They, too, are blood-suckers, and rapidly deplete the health and strength of the fowl. To destroy them, a liquid is much better than a powder. Paint the roosts and spray the dropping-boards and walls with a preparation of crude carbolic acid and coal oil (kerosene), mixed half and half.

There is another parasite belonging to this family, called the depluming mite. It usually appears in the spring and summer, and attacks the roots of the feathers, causing them to break off and leave a bare spot.

The mite is quickly passed from fowl to fowl, and soon spreads through the entire flock. You will not see anything suspicious on the bare spots, but if you will pull out some of the feathers and examine the roots, you will see these mites.

Spray the houses as for the other mites, and rub carbolated vaseline into the roots of the feathers. It is also a good treatment to dip the fowls in a tea made from tobacco leaves.

The stick-tight, or hen flea, is a great pest in some of the southern states. It generally attaches itself to the comb or wattles of the fowl, burying its head in the flesh. Sometimes they crowd around the eyes, and cause blindness until removed. They stick so tightly that they cannot be pulled out. Mix ten drops of carbolic acid and some sulphur with a teaspoonful of vaseline, to make a soft paste. Rub this well into the feathers and skin of the head and wattles of the fowls.

The premises must be cleaned of the fleas also. Burn all litter and trash, and spray the ground, nests and houses with the coal oil and crude carbolic acid preparation.

There is another parasite that causes the disease called scaly leg by boring under the skin of the feet and legs of the fowls. They cause a powderous secretion which enlarges the feet and legs of the fowl, giving them a rough, ugly appearance. Dip the feet and legs in coal oil, rubbing with the hand, and allowing it to soak well in.

You cannot make a success of your poultry if they are troubled with lice. To be a good layer, a hen must be kept comfortable and happy. This is impossible if she is fretted and annoyed by these pests. Imagine a flock that fights head lice and body lice all day, with perhaps hen fleas and scaly leg in addition, going to roost at night, to be tortured by mites which swarm from the hiding places and cover them. These are apt to be the conditions in a dirty poultry house, where the filth is allowed to accumulate under the roosts and in the corners. The fowls, with their vitality weakened and their strength sapped by these parasites, take cold easily, and quickly succumb to disease. They are always in poor health, although eating heartily; and the poultryman finds that while his feed bill is no less, he gets no eggs, his poultry does not sell well because it is poor, and his young chicks die. Such a man says there is no profit in the poultry line, and indeed there is none for him.

Cleanliness is one of the greatest aids in bettering this condition, for these parasites breed in the filth and dirt. Give the house a thorough cleaning. Burn the old litter and nests, scrape the floors clean, paint the roosts and nest boxes, and spray the walls and floor with crude carbolic acid and coal oil.

Put insect powder on the fowls, grease their heads, and dip their feet and legs in coal oil. It will be time well invested.

The hens will help you in this work of extermination, if you will see that they are kept supplied with a good dust bath. Mix ashes with the dirt for the bath. All this may seem like a great deal of trouble, but success is never attained in any business without painstaking care and faithful work.

In the matter of diet, the first thing needed is water, and it must not be chilly. Some coarse, clean sand should be placed in the water each time, or in some shallow vessel near the feed or water. They need both grit and water while eating.

Hens that have been confined closely for months, and have been laying in the winter months, or that are poorly fed, and are kept in dirty houses, where lice and mites prevail, cannot produce healthy eggs, and will produce only poor, weakly chicks.

Poultry Diseases and Remedies

WHEN fowls are closely grouped or kept in filthy or draughty buildings there is apt to be a development and rapid spread of destructive ailments. Climatic changes, floor dampness and wet grounds are severe on chickens. Attention to health and feeding will not only prevent losses but will bring profits.

Usually the first symptom of tuberculosis noticed is emaciation, or "going light," accompanied often though not always with a pale appearance of the comb and wattles and the skin about the head. There is frequently, though not always, a persistent diarrhœa, the droppings appearing of a green or greenish-white color. Lameness in one or both legs may occur, due to infection of the joints. In the latter stages of the disease, the feathers become dry and ruffled, the bird becomes weak and mopy and moves but little. The eye is bright and the appetite is usually good throughout the sickness and the affected fowls may eat ravenously until a few days before death occurs.

Probably the commonest method of spread of tuberculosis from flock to flock is by the transfer of infected birds. A hen may be quite seriously affected without showing any external symptoms of the disease, and such an individual when introduced into a flock can serve as a source of infection for other fowls through the medium of the droppings.

To guard against tuberculosis give the best care to all fowls that can reasonably be given. Keep their houses clean, well ventilated and free from draughts. Furnish a regular supply and good variety of food. See that they exercise sufficiently and have a healthy, vigorous appearance. Use only sound stock for breeding, and try to select a line of birds possessing superior qualifications. This is the only way to handle poultry for success, and such management will ward off nearly all diseases.

Asthemia, or "going light," has symptoms like tuberculosis. If the owner of the flock is in doubt and cannot get an expert's opinion it will be safe to give quarter-grain doses of calomel three times a day in mash. Instead of this castor oil may be given three times a day in tablespoonful doses. Two days of this treatment or a week of the calomel treatment ought to suffice for clearing out the bacteria, and afterward the food should be more than ordinarily stimulating.

Cholera is first detected by noticing yellow excrement. This is a deadly infection and goes rapidly through a flock. Birds with cholera have a high fever and become thirsty. They soon become weak and in three or four days expire. When cholera gets into a flock the first move should be to separate the well from the sick. Thoroughly disinfect all buildings. A pound of sulphuric acid in fifty quarts of water makes a good disinfectant. For medicine a tablespoonful of carbolic acid for each quart of water in the drinking vessels may prove efficacious. For flocks of any size the following cholera remedy should be procured as soon as possible after the disease appears: One ounce capsicum, one ounce asafetida, one ounce pulverized rhubarb, one ounce sulphur and three ounces Spanish brown. Mix and place in an air-tight can. Twice a day feed an ordinary warm mash in which there is a teaspoonful of the mixture for every quart of the food.

When white diarrhoea appears the worst cases should be killed and burned, any seemingly affected removed from the well ones, the quarters cleaned and disinfected and a very little creolin given in the drinking water. Two drops of creolin in a teaspoonful of water is recommended. However, a somewhat weakened solution will prove effective in slight cases. Another good remedy is to scald a cupful of sweet milk to which has been added a pinch of black pepper. Allow it to cool and give nothing else to drink until all of the birds have had a drink of it.

When blackhead attacks a flock of turkeys the sick birds will have to be killed and burned and all buildings and feeding vessels disinfected. Turkeys exposed to the disease may be saved by giving them a few doses of pepper and ginger in sour milk or Dutch cheese.

Gapes in chickens are caused by worms in the windpipe. These worms may be removed by using the tip of a feather which has been moistened with oil of cloves and sweet oil. Insert the feather in the windpipe, twist it around several times and then withdraw it. Clean and disinfect the premises.

Roup is a common ailment among chickens, and resembles a severe cold in a human. A simple remedy is a little kerosene placed in the nose passages. Carbolic acid may be used in the same way—one part of the acid to fifty parts of water. Use the Douglas mixture in drinking water. This Douglas mixture is made as follows: One-half pound sulphate of iron, two ounces sulphuric acid and two gallons soft water. After this has been mixed let it settle overnight and then pour into bottles. Add a tablespoonful to each quart of drinking water. This is a good general tonic as well as a preventive of disease.

Venetian red placed in drinking water is of great value in the poultry house. Use a tablespoonful of this powder in two quarts of drinking water. The water can be renewed from day to day without using any more of the venetian red until it has all disappeared from the bottom of the vessel.

Owners of poultry must provide dust heaps and change the dirt as it seems necessary to do so, using a considerable amount of wood ashes with the dust if obtainable. Tobacco in nests and whitewash around buildings help to destroy vermin. Put a little carbolic acid in the whitewash. An occasional fumigation with sulphur is good. There are efficacious insect powders for sale at drug stores. If lice are on the premises rub vaseline or lard on the heads and under the wings of young chickens as a preventive. This or insect powder should also be applied where vermin are observed on the birds. Keep buildings and yards as clean as possible, using considerable slaked lime on floors and throughout the yard.

Nor can there be success if poultry is so housed that the birds cannot escape taking cold, the common causes of which are dampness and draughts. The ordinary attacks of cold and influenza develop into various fatal diseases unless they are properly treated. Instead of using the roup remedy, as many do, owners of large flocks ought to keep on hand the following: Prepare a solution of two per cent permanganate of potash, by dissolving two ounces of the permanganate crystals (bought at any drug store at about thirty cents per pound) in three quarts of water. Keep this solution ready, and when a bird shows the first signs of nose or throat trouble take enough of the solution to allow the head of the fowl to be submerged and put it under until the bird nearly chokes. Remove the bird's head from the liquid and allow it to sneeze and sputter, forcing the liquid into all the air passages. Repeat this three times before you let the bird go, and repeat it twice a day until the fowl no longer shows signs of disease. The operation is simple and in the majority of cases entirely sufficient. Potassium permanganate is an excellent disinfectant and can be given to the birds to drink with the result that many other cases will be warded off. When given in drinking water, only enough should be placed in the water to give it a claret color. The birds can be given water thus treated for three or four days at a time. No other water should be placed where they can get it, otherwise they will prefer the untreated water to that containing the drug.

The greatest advantage that I see in raising chickens artificially is that the chicks can be kept free from lice from the moment they are hatched until they are full grown, provided the poultry raiser will exercise cleanly methods of management. By this means, the loss of chicks from lice can be reduced to nothing and the fowls will be stronger and healthier than when their blood is pumped out by parasites. The ordinary nest in which chickens are hatched under hens is usually so foul with parasites that chicks have small chance to live.

In order to facilitate cleanliness in the poultry house and to greatly reduce the amount of filth, dropping boards should, by all means, be used. By using a little precaution in placing the dropping boards so as not to obstruct the light the entire floor space beneath can be utilized for a scratching floor. At least six inches should be allowed between the dropping boards and the roosts, the distance depending entirely upon the arrangement of the roosts. If the platform is made in sections it can be handled much more easily, as it is frequently found desirable to remove them in cleaning. Smooth boards are the most desirable to use.

Poultry is subject to the same general laws of health as human beings are, and we should not overlook this fact in caring for them. Pure air, pure water and pure food, as well as thorough cleanliness, are all essential. The fowl's power to resist disease is due to these.

Neighborhood Social Centers

A NATURAL social center is the district school, and adjacent to or convenient to nearly every school there ought to be a neighborhood playground and club building. It is not best to use the schoolhouse for social gatherings as a regular thing. There ought to be weekly meetings of farmers and their families most of the year. Perhaps in midsummer they should be suspended, although I have noticed that farmers enjoy ice cream socials as well as other people.

Debates on political and agricultural topics, and all manner of literary and musical exercises, should be conducted in connection with the weekly socials. As many fun-making games as possible should be introduced. To give a practical turn to such affairs and to still further vary the entertainment there could be an occasional demonstration of seed testing, farm bookkeeping, etc., together with an exchange of experiences.

These social centers have already been established in a great many places, but thousands more are needed. The cost of a suitable building and a few acres of ground is readily subscribed in any neighborhood. The better the building, the more enjoyment it will bring—the more good will it do the rising generation. It should be large enough to contemplate simple courses of domestic science, manual training and indoor athletics. The property needs to be under the control of an association, or the subscribers can merely vote to place it in the care of a trustee. A public-spirited school teacher is of great assistance in such matters. The playground should include a tennis court, baseball diamond, grove, etc. This is only intended to be a suggestive outline as to what a farming community should do to provide a central meeting place and stimulate the pleasure of country life. Almost anybody taking up this subject will have practical ideas on carrying forward such a project. Where there is no church in the neighborhood, it is sometimes found desirable to establish a Sunday school in these community centers, and the buildings may be used for preaching services when desired.

Plans for ornamentation will suggest themselves. Nearly every woman in the community would feel able and willing to contribute plants and assist in their harmonious arrangement about the building and ground. Experiments in flower growing could be taken up and made exceedingly practical, besides beautifying the grounds. There might also be room enough for other experiments in seed germination or the production of novel plants.

Society in the country fails to receive from its schools the results which it needs. This deficiency is recognized by all of the larger schools and the farmers' institutes, which today are giving a great deal of attention to the social life of agricultural communities. In fact, the government itself has recognized the menace to the nation in the old conditions and is inquiring for a remedy.

Farmers' institutes, granges and colleges are among the leading agencies which are applying remedies for the defects in our rural schools and in the social conditions surrounding them. While they are still far short of attaining sufficient results, they are progressing along right lines.

Selecting and Testing Seed Corn

THE time to select seed corn is in the fall after the grain is thoroughly ripe, and the selection should be made in the field. This method enables one to know exactly the kind of stalk which produced the ear and to avoid those stalks which, although they may have borne one good ear, indicate by their general appearance that they would not reproduce a perfect stand the next season.

Seed corn selection is one of the most important details of growing the crop. It must be undertaken in a systematic manner, because slipshod and uncertain methods will only result in disappointment and failure.

Really seed corn should be raised on specially prepared ground from pedigreed seed, and this work should be undertaken at planting time.

When the corn is thoroughly ripe in the field the selection should be made by taking a row at a time and picking only those ears which come up to a certain standard fixed beforehand.

In the selection of the standard the farmer must make up his mind in advance whether he wants a large, coarse stalk with the ear high from the ground, or a smaller, stout stalk with the ear lower down.

If he desires a large ear with coarse grains, or a medium-sized ear with the grains compactly set, he must make his selections accordingly.

Right here, however, the selector is warned against a very common mistake—that is picking ears of abnormal size or appearance. If he wants a large ear with coarse and loosely set grains he may find an occasional ear bearing these characteristics in a very marked degree, abnormally so in fact, but it would be a mistake to select such an ear, because the tendency will be to increase variation and when these variations run to excess they are pretty sure to produce undesirable qualities.

It would be just as great a mistake if the selector is looking for a medium-sized ear with closely set grains to select an undersized ear with the abnormally sized grains.

It is a good plan to select seed from stalks of stout, healthy growth which have made uniform progress during the season and that are well provided with leaves so as to provide plenty of fodder. It is important to observe the tassel of the stalk to see that it is strong, symmetrical, well developed and free from any evidence of disease.

The stalk from which the ears are taken should be well rooted in the ground, upright, strong and vigorous, and any evidence of disease or abnormal growth should at once condemn it.

Only ears that are well silked and that are thoroughly covered with the husk from tip to tip should be selected. Here again it is a mistake to select ears bearing abnormally developed husks or husks that are too little developed.

If the ear contains an unusual amount of husk it is a sure sign of coarseness and will show up badly in next year's crop.

The shank bearing the ear should be short and not over an inch or an inch and a quarter in diameter, and the ears pointing downward are the most desirable. These shed the rain and thus preserve the grain while those ears which stand upright, or nearly so, naturally catch moisture which trickles down into the grain and causes it to rot.

As to the number of rows and grains on the ear, these will vary with the variety, but in most standard varieties they run from 16 to 20, although they may run as high as 24 and still conform to standard.

If the number runs below 14 the ear should be dis-
carded.   The rows should run straight from butt to tip
and those ears containing wavy rows or rows that become mixed at any point and lose their identity are not
to be taken.

Do not select ears that are much larger at the butt
than at the tip.   The cob of the perfect ear should be perfectly straight and uniform in circumference.

The grain should be rather wedge-shaped but symmetrical and well formed and not too long.   The tip of
the ear should be perfectly covered with corn, as well as
the butt.   Not many ears containing these characteristics
will be found in a random selection the first season; but
by careful breeding, ears may be produced which will be
perfectly covered at both ends and symmetrical in appearance from butt to tip.

In selecting seed corn it is necessary, of course, to aim
at the perfect standard and not be content with anything
else.   If one goes to the trouble of making any selection,
why not carry it out to its conclusion and strive to produce perfect grains instead of one half or three quarters
perfect?   Only the perfect grain is worth striving for.
The selection of seed corn in the field is not any easy job
or one quickly accomplished.   It cannot be done in the
usual corn picking way, but must be done with basket
on arm and in a spirit of calm contentment even though
a whole day's work brings no more than a dozen perfect
ears to the seed bin.

If the work is hastily done the chances are largely in
favor of a poor crop the following year.   What is a day
or two spent in the selection of seed as compared to the
increase of a year's crop resulting from careful and wise
selection?

The ears selected for seed should each be carefully
marked and labeled and it is a good plan to make the
label explicit.   For this purpose a card two or three

inches long may be used, upon which should be noted
the character of the stalk, the quality of the tassel, the
condition of the root, and other items necessary to a
complete understanding of the nature of the plant which
bore the seed.

These details are not likely to remain in one's mind
between the time of selection and the planting, and it
is well to keep all these facts constantly noted.

The seed ears should be stored in a rat-proof room,
not too cold nor warm enough to start germination in
case of damp weather at any time during the winter.
After the ears have dried a few days they should be
husked and placed in racks, that they may cure uniformly.

Of course in the spring, two or three weeks before
planting time, the seed must be thoroughly tested for
germination power. This is as important as selection and
even more so, because it is useless to go to the trouble
of preparing ground and planting seed unless you know
it will grow. Make sure that the seed corn has not been
damp or frozen.

One of the simplest devices for testing seed corn is
what is known as the "cloth roll" method. This was devised by a corn grower in Iowa and is now in quite general use in that state. It is especially valuable where a
large amount of corn is to be tested.

All the apparatus needed is a knife and a few strips of
muslin about six inches wide and 4 or 5 feet long. The
ears to be tested should be laid out in rows where they
may be gotten at conveniently. Wet one of the strips
of muslin with warm water and lay it down in front
of the row of corn. Begin at one end of the row of
corn and take out 6 kernels from each ear. Place them
on the cloth, beginning at the upper left hand corner
and working across from left to right. Two rows down
the strip of cloth are enough.

Mark off the cloth into squares and place the kernels from the different ears well apart. When the cloth is full begin at the upper end and roll it up carefully. Keep it stretched tightly crosswise while rolling and there will be little danger of the kernels getting out of place. After the cloth is rolled up you have the kernels from 50 or 60 ears in a compact roll.

As many of these rolls can be prepared as desired, the ears being tied up as the kernels are taken from them. On the outside of the roll mark the number of the last ear from which kernels were taken. This can readily be done with a soft pencil. It is not necessary to tie up the rolls, as the wet cloth will stick enough to hold them. Wet the rolls from time to time with warm water and keep up an even temperature until the germination is completed.

After the kernels have germinated enough so that the sprouts begin to appear at the end of the ears, the test is ready to read. Begin with the last roll. As it is unrolled the kernels in the lower right hand corner will represent the last ear in the pile. It is a short job to go over the corn, compare it with the tested kernels and throw out the dead and weak ears. The work is simplified by having three barrels, one for the good ears, one for the poor ones and one for the weak ones. As soon as all the ears tested on the first roll have been checked, take the next one in order, etc. If ordinary care is exercised there is little danger of making mistakes. The work can be done very rapidly. Every dead ear thrown out and replaced by a good one means something like 8 bushels more corn the following year, or $4 more profit.

If a person will go to the trouble of making a frame resembling a kitchen table it is easy to arrange another method of testing seed corn, and one that will be quite satisfactory. Nail a cleat around the edge of the table and put on about an inch of earth or sawdust. Mark

fifty or one hundred squares on a sheet of muslin large
enough to cover the table, numbering the squares from
one up. On each square place three or four kernels of
corn from ears which are numbered with tickets to correspond with the squares. Cover the whole batch on
the table with a cloth pad or several sheets of muslin and
keep moist until germination is completed. The table
should stand in a warm room.

Farm Bookkeeping

Vegetable Garden Account

In this illustration of a garden account the figures may
not tally with actual experience. Expert gardeners often
realize much more than $435 net profit from three acres,
and yet this conservative figure will be found close to
what the average person can accomplish. The item of
$200 is hardly enough for labor, but there is this con-
sideration—if the labor is highly skilled and worth more
than $200, the net profits will also be more than are
shown in the table:

1913	DEBIT	
Interest on $500, value of 3 acres	$	30
Fertilizer		100
Labor		200
Yearly value of tools, etc.		25
Seeds and plants		35
Miscellaneous		25
	$	415

CREDIT		
Cabbage, 1 acre, sales	$	250
Sweet corn, ½ acre, sales		100
Tomatoes, ½ acre, sales		150
Celery, ¼ acre, sales		100
Onions and cucumbers, sales		150
Lettuce and radishes, sales		100
	$	850
Expense		415
Net profit	$	435

Specimen of Labor Account

1912   George W. Smith   Cr.   Dr.

March 15. Began work at $30 per month.
April 1. To cash $10.00
April 30. To cash 30.00
May 31. To cash 35.00

May 31. By 2½ months' work......$75.00 $75.00

A yearly labor account may be kept in precisely the same way.

Illustration of Poultry Account

1913   DEBIT

Interest on investment of $800..................$ 40
Cost of feeding 1,000 chickens................. 350
Value of labor............................. 150
Cost of maintenance........................ 50
Miscellaneous 25

$ 615

CREDIT

3,000 dozen eggs.............................$ 600
1,000 broilers 300
Other poultry 250
Value of fertilizer 100

$1,250
Expense ....$ 615

Net profit ....$ 635

In illustrating a simple method of account keeping it does not matter whether these figures are too high or too low. The main items to be put down in the debit and credit columns are shown, but the account can be changed as experience demands. It is safe to say that a well-managed poultry plant of this kind will pay more than $635 net.

Financial Statement of the Chicken Flock

This table gives an illustration of one simple method of telling what a flock of 200 chickens is paying:

	Eggs and Poultry	Feed and Labor	Profit
January	$ 74.00	$ 34.44	$ 39.56
February	80.60	26.00	54.60
March	84.50	21.55	62.95
April	92.00	18.46	73.54
May	78.90	24.15	54.75
June	58.00	24.80	33.20
July	47.60	20.00	27.60
August	57.00	21.20	35.80
September	61.80	22.00	39.80
October	88.40	33.30	55.10
November	64.60	31.20	33.40
December	71.70	32.60	39.10
	$859.10	$309.70	$549.40

Illustration of Egg Account for Week
12 Birds in Pen

Pen No. 1	....	Pen No. 9	....
" " 2	....	" " 10	....
" " 3	....	" " 11	....
" " 4	....	" " 12	....
" " 5	....	" " 13	....
" " 6	....	" " 14	....
" " 7	....	" " 15	....
" " 8	....		

Total ....

Total value of food........................... ....

Net profit for week...................... ....

Trap nests will prove the merit of each hen. This helps to build up a good flock, and the total or individual profits are shown.

Table Showing Cost and Profit of Raising Potatoes
Illustration on Basis of One Acre

Rental value of land as plowed	$ 10.00
Value of 50 tons of manure applied	50.00
Harrowing and subsequent cultivation	10.00
Cost of seed and planting	6.00
Digging and marketing	8.00
Spraying and incidental expenses	5.00
	$ 89.00

Total receipts for 245 bushels	$171.50
Expenses	89.00
Net profit on land, labor, etc.	$ 82.50

A farmer who keeps his soil up by growing clover and other legumes, as well as by the regular application of manure, and who manages his work well, will reduce this expense about $25, thus running his net profit above $100 an acre. This simple method of keeping the account will answer the purpose for that part of the farm.

Table Showing Net Assets of Farmer
Inventory Year by Year
1912

Farm of 100 acres, value.....................	$ 6,000
Dwelling and other buildings.................	3,500
Four work horses and 2 colts.................	700
Eighteen head of cows and heifers.............	900
Fifteen hogs, varying........................	150
Sixty chickens and ducks.....................	60
Machinery, harness and vehicles...............	350
Pumps, engine and windmill..................	300
Miscellaneous equipment	40
Cash on hand	600
Total assets	$12,600
Less mortgage of......................	3,500
Net assets at end of year.............	$ 9,100

1913

Farm of 100 acres, value.....................	$ 6,500
Dwelling and other buildings.................	3,250
Six head of horses..........................	800
Twenty head of cows and heifers..............	1,000
Twelve hogs	125
One hundred chickens and ducks..............	100
Machinery, harness and vehicles...............	325
Pumps, engine and windmill..................	275
Miscellaneous equipment	50
Cash on hand..............................	375
Total assets	$12,800
Less mortgage of......................	3,000
Net assets at end of year.............	$ 9,800

These figures show an increase of $500 in the value of the land and a slight decrease in the value of buildings and machinery. They also show a decrease in the debt and a gain in the net assets. Such an account is easily kept and it gives the man of the soil a good working basis and something to be guided by. It would not add much labor to itemize the inventory more fully, putting in a few more particulars respecting animals and machinery.

Illustration of Milk Report for Week

Name—	Sun.	Mon.	Tue.	Wed.	Thur.	Fri.	Sat.	Total.	
				Pounds and Tenth-pounds					
Ada—									
A. M....	11.7	11.6	12.0	11.4	11.2	11.4	11.6	80.9	
P. M....	10.2	9.8	8.7	9.0	9.4	9.2	9.1	65.4—	146.3
Blossom—									
A. M....	13.2	12.8	13.6	13.4	12.7	13.3	13.0	92.0	
P. M....	7.4	7.5	8.0	6.9	7.7	8.2	6.8	52.5—	144.5
Dinah—									
A. M....	...	...	...	9.3	9.5	9.2	8.9	36.9	
P. M....	...	...	...	9.0	7.3	8.0	7.7	32.0—	68.9
Hilda—									
A. M....	11.3	11.5	12.0	11.8	12.2	11.9	11.8	82.5	
P. M....	10.6	10.8	10.0	11.2	10.7	11.0	11.3	75.6—	158.1
Ida—									
A. M....	12.0	12.4	11.9	12.3	12.6	11.8	12.2	85.2	
P. M....	10.2	9.6	10.0	9.8	10.3	9.3	9.9	69.1—	154.3
Julia—									
A. M....	12.5	11.9	12.2	12.0	12.4	12.6	11.8	85.4	
P. M....	12.0	11.6	11.3	11.7	10.9	11.2	11.4	80.1—	165.5
May—									
A. M....	13.0	13.5	12.9	13.2	12.8	13.4	12.9	91.7	
P. M....	13.6	12.7	13.1	13.0	12.7	13.2	12.8	91.1—	182.8
Peach—									
A. M....	11.5	11.8	11.2	12.0	11.6	11.4	12.2	81.7	
P. M....	10.7	11.0	10.9	10.6	11.2	10.4	11.3	76.1—	157.8
	159.9	158.5	157.8	176.6	175.2	175.5	174.7		—1,178.2

After keeping such an account as the above for two weeks an owner can tell whether any cow is worth feeding or not. Make such a record about twice a year.

Ledger Account for Month or Year

This Page Shows the Two Sides of the Account

Dr.				Cr.		
1912. Cash.			1912. Cash.			
To inventory cash on hand......	B. 1	$ 378.40	By cash farm products	B. 1	$	6.75
To cash from John Rice....	B. 1		" " shoeing bill	B. 1		8.25
" " for apples	B. 1	5.40	" " seed wheat	B. 4		15.00
" " milk	B. 2	42.36	" " Peter Brown	B. 2		10.00
" " colts	B. 2	96.00	" " repairs	B. 2		4.29
" " horse	B. 2	160.00	" " harness	B. 2		3.68
" " eggs	B. 3	21.50	" " bills of Bell & Bessy.	B. 2		107.00
" " wheat, farm			" " J. Smith	B. 2		20.00
products ...	B. 3	232.50	" " threshing bills	B. 3		21.00
" " wheat, 1900 ...	B. 3	240.00	" " repairs	B. 3		29.00
" " Burroughs' note			" " John Doe	B. 3		33.75
paid	B. 3	163.25	" " P. Handy, labor.....	B. 4		15.00
" " 10 cords wood..	B. 3	30.00	" " D. Hill	B. 4		3.00
" " 96 bbls. apples.	B. 4	120.00	" " span fillies	B. 4		275.00
" " 60 bbls. corn....	B. 4	24.00	" " Peter Brown	B. 4		17.00
" " 200 qts. cream..	B. 4	70.00				
						$ 568.72
$1,583.41			1913.			
			To balance cash on hand (to			1,389.69
$1,958.41			1913 cash account)............			$1,958.41

Useful Hints for Everyday Farm Life

HENS are helping to lift a good many mortgages nowadays.

––––––––

The lack of organic matter is the greatest trouble we have in the vineyard.

––––––––

The finer the soil the better the vegetables, both in quantity and quality.

––––––––

Dry air, good feed and plenty of exercise are necessary for winter eggs.

––––––––

Work the surface soil over after each rain, and thus retain all the moisture.

––––––––

Fowls need plenty of fresh, pure water. Thoroughly wash their dishes every day.

––––––––

As a rule, hens that lay steadily during cold weather are indifferent hot weather layers.

––––––––

Winter eggs do not come by chance. It takes planning and work to get them, but it pays.

––––––––

Make a hot bed and have some early plants ready to set out when the weather is warm enough.

––––––––

If you think of setting out an orchard and have had no experience, hire a good man to show you how.

Vegetables delight in having warm, deep, rich and mellow soil and will pay generously for the privilege.

Saltpeter water—one ounce of saltpeter to a gallon of water—is a good spray for rust on bean vines and bushes.

Some day we are going to find that as good a way as any to use the surplus sour milk is to give it to the hens.

Three rules for success in gardening are: Freedom from weeds, thinning out, and keeping the ground mellow.

Do not forget that the fowls need green food. If a change of yards is not possible see that some is fed them daily.

A few bad eggs in a case is sufficient to give the whole lot a bad name. Be careful that every egg is strictly fresh.

Poultry raising offers to women an excellent means of making money because the work is not too taxing for their strength.

Don't crowd the chicks. Give them room to exercise and grow in. See that they are kept comfortable and well fed.

Much can be done to prolong the life of trees. Fill up the decayed places with cement after scraping out all the decay.

The ground should never be allowed to become baked, as in this condition a great deal of moisture is lost unnecessarily.

Are there any old apple trees in your orchard bearing undesirable fruit? It is easy to graft good varieties upon them.

———

Give the hens plenty of lime and charcoal. A dishful kept where they can help themselves is a valuable addition to the houses.

———

Money can be made from small fruits. The area is decreasing year by year, and this means the prices will keep getting better.

———

Cultivation is a moisture conservator, but if the ground is dry, don't run the cultivator teeth deep. Keep the top soil stirred only.

———

Keep an egg record and do not fail to make entries daily. The successful poultryman must be business-like in every respect.

———

The poultryman who fails to keep an accurate account of his transactions is traveling over the road of uncertainty that leads to failure.

———

It is poor economy to feed spoiled food to the poultry. They may contract disease or become poisoned. Burn all decomposed food stuff at once.

———

The old family orchards are rapidly disappearing, so that in the future commercial orchardists will supply the rural as well as the city population.

———

Truck crops suffer least from fungi in seasons that open with a cool spring and end with a very hot summer, with a rainfall below the average.

No more simple or efficient method for the improvement of the egg supply of the country could be adopted than the production of infertile eggs.

We prune grapevines to produce larger and better fruit, maintain vigor, to keep vines within limits, and to cause ease of cultivation and spraying.

It is useless to try to grow vegetables upon ground that is poorly drained. For this reason a clay loam with a goodly portion of sand is to be desired.

It pays better to milk a four-gallon cow and sell her when dry for two cents a pound than to milk a two-gallon cow and sell her for four cents a pound.

It would not be easy to find a fruit that can be more rapidly improved by careful selection, or run out more rapidly by careless handling than the tomato.

Whey is a by-product of cheese, and possesses more or less feeding value when fed to swine in a judicious manner. Most feeders prefer to feed it sweet.

Ducks are great feeders and they are also great growers, so where does the loss come in? A few ducks will help keep the income up to the required standard.

The farmer not prepared with woven wire fencing, with ample alfalfa or clover pastures, is not properly prepared for the economical production of pork.

The fact that eggs are cheap at any season of the year does not lessen their value for the family table. Even when the price is high they are cheaper than meat.

When you have found for a certainty that a hen is unprofitable dispose of her at once. Some hens are never good layers but they eat as much as the best of the flock.

———

Some farmers demand upon the table—at least once a week—a good old onion stew—to keep them healthy. The chickens will be all the better for just the same every week.

———

Keep the poultry out of the barn. As well turn a pig into the parlor. Many men allow fowls to find their own quarters, and then they wonder why they are not a good investment.

———

The best work that can be done for fowls in winter is to lay in a good supply of litter and dry dirt under shelter. It is scratching in the winter that keeps them in best laying condition.

———

Don't confine ducks to one kind of feed. They like a variety. Cornbread is good for young ducks, but it is fattening, and the wisest thing is to mix it with oatmeal, bread crumbs or potatoes.

———

Perhaps you have heard an undue commotion among the hens at roosting time. They were scrapping for the higher places, so build them on a level, and never have one placed over the other.

———

If you have not found pork production profitable, buy some woven wire fencing and make a hog pasture in your alfalfa field where there will be shade and water, and no longer say it don't pay to keep hogs.

———

The hens need plenty of shade. Keeping them exposed to the scorching rays of the sun is little short of cruelty.

A shelter can easily be rigged from old burlap or a few armfuls of fir boughs, if there is no natural shade.

It often is your fault that hens get to eating eggs; but after they do contract the habit, lay the axe at the root of the tree—in other words, stop the business, short off. Then change your bill of fare. Something is lacking in the feed.

Vaccine is effective in guarding against hog cholera. The common vaccine is blood serum from the body of an immune hog. The double vaccine treatment is the use of virulent blood serum from the body of a hog in the last stages of cholera.

It may be possible to have poultry live without any animal matter, but for profit and thrift it is necessary that they receive a certain per cent of meat in the daily bill of fare, especially when they are confined to runs, or to houses in winter.

One reason why women usually succeed with poultry is because they are considerate of the wants of the fowls. Women have more patience naturally than men, and it requires a great deal of patience to make a success of poultry raising.

If farmers and others engaged in the production of eggs would market their male birds as soon as the hatching season is over, a large saving would be made, as practically every infertile egg would grade a first or second if clean and promptly marketed.

The fact that dairymen have devoted more attention to other phases of their dairying than to the breeding and development of the cow is one of the reasons why so many of our dairy herds are not capable of returning a profit from their food and cost of care.

The average hen outlives her usefulness in two years and is more profitable sent to market. There are at times good hens in the third and even fourth year, but the average limit is two. Old hens are more likely to contract diseases than the younger ones.

More chicks are killed every year by coarse food than in any other way. Their bowels are tender, so give food that will be easy to digest. Well-dried and crushed bread crumbs, lightly moistened, are as good as anything. Mix in a bit of fine-cut lettuce or onion.

Pick grapes, if possible, during the heat of the day, for then the stems are less brittle and fewer berries will split and be torn from the branches. Never pick them after a rain and before the bunches have dried out, if you can avoid it, for that tends to cause the fruit to mold badly.

Ten grains of nitrate of potash in a little milk (warm), three times each day will greatly assist in overcoming rheumatism in hogs. This dose is for the grown hog. If given to pigs or growing shoats, about three grains for each hundred pounds of live-weight will be sufficient.

A large part of the heavy loss from bad eggs can be obviated by the production of infertile eggs. This has been demonstrated beyond a doubt by the investigations concerning the improvement of the farm egg which during the past two years have been conducted in the Middle West.

It is an invariable rule that animals receiving proper care are much better able to resist disease than are those which are poorly housed and improperly fed. Cleanliness is of first importance with all live stock. Next are clean water, a variety of wholesome food and comfortable beds.

Eggs contain all the elements necessary to supply the human body with nourishing food. This is not true of any other article of food. One-half of an egg is nutriment, while not more than one-fourth of meat is so; thus it will be seen that one pound of eggs is equal, in food value, to two pounds of meat.

Ireland is the greatest poultry growing country in the world. It is far ahead of France, though we have always adopted the latter as the leading country in this industry. Ireland, with a population of not quite 5,000,000, has 14,000,000 fowls, while France with a population of seven times greater has only 40,000,000.

When pigs are once afflicted with "bull nose" there is no cure. The disease may be arrested by smoking with camphor-gum. This is done by confining the animals in a tightly covered box, and placing a little camphor-gum on a red-hot stove-lid. They will inhale the fumes. The trouble is, no doubt, infectious.

There is an insistent market demand for high-class horses, especially for draft horses, that cannot be supplied. On the other hand, the country is flooded with common ordinary "plug" horses. They do not fill any particular requirement or demand, hence the very low and profit-killing prices for which they must sell.

Northern Minnesota is fast becoming a dairy section and the raising of hogs is receiving increased attention. Conditions that are favorable to the dairy industry are favorable to hog raising. Clover that produces milk so abundantly produces meat equally well and the dairy farmer can produce no meat so profitably as pork.

———

Hiccoughing in pigs is caused by a derangement of the stomach. One of the best ways to correct the trouble is to change the sow's ration, feeding less corn and more of such feed as ground oats and bran. If the trouble does not cease, give each pig eight drops of tincture of asafoetida twice a day till the hiccoughing ceases.

———

For colic in horses: Chloroform, one ounce; laudanum, eight ounces; sulphuric ether, two ounces; Jamaica ginger, eight ounces; raw linseed-oil, two pounds. Mix well and divide into ten doses and give one each hour until relief comes. This remedy is used at the fire sta- tions in a number of the cities, and has rarely been known to fail.

———

A successful sheep grower writes: "I have found that the great trouble with most sheep-dips is, they are too strong, and cause irritation of the flesh. For each 10 sheep I use only one-fourth pound of plug-tobacco. This I boil in about 30 gallons of water, and dip the sheep therein as soon as cool. I make an application once each week until the trouble is overcome."

———

As a stock food we have found buttermilk better adapted for pigs than for any other animals; but would not advise feeding it to very young pigs. As a feed for swine our experience has led us to believe that it has about the same feeding value as skim-milk. We would, however, prefer skim-milk on account of its being less liable to derange the animal's digestive system.

———

The following is an excellent remedy for a cough that follows distemper in horses: Granulated sugar, one pound, in which mix powdered chlorate of potash, eight ounces, and powdered lobelia, two ounces. Mix well together, place a teaspoonful in the ·feed-box before feeding, and place the grain-feed on top of it, or, if you are feeding meal mixed with the hay, mix it with the ration.

For the first twenty-four hours to thirty-six hours after they leave the shell little chicks want warmth sufficient for comfort, fresh air to breathe and a chance to sleep without being disturbed. When they are sufficiently rested and thoroughly dried out and fluffy, stand strong on their legs and begin to persistently make the "hungry cry," they are ready to go to brood coop or brooder for their first feed.

It will surprise most dairymen to learn that carefully kept cows are given four ounces of salt each, daily, mixed with their feed. They eat their food better, and the owner thinks they do better when given this amount than when the allowance is smaller. The cows are fed three times a day, and the salt is divided between the three feeds. Fine table salt is invariably used; the cows prefer it to coarse salt.

A hog coming down with cholera is sluggish and refuses food. The eyes are inflamed and the hair becomes rough. A cough and weakness are other symptoms. An inexperienced owner needs the help of an expert in such cases. Veterinarians usually know how to procure and use the serum, and it is best to employ them if they can be reached. Nearly all states have public veterinarians

The guinea fowl is a native of warm countries and has a natural fear of snow, so when guineas are caught out in a storm there is a good chance for trouble if we undertake to force them to walk through snow to the poultry house. The guineas will take to flight rather than wade in snow and rather than light on the ground when covered with snow they will alight in trees, or if there are no trees they will light on the tops of buildings.

———

Many times a severe cough in a horse can be corrected by the use of the following remedy: Nitrate of potash, three drachms; tartarized antimony, one drachm; powdered digitalis, three-fourths drachm; camphor, three drachms. Mix well, divide into two equal parts, and make each into a ball with a little raw linseed-oil. Give one dose in the morning and the other in the evening. Continue each alternate day until relief is noticed.

———

To rid swine of worms, give one dose made up of 4 tablespoonfuls of oil of turpentine, one-half teaspoonful of liquor of erri dialysatus and 6 ounces of raw linseed oil. This is suitable for an animal weighing 100 to 150 pounds; for larger or smaller stock change the dose. Repeat in four days if necessary. Kidney worms are not directly reached by any known remedy, but the treatment and management outlined above will have a good effect.

———

One of the best methods to take care of the steel plow is to grease the mold board, share and land slide just as soon as the plowing is done. Leaving a highly polished surface exposed to the weather for one night starts a rust. Paint must be scraped off with some sharp instrument, while grease can be wiped off with a cloth, or not infrequently the farmer can hitch to the plow without touching the share, the dirt pushing off the grease. Paint is a good preservative of wood, but should not be applied to metal which has wearing or bearing surfaces.

People ought to know that the very best thing they can do is to eat apples just before retiring for the night. Persons uninitiated in the mysteries of the fruit are liable to throw up their hands in horror at the visions of dyspepsia which such a suggestion may summon up, but harm can seldom come by the slow eating of ripe and juicy apples before going to bed. The apple is excellent brain food because it has more phosphoric acid in easily digested shape than any other fruit.

The first step in determining the freshness of an egg is to know that the hen that laid it was not mated while the egg was in the oviduct; to be sure about this, separate from laying hens all male birds at the close of breeding season. Each egg should be candled. In candling, a fresh egg appears unclouded, almost translucent; if incubation has begun, a dark spot is visible. A rotten egg appears dark colored. A settled egg is one in which the yoke appears attached to one side of the shell. With interested observation one may become expert in selecting fresh eggs in a short time.

Wean pigs when eight to ten weeks old. After weaning, feed the following ration: Soaked corn, two parts; barley, two parts; middlings, two parts; meat meal, one-half part, and roots in liberal quantities. When the weather becomes cold feed dry corn and barley. Make a thick slop of middlings, meat meal and water, but use milk instead of water if you have it. The farmers of the United States have not yet appreciated the value of roots, such as mangels and sugar beets. Next year try an acre; you will grow more afterwards. For pigs they should be cut up with a pulper. The chief value of roots lies in their succulence. They are a substitute for grass.

To develop a laying strain of hens a fancier says that owners must not keep fowls in large flocks; not over fifteen to the flock, and each of these must be known individually by toe marks, leg bands and trap nests. He says that the hen which often gets broody is most often the hen that lays most eggs, if you break her up immediately she gets broody. The laying hen carries a business air that soon shows her worth. The laying strain must be pure-bred; the male of this strain and for this strain must have comb well developed and large for his breed, and be an early and persistent crower, both showing extra good development.

Speaking of lumpy jaws in cattle, G. G. Graham says: "The most satisfactory way is to remove the growth with the knife when in the tissues only. The animal is thrown; the head then held in a favorable position, the skin is cut over the tumor, and the swelling removed by cutting around it in the healthy tissues." If hemorrhage is large the vessel may be tied or taken up with the forceps; bleeding from smaller vessels may be seared with a red-hot iron. The wound should be washed with an antiseptic in 1 per cent solution after the tumor is removed, and then packed with antiseptic gauze or cotton, and the wound stitched up. The next day remove the stitches, and treat as an open wound.

When the goose becomes broody, if I wish her to lay another litter I shut her up a few days, and in the course of two weeks she will generally commence laying again. If I wish to set her on the first litter I give her not more than 15 eggs. At the same time I replenish the nest with straw, and then keep away. If she has free range and plenty of water, she will need no other care. In about 30 days she will come off with the goslings. These I keep close at hand for a few days, until they get

strong, but allow them to nip the tender grass at will. A
shallow dish of water is given them to drink from. They
are kept out of rains until they are well feathered. I
feed a little cracked corn at night to coax them home.

The amateur farmer does not need expert advice to enable him to keep his hogs in clean yards and buildings.
Without much scientific knowledge he can see the wisdom
of allowing them to range in grass or clover. They need
a change of pasture and grounds now and again. It takes
only a little systematic effort to provide clean troughs
and fresh water. A shed is needed for shade in summer
unless there are trees, and winter pens and yards should
be kept in a sanitary condition. All these things count
largely in warding off disease and in making a good
quality of pork. The charcoal and wood ashes which are
valuable aids to the health of swine, will help to a great
extent in warding off cholera. Corn given in a green
stage is one of the causes of cholera and this kind of
feeding should be avoided.

Sheep are easier to winter than any other stock. That
is, of course, providing they have sufficient shelter and
plenty of fresh water. The barn in which I keep my
sheep is completely inclosed, and as warm and tight as
any of the buildings for the rest of the stock. It has
plenty of windows, and openings in the windows for
ventilation. I feed timothy or upland hay at night, and
straw liberally during the day, with a little ground oats
and shorts, mixed, in the morning. My feed racks are
built a foot from the floor. They are a foot wide at the
bottom, 2½ feet high and 2 feet wide at the top. The
sides are made of boards 8 inches wide and 6 inches apart
up and down. Besides a system of window ventilation,
I have ventilators in the roof, so that I am sure at all
times of the sheep having plenty of fresh air.

At the Missouri Station bone meal was fed with corn to hogs in a fattening test with very good results. About an ounce of the meal was fed to each hog per day. At the Nebraska Station four lots of pigs were fed to determine the value of wheat shorts, tankage and steamed ground bone, as supplements to corn meal. These hogs were pastured on alfalfa, and for this reason the lot fed on corn alone made about as satisfactory gain as any, although the lot which was fed bone meal in addition to the corn had the strongest bone. Shorts strengthened the bones some, and tankage with corn produced much stronger bone than corn alone. Where mixed grain rations are given, or skim milk or good pasture, all of which supply ash material, it is doubtful whether bone meal is of much value other than for the purpose of strengthening the bones.

———

Measles are common with small pigs. Since it is a contagion, it spreads very rapidly when once there is an outbreak in the herd. Some of its more common symptoms are coughing and sneezing. The eyes are red and watery, and there is generally a discharge from the nose. The appetite is generally impaired, and there is a desire to remain in the nest or bed. On the fourth or fifth day a red rash appears on the skin, first in small pimples and later in large spots, which rise above the surrounding surface of the skin. The elevations are the same on infected pigs whose skins are white as on the dark-skinned animals. The pig should have a dry bed in which to sleep. Perhaps the most simple remedy is a half pint of boiled flaxseed with the soft feed, once each day. Ten grains of nitrate of potash in the drinking water is also good.

———

Many experts claim that the open-front house will give the best results in ventilation, although it seems hard to convince the average poultry owner of this fact, in spite of the proof in the operation of the same by some of the largest commercial plants in the country. With the north, east and west side bottle-tight, the south side open from two to three feet from the door, so that no drafts will hit the fowls and with muslin curtains to lower on stormy days, there is no need of ventilators. This type of ventilation is fast coming to the front as the most practical. A house sixteen feet wide and eight feet high in the front, which faces the south, or as near south as possible, and five feet high in the rear, allowing the sun to reach the back sill of the sixteen-foot floor some time during the day, offers ideal conditions. With such a house, properly managed, there will be no colds or roup to cause failure.

———— .

Special thermometers fixed in the ground a few inches deep show that an orchard cover crop keeps the soil several degrees warmer than a bare soil close by, in an experiment now going on at Indiana Agricultural College. It is also being found that there is more moisture under the crop than there is where no crop has grown. Rye, millet, wheat, rape, crimson clover, soy beans, cowpeas and vetch have been planted over different orchard acres to see which gives best results for the cost of planting, which, if any, is most practical. So far vetch has given excellent results but the seed is pretty expensive. Cowpeas will not grow unless they are put in early, in an average year. Rape grows well after frost, and seems to be a good practicable crop. Millet, because it is inexpensive to put in, is considered one of the most practicable. Chickens, calves and pigs may be pastured safely in the orchard, but other stock are liable to injure the trees.

Dates for Planting Vegetables

Asparagus. Plant between 20th of March and 15th of April, according to locality and season. Plant in trenches with rich soil, placing roots three feet apart.

Beans, Lima. Plant April 10th to 25th. Plant 2 inches deep, 6 inches apart, in rows 2 feet apart. This is for bush beans. For pole crop set poles 4 feet apart and plant 5 beans to each pole. Pinch off when vines reach top of poles.

Beans, String. Plant 1st to 15th of April, in rows 2 inches deep, about 4 inches apart in row. Plant frequently a few at a time to extend crop over the season.

Beets. Plant April 1st to 15th, placing seed thinly in drill 1 inch deep. Thin out as needed.

Cabbage. Set plants May 1st to 15th. Can buy plants as needed or start seed indoors a month earlier.

Cauliflower. Plant early in May. Buy plants or start seed indoors.

Carrots. Plant April 1st, thinly, ½ inch deep in rows. Thin out as needed by pulling largest.

Celery. Plant seed in hot-bed during early spring; transplant when season is well advanced. Plants can be set out in July or August for fall and winter use.

Corn. Early and late varieties can be planted beginning about the middle of April, the later kind up to the middle of July.

Cucumbers. Plant April 20th to May 1st, in hills 4 feet apart, a number of seeds in each hill.

Eggplant. Plant any time in May, according to weather, plants 2 feet apart.

306

Lettuce. Plant early varieties about April 1st, and late about July 1st to August 1st, and pick as required for table or market.

Melons. May 1st to 15th. Plant in hills 4 feet apart each way, 12 seeds to hill. Thin to 2 vines to hill. To check striped beetle cover each hill with box cheesecloth top, or plant radishes with melon seeds. To guard against insects spray with arsenate of lead every two weeks. Pinch vines back when 3 feet long.

Onions. About April 1st. Plant sets 2 inches deep in rows 2 feet apart.

Parsley. April 10th to 20th. Soak seeds, cover lightly with soil.

Parsnips. April 1st to 15th. Scatter seeds thinly in rows.

Peas. Early varieties about April 1st. Scatter manure in trench, sow peas directly on this and cover 3 inches deep. Plant late crop June 15th to July 1st.

Pumpkin. Plant May 15th in hills 6 feet apart.

Radishes. April 1st and every 2 weeks, planting seed ½ inch deep.

Spinach. Plant about April 1st, 1 inch deep, rows 1½ feet apart.

Squash. Plant early in May in hills 4 feet apart, 12 seeds to hill.

Tomatoes. Plant early in May, setting plants 3 feet apart. Pinch back to 1 stalk; tie to stake or trellis.

Turnips. April 1st to 15th. Plant seed ½ inch deep.

Insecticides and Fungicides

Approximate Cost Is Given

Ant Exterminator. A powder. 25 cts., 50 cts. and $1.00.

Aphine. The insecticide that kills plant lice of every description; a strong nicotine extract. 1 qt., $1.00; 1 gal., $2.50.

Aphis Punk. A nicotine paper. For fumigating. Box, 60 cts.; 12 boxes, $6.50.

Arsenate of Lead. For elm-leaf beetle and caterpillars. 1 lb., 25 cts.; 5 lbs., 90 cts.; 10 lbs., $1.65; 25 lbs., $3.75; 100 lbs., $14.00. 1 oz. to 1 gallon of water.

Bordeaux—Arsenate of Lead Mixture. A combined fungicide and insecticide. For plants, trees and shrubbery. Three ozs. to 1 gal. of water. Apply as a spray. 1 lb., 15 cts.; 2 lbs., 26 cts.; 5 lbs., 60 cts.; 10 lbs., $1.15; 20 lbs., $2.15; 50 lbs., $5.12; 1000 lbs., $10.00.

Bordeaux Mixture Paste. The supreme remedy against fungus, rust and all kinds of rot. Five ozs. to 1 gal. of water is standard strength. 1 lb., 11 cts.; 2 lbs., 18 cts.; 5 lbs., 40 cts.; 10 lbs., 75 cts.; 20 lbs., $1.35; 50 lbs., $3.12.

Bordeaux Mixture (Liquid). By simply adding water and stirring it is ready for use. 1 qt., 40 cts.; 1 gal., $1.00; 5 gals., $4.50. One gallon will make one barrel of liquid.

Bordeaux Mixture (Dry). For dusting plants affected with mildew and all fungous diseases. 1-lb. box, 20 cts.; makes 5 gallons spray; 5-lb. box, 90 cts.

Copper Sulphate. For early spraying and making Bordeaux. Lb., 15 cts.; 10 lbs., $1.25; 25 cts., $2.25.

Kerosene Emulsion (Concentrated, Liquid). For plant lice and aphis. 1 qt., 40 cts.; 1 gal., $1.00; 5 gals., $4.50.

Kerosene Emulsion (Paste). Used as a summer wash against scale, plant lice and aphis. Ready for use by simply adding water. 1-lb. can, 15 cts.; 5-lb. can, 60 cts.; 25-lb. can, $2.50.

Lemon Oil. For all insects and soft scale; one of the best-known Insecticides. ½ pt., 25 cts.; pt., 40 cts.; qt., 75 cts.; ½ gal., $1.25; gal., $2.00; 5 gals., $9.00.

Lime Sulphur Solution. A perfect scale and fungus destroyer; special for plum and peach trees, which need fall and spring treatment; cures peach leaf curl. Use during dormant period. Protect the hands with gloves when applying. Dilute with 10 parts of water. 1 gal., 75 cts.; 5 gals., $2.25; 10 gals., $3.75; half-bbls., $6.00; bbls. of 50 gals., $10.00.

Nicoticide. Fumigating compound. 1 pt., $2.50; ½ pt. $1.25; 4 ozs., 70 cts.; vaporizing apparatus, 50 cts.

Nikoteen. An economical and powerful nicotine extract. One part to 600 of water is sufficiently strong to kill all insects except scale, for which use 1 to 400. Pt. bottle, $1.50.

Pruning Compound. A specially prepared thick paint, with a rubbery, elastic film. Just the thing to use after pruning trees. 1 qt., 40 cts.; 1 gal., $1.20.

Rat Corn. Sure death to rats and mice. A new scientific discovery; not poisonous to other animals. 25 cts., 50 cts. and $1.00 size cans.

Scalecide. Recommended for scale as a winter spray. Dilute 1 gal. to 20 gals. of water. 1 gal., $1.00; 5 gals., $3.25; bbl., 50 gals., $25.00.

Slug Shot. One of the cheapest and best powders for destroying insects. 1-lb. carton, 15 cts.; 5 lbs., 30 cts.; 25 lbs., $1.40; 50 lbs., $2.75; 100 lbs., $5.00.

Soluble Oil. An excellent scale remedy. Specially good for lawn trees and hedges, as it will not stain. Mixes perfectly with water. Use during dormant period. Dilute with 15 to 20 parts of water. 1 gal., $1.00; 5 gals., $3.65; 10 gals., $6.65; half bbl., 60 cts. per gal.; bbl. of 50 gals., 50 cts per gal.

Sulphur, Powdered. For mildew. 1 lb., 10 cts.; 5 lbs., 40 cts.; 10 lbs., 60 cts.; 50 lbs., $2.50; 100 lbs., $4.00.

Tobacco Dust. 1 lb., 10 cts.; 5 lbs., 25 cts.; 100 lbs., $3.50.

Tobacco Soap. For plants, trees, cattle and all insect infested animals. ½ lb., 25 cts.; 10 lbs., bulk, $3.00.

Tree Tanglefoot. (Caterpillar Paste.) A remedy against caterpillars and all tree-climbing insects. 1 lb., 30 cts.; 3 lbs., 85 cts.; 10 lbs., $2.65; 20 lbs., $4.80.

Fertilizers for Farm and Garden

Approximate Cost Is Given

Animal Base and Potash Compound. For all crops. Superior for broadcasting in spring prior to harrowing. 2 per cent. ammonia, 8 per cent. Av. Ph. Acid, 2 per cent. potash. Per sack, 200 lbs., $3.00; per ton, $23.50.

Bone Flour. Ground fine; excellent for pot plants or beds where an immediate effect is wanted. 5 lbs., 25 cts.; 100 lbs., $2.50; bbl. of 200 lbs., 4.50; ton, $40.00.

Pure Bone Meal. A standard fertilizer for all purposes, safe and effective. 3 lbs., 15 cts.; 5 lbs., 25 cts.; 25 lbs., 75 cts.; 50 lbs., $1.25; 100 lbs., $2.00; 200 lb. sack, $3.50; per ton, $33.00.

Ground Bone. A little coarser than above; excellent for grass plots, gardens, etc. Apply 400 to 600 lbs. to the acre. 5 lbs., 25 cts.; 25 lbs., 75 cts.; 50 lbs., $1.25; 100 lbs., $2.00; sack of 200 lbs., $3.50; per ton, $33.00.

Coarse Bone. Ground coarse, for grape borders and poultry. A superior fertilizer to use when planting shrubbery and trees. 5 lbs., 25 cts.; 50 lbs., $1.25; 100 lbs., $2.25; 200-lb. sack, $4.00; per ton, $35.00.

Fine Ground Bone. Contains 3 per cent. ammonia, 16 per cent. phosphoric acid. 100 lbs., $1.75; 200-lb. sack, $3.25; per ton, $30.00.

Cattle Manure, Shredded. For garden, lawn and greenhouse, and especially good to mix with compost and for water lilies. 100 lbs., $2.00; 500 lbs., $9.00; 1,000 lbs., $16.00; per ton, $30.00.

Hard-wood Ashes. Indispensable as a lawn dressing, or to apply to orchards. Should be applied late in fall or early spring at the rate of 1000 to 1500 lbs. per acre. 5 lbs., 20 cts.; 10 lbs., 35 cts.; 25 lbs., 60 cts.; 100 lbs., $1.50; per bbl., $2.50; per ton, $22.00.

Kainit (German Potash Salt.) Analysis: 12 per cent. actual potash. Excellent to apply in fall or winter on lawns or vegetable garden. Apply at the rate of 1000 lbs. per acre. 100 lbs., $1.25; 200 lbs., $2.00; per ton, $15.00.

Land Plaster. Much used in composting or mixed with guano, etc. 100-lb. bag, $1.00; 200-lb. bag, $1.50; per ton, $10.00.

Muriate of Potash. 80 per cent. pure, equivalent to 48 to 50 per cent. actual potash. A high grade fertilizer, and one of the best orchard fertilizers known. 25 lbs., $1.00; 50 lbs., $1.75; 100 lbs., $3.00. Original sacks of 200 lbs., $5.50.

Nitrate of Soda. A fertilizer for all crops. It is very quick in action and hastens maturity of crops fully two weeks. Being quickly soluble, it should not be applied until the plants are above ground, when 200 to 300 lbs. mixed with land plaster is sufficient per acre. Nitrate of Soda does not exhaust the land. 5 lbs., 25 cts.; 25 lbs., $1.25; 50 lbs., $2.00; 100 lbs., $3.50. Large quantities, prices on application.

Peruvian Guano Substitute. For potatoes and all vegetables. Since it is difficult to procure pure Peruvian Guano, we recommend this brand as a good, all-round fertilizer. 5 per cent. ammonia, 6 per cent. available phosphoric acid, 7 per cent. potash. 50 lbs., $1.50; 100 lbs., $2.50; sack of 200 lbs., $4.00; ton, $36.00.

Potato Manure. One of the most successful potato manures ever put on the market. Its great potash content makes it valuable for use on all root crops, also on fruit lands. It works well on grass and fruit in connection with bone meal, and makes a valuable and lasting top-dressing. 2 per cent. ammonia, 5 per cent. Av. Ph. Acid, 10 per cent. potash. Per sack, 200 lbs., $3.50; per ton, $28.00.

Sheep Manure, Pulverized. A pure natural manure, unequalled for mixing with potting soil for lawns, general vegetable and flower garden fertilizer, for making liquid manure water or for any purpose where quick as well as lasting results are wanted. 2-lb. package, 15 cts.; 5 lbs., 25 cts.; 10 lbs., 40 cts.; 25 lbs., 75 cts.; 50 lbs., $1.25; 100 lbs., $2.00; 500 lbs., $9.00; 1000 lbs., $16.00; ton, $30.00.

Tobacco Stems. An indispensable lawn covering for winter. It not only acts as a protector, but imparts large quantities of ammonia and drives away insects and moles. Bbl., $1.00; bale, $2.00; ton, $12.00.

Wheat Fertilizer. This brand combines in available form the necessary elements for the growth of all grain and grass. Ammonia, 2 per cent.; phos. acid, 8 per cent.; potash, 2 per cent.; nitrogen, 1.65 per cent. Sacks of 200 lbs., $3.00; ton, $23.50.

INDEX

PAGE

A

Advantages of farm life............................... 30
Agriculture to be more profitable............10, 20, 27, 35
Aim to exceed the average........................... 25
Alfalfa; hardy varieties..............................118
Apples; market demands; storage..................185, 186
Arguments for mixed farming..................11, 16, 159
Avoid Single Crops................................... 51

B

Bacteria of the soil................................. 87
Beef production 26
Bookkeeping for farm................................283
Broomcorn 139
Butter marketing..................................... 27

C

Cabbage raising...................................... 32
Cattle feeding....................................... 51
City men as farmers........................29, 46, 66, 68
Chemical elements for plants......................... 85
Cherries—Late varieties safest......................183
Community Social Centers............................275
Concrete on farm....................................151
Co-operation among farmers.......................... 27
Corn, how to obtain good crop....................134, 277
Cow testing.....................................127, 129
Crop combinations and diversity............18, 21, 36, 118
Crop rotation...............................19, 34, 82

PAGE

Crop succession 38
Crops—relative value 14

D

Dairy by-products 130
Dairy cows compared................................129
Dairy management and profits..........25, 37, 114, 124, 127
Dates for planting vegetables......................39, 291
Deep plowing 100
Diversity reduces risk.............................17, 20
Duck raising 259

E

Earning capacity of land.....................18, 40, 53, 72
Education for the farm............................. 23
Egg preservation 256
Egg production 244, 249
Egg type in hens...................................252
Exports and prosperity............................. 12

F

Farm facilities improving.......................... 10
Farm home betterment..............................10, 33
Farm hours too long; labor.............15, 17, 22, 31, 35
Farm improvements a vital question................ 12
Farm life more hopeful............................. 22
Farm work irksome.................................9, 10
Farmer lacks selling knowledge........9, 26, 27, 70, 76, 115
Farming opportunities 9, 30, 46, 63
Farms are too large...............................12
Fertilizers 295
Floriculture; commercial value.............31, 61, 214
Fodder crops; new 122, 123

PAGE

Forage problem ....,...........................117
Fruit farming; suits amateurs........48, 56, 65, 171, 176, 183

G

Gardening a source of profit.......................21, 200
Grain yield in Europe.......................24, 36, 80, 143
Grain yield low...................................24, 36

H

Honey production 50, 235
Hotbeds and coldframes............................221
Humus for land betterment........................... 81

I

Insect pests; remedies. 225, 232, 293
Insecticides 293
Investments in the country........................... 30
Irrigation by wells...................................148

L

Labor problem on farm................15, 17, 21, 22, 31, 35
Legumes benefit land..........................85, 96, 122
Lime a farming adjunct............................... 81
Little farms of Europe............................... 53
Location important 20

M

Manure; value of liquid............................45, 93
Moneymaking ideas 25

O

Onion growing 168
Orchard heating 183

P

Parasites cause loss....................................266
Parcels post aids farmers........................... 77

PAGE

Pasture waste 41
Phosphorus an essential................................. 83
Pickles 164
Population changes 36
Pork production 25, 26, 108
Potatoes 36, 102, 202
Poultry diseases and remedies........................270
Poultry management 49, 244, 274
Prices of farm products................................ 11
Profit sharing 61, 64
Profits in novelties...................................159
Pruning important 176

S

Silo construction and use............................155
Small fruits pay 187, 196
Soil improvement 80, 98
Strawberries, early and late...................192, 197
Sugar beets 142
Sweet potatoes 106

T

Turkey raising 263

W

Weeds cause work and loss.............................. 24
Weeds have market value..............................163
Women farmers 73

Y

Young people on farm.............9, 12, 22, 33, 57, 67, 161